DATE DUE

~~NO 1'00~~		
OC 6'00		
~~JE 8'05~~		

DEMCO 38-296

The Strengths Model

The Strengths Model

*Case Management with People
Suffering from Severe and
Persistent Mental Illness*

Charles A. Rapp

New York   Oxford
Oxford University Press
1998

Oxford University Press

Oxford   New York
Athens   Auckland   Bangkok   Bogota   Bombay   Buenos Aires
Calcutta   Cape Town   Dar es Salaam   Delhi   Florence   Hong Kong
Istanbul   Karachi   Kuala Lumpur   Madras   Madrid   Melbourne
Mexico City   Nairobi   Paris   Singapore   Taipei   Tokyo   Toronto   Warsaw

and associated companies in
Berlin   Ibadan

Copyright © 1998 by Oxford University Press, Inc.

Published by Oxford University Press, Inc.,
198 Madison Avenue, New York, New York 10016

Oxford is a registered trademark of Oxford University Press

Library of Congress Cataloging-in-Publication Data
Rapp, Charles A.
The strengths model : case management with people suffering from
severe and persistent mental illness / Charles A. Rapp.
p.   cm.
Includes bibliographical references and index.
ISBN 0-19-511444-2
1. Psychiatric social work—United States. 2. Social case work-
-United States—Methodology. 3. Mentally ill—Rehabilitation-
-United States. I. Title.
HV689.R36 1998
362.2'0425—dc21   96-50963
                                   CIP

1 3 5 7 9 8 6 4 2

Printed in the United States of America
on acid-free paper

For my sons, Justin and Devin,

and

Linda, my wife, who also is the best strengths practitioner
I have known.

Thank you for all you have given me.

CONTENTS

FOREWORD

In the fall of 1982, as a part of my M.S.W. practicum requirements, I was assigned to a special project at the Bert Nash Mental Health Center in Lawrence, Kansas. I was still working full time at the Menninger Foundation Children's Residential Treatment program, a job I had held since earning my Bachelor's Degree in Social Work. This new project was headed by a doctoral candidate, Ronna Chamberlain, and featured an outreach case management project serving those we then called the chronically mentally ill. In this project, we were to visit people in their homes, assist them with the problems of living they faced, and help them reach their goals by focusing on personal and environmental strengths.

I could not have been operating in more contrasting worlds. In my job, I was spending a considerable amount of time in a hospital setting, operating from a psychodynamic orientation, with great emphasis placed on accurate diagnosis and treatment. In my educational experience, we were operating freely in the community and we were intentionally not told the diagnosis of those with whom we worked. At first, I and others found the work a bit confusing. The professionals who surrounded us had a more sophisticated lexicon to describe their work, and there was a great deal of concern about very lofty issues like professional boundaries, creating false expectations among "the patients," and such.

Yet, as the project expanded to other sites, it became clear that consumers were accomplishing things that certainly were unexpected. First, they were staying out of the hospital despite the fact that many were referred with the stated belief that it was only a matter of days before another hospitalization would be necessary. Beyond this, consumers and case managers began talking about finding jobs, making friends, and living independently. Interestingly, when case managers brought these goals to treatment team meetings, they were met with a wide range of reactions, from amazement to ridicule, but most often we were subjected to a lecture about our naiveté and the true nature of serious mental disorders.

The work itself was hard but fun for many of us—but utterly distasteful to others. This has not changed. For those of us who enjoyed the work there was a real sense of being a mental health maverick, and this created a sense of purpose. You spoke so differently about these folks than did other staff. You seemed to know so much more about their lives and what they still dreamed for. I remember an early attempt to learn from the consumers about case management: what they saw as helpful or not helpful. It seems funny to look back now and recall that we were a bit disappointed by the early returns. The consumers said that they appreciated that the case manager helped them rearrange furniture, structure their day, or cooked a meal with them. They didn't discuss feeling empowered, or how completing the strengths assessment improved their self-esteem. Yet, they were taking more control over their life and they did seem to feel better about themselves.

Herein lies the dilemma that case managers so often face. Case management is so practical that some, even case managers themselves, devalue the importance of it. We know now from consumers that the fact that the service operates where the rubber meets the road is why it matters so much to them. The power lies in the practicality.

By focusing on real-life goals in real-life settings, strengths-based case management predated by 15 years the current interest in recovery as a mission of our work. Implementing the strengths model elevates the consumer from a passive recipient of services to the director of the process. It affirms the person not as a patient, or client, or even a consumer but instead as a citizen. Case managers working from the strengths model help others reclaim full citizenship, replete with all the rights and responsibilities that come with citizenship. Case managers also challenge our communities to move beyond the segregation impulse to embrace instead those who face serious challenges and to allow them to make their contribution to the human enterprise.

In the early days little time was spent considering the power and potential of the strengths perspective in other realms of social work practice. Instead, work began with professionals and officials in other states to understand and implement case management in mental health. This would require plodding through predictable skepticism and scorn, but slowly but surely the model took hold. This effort has never lost steam. Training and technical assistance have occurred in over 40 states and internationally. This fact alone makes this one of the most eagerly awaited books in our field. Charlie Rapp and others have been just too busy to write it all down until now.

The concepts and principles that underpin the strengths model have stood the test of time. This model is based on humanism and pragmatism—

a wonderful combination. The growth of case management and other helping modalities in mental health have had an enormous impact on the field. Today, state hospital roles are shrinking, hospitalizations are of shorter duration, and we have not only specialized housing and work programs but we have consumers running such programs. Better still, we have consumers living and working in normalized settings, drawing on the supports of friends and, at times, professionals. The technology has changed but is still centered on a person who listens, cares, and helps people with the practical issues they face in daily life. We call these people case managers.

There is great danger in reading this book too narrowly. The power of this method of helping is only underscored when one considers that the successes recorded here were with those considered among the most disabled, the most impaired, and those least likely to approach normalization. This model suggests that individuals and communities have strengths that can be called forth, expanded, and matched to help people reach their potential. These same processes can help all of us lead successful and satisfying lives.

There is also danger that readers will dismiss this work as simply good social work practice—the way, in fact, most professionals operate on a day-by-day basis. To embrace the strengths perspective requires that all aspects of practice must be examined and challenged. This text makes clear that all key phases of social work practice, from engagement and assessment to the evaluation of outcome, look different when the strengths perspective is employed.

There were precursors to this work, of course, such as White's pioneering work on competence and Maluccio's application of the principles of competence in social work practice. However, the interest in strengths-based practice models, particularly in case management, has led to applications in alcohol and drug treatment, public assistance programs, older adults, and children. Indeed, the strengths perspective has reenergized all facets of social work including direct practice, public policy, and research. Accordingly, the principles and methods in this book have wide application on the streets and in the classroom.

W. Patrick Sullivan, Ph.D.
Director
Indiana Division of Mental Health

Associate Professor
Indiana University
School of Social Work

PREFACE

This is the first text published on the strengths model of practice despite its growing popularity over the last decade. The model is comprised of a theory, a set of values and principles, and explicit practice methods that have been developed and refined over the last 15 years. The empirical testing of the model has shown consistent results that are superior to traditional approaches to serving people with severe and persistent mental illness.

Having said this, much work is yet to be done. Too often, achievement and the quality of life of people suffering from severe and persistent mental illness remain inadequate. Unemployment is between 70% and 80%, loneliness dominates many lives, much of their time is spent segregated from "non-clients," poverty places a pall on their being, and options are severely constricted. While the strengths model is not a panacea for this oppressive situation, it has demonstrated its ability to make a positive difference in the lives of people we are privileged to serve.

This book is primarily a practice text. It is the first attempt to translate systematically the ideas and conceptions about the strengths model into a set of empirically derived practices. While the first three chapters are more conceptual in nature and Chapter VIII discusses the organizational and managerial context for practice, the guts of the book is strengths model practice: engagement, strengths assessment, personal planning, and resource acquisition. The myriad of case vignettes attempt to make the practice "come alive" for the reader.

Given this purpose and feedback received from a wide variety of people, I have come to believe that this text has relevance for multiple audiences. For social work students (B.S.W. and M.S.W.) the book should be directly applicable for any classes devoted to case management or mental health practice. It could be a useful supplement to undergraduate or graduate social work practice classes. Some universities have begun elective courses on the strengths model. For these courses, the fit seems to approach the ideal. I have also been told that the book would also have relevance in some university curricula in psychology, nursing, psychiatry, vocational rehabilitation, and occupational therapy.

The book was also written with current mental health professionals in mind. Case managers should find this volume directly relevant to their practice. Team leaders, supervisors, and administrators would benefit from the detailed explanation of methods as well as the chapter on creating a supportive case management organizational context. The behavioral listings of strengths-oriented practice following each of the practice chapters are currently being used by quality assurance personnel. For people responsible for staff development and training, the book should provide a blueprint for organizing and implementing training for case managers.

The sole authorship of this book camouflages the fact that no book owes more to more people than this one does. Unless the editors from Oxford take it out, you will find the pronoun "we" used throughout although it's not clear who "we" is. I would like to use this preface, then, to define "we."

The book started in 1982 when the University of Kansas School of Social Welfare was awarded a $10,000 contract to provide case management services to a group of people, at that time, referred to as chronically mentally ill. With good fortune that only could have come from a higher being, Ronna Chamberlain, a new Ph.D. student, was assigned to me as a research assistant to design and mount this project. We identified the desired client outcomes (e.g., community tenure, independent living, work, leisure time activities) and were befuddled by how existing case management approaches with their emphasis on linking clients to formal mental health services would be able to achieve them. Discarding the current approaches, we began identifying the elements of practice that we thought would make sense. The notion of individual and community strengths was central to this initial formulation. We selected four students who were then assigned to the project to meet their field practicum requirements for their B.S.W. or M.S.W. degrees. Ronna acted as their supervisor and field instructor.

We evaluated the work as best we could. Given that the intervention was new and quickly put together, that we were using inexperienced students to actually deliver the service, that the host agency was not always supportive of our efforts, and that very few approaches with this population had demonstrated success, we were at best hopeful that the data would show some areas of success and provide direction for improvement. We found, much to our surprise, that on 19 of the 22 indicators we assessed, the results were positive (Rapp & Chamberlain, 1985). We could not really believe it, but the next year we mounted three other projects in three different mental health centers. Matt Modrcin, Dick Wintersteen, and Jim Hanson joined the team. Refinements were made in the approach, the evaluation was made more rigorous, and once again, positive results were found. Based on this work, we put together a training manual.

By the mid-1980s case management was becoming the centerpiece of community support services and states were devoting considerable effort to developing case management "systems." We were asked to provide consultation and training in Kansas and several other states. It was at this time that we became acutely aware that this "strengths approach" was a dramatic shift from the past. In a typical group of trainees, it seemed half the people said they were already doing it, and the other half said we were crazy for thinking it. I wish I had been smart enough at the time to let them battle it out instead of trying to convince each half that they were wrong. To be fair, even in the earliest training groups, there were always a few people for whom the approach resonated. It put into words and methods what their own practice sensed was right. These people became the "champions" of the strengths approach.

By the late 1980s, the strengths approach was benefiting from the attention of an increasing number of faculty members and Ph.D. students at the School of Social Work. Liane Davis and Sue Pearlmutter applied the model to AFDC recipients in the JOBS program, Becky Fast applied it to work with the elderly in long-term care, Dennis Saleebey sought to tailor the model to an approach to community development, John Poertner applied it to work with youth and families, and Rosemary Chapin sought application of strengths to social policy analysis and development. Ann Weick, Jim Taylor, and Dennis Saleebey applied their intellectual energy to developing a richer conceptual understanding of the model. Ed Canda, Alex Westerfelt, and Mahasweta Banajee joined the struggle of understanding. In 1993, as part of the CSWE reaccredition study, the School adapted the strengths perspective as one of its guiding curriculum themes. It is rare in social work and other disciplines for a whole school to be so identified with a particular innovation. To be a part of such an experience is a source of great pride and joy.

So, the "we" is the faculty and PhD students of the KU School of Social Welfare. The "we" is also the myriad of people in practice and administration who based their practice on the model—who were able to show us where further work was needed but whose work gave the model a credibility it would never have achieved if relegated to academics. Among the "we" I am indebted to are Leslie Young, Estelle Richman, Kevin Bomhoff, Marti Knisely, Tom Wernert, Martha Hodge, Linda Carlson, Coleen Kessler, Diane Asher, Diane McDiarmid, and Kristin Bertonsin.

The "we" also includes those people from other universities whose work has mightily influenced the approach. This includes Julian Rappaport, Steve Rose, Wes Shera, Cathleen Macias, Pat Deegan, Paul Carling, and Peter Ryan.

There are three special "we's." The first and foremost is Ronna Chamberlain. Her ideas at the start and throughout its development have comprised the core ideas of the strengths model. Since she does not like to write, although she does it well, or speak publicly, although she is quite articulate, her contribution is hidden from most people. Without her, this book would not be.

A second special "we" is Wally Kisthardt. While his writing and research has added much to the development of the strengths model, it has been as the principal trainer and presenter on the strengths model that special recognition is warranted. Wally's ability to make this "radical" approach accessible to the masses has been indispensable. Whether through demonstrations, poetry, songs, or articulate presentations, his ambassadorship has reached thousands in the United States, England, and Ireland. He has also served as my aide-de-camp for so many years, I cannot fathom working without him.

The third special "we" is Pat Sullivan, currently Director of Mental Health for the State of Indiana and Associate Professor of Social Work at Indiana University. Pat was a student case manager in our first project in 1982, was a supervisor of one of our special student units, supervised the supervisors of other projects, helped design the early training, was a trainer, ran a CSS program based on the strengths model, and provided technical assistance to CSS programs trying to implement the strengths model. He extended the model to work with substance abusers and employment assistance programs. Pat has done more to conceive of and articulate the role of environment in the strengths model than anyone else. I am honored that Pat agreed to write the foreword for this book. In a sense, the circle has been completed.

I would like to express appreciation to Wanda Buck for typing, retyping, retyping, and retyping the manuscript over the last year.

A significant debt is owed to John Poertner, who sacrificed his own professional preferences to allow me a sabbatical to write this book.

A FEW COMMENTS ON LANGUAGE

In this book, I have used various terms to refer to people with serious mental illness. Occasionally I used the term "consumer," which had currency in the late 1980s and early 1990s as the preferred term but which is now losing favor. Often I use "client." I wish I could just use "people" but it would be less clear who I was writing about at a particular time. Please understand, the use of each term is a rhetorical convenience. I find no term that separates the people afflicted from the rest to be acceptable. The entire strengths approach is about personhood, not patienthood or clienthood or even consumerhood. Their courage, resilience, and, yes, their strengths in the face of a mean-spirited disease and an often unresponsive and oppressive society have taught us more about being human than anything else. So I end this preface with a favor to ask of the reader. If any of terms used have negative connotations to you, or even if they do not, read "client" or "consumer," but think Alice, Joe, Joan, and Bill. People, just like you and me who are striving for the same things we are, who are both flawed and flawless, who have struggles and difficulties, who valiantly fight every day, who can experience joy and satisfaction. In other words, they are you and me.

Charles A. Rapp

August 1996

CHAPTER 1

History, Critique, and Useful Conceptions: Toward a Strengths Paradigm

The strengths model represents a paradigm shift in mental health, social work, and the other helping professions. A paradigm is a model or way of perceiving the world and solving problems. The current paradigm, which has continued for over a century, has been found wanting. The lives of people with severe mental illness continue to be marked by poverty, loneliness, limited opportunities for achievement, pain, and suffering. As Saleebey (1996) writes:

> The impetus, in part, for the evolution of a more strengths-based review of practice, comes from the awareness that our culture and the helping professions are saturated with an approach to understanding the human condition obsessed with individual, family, and community pathology, deficit, problem, abnormality, victimization, and disorder. (p. 1)

This chapter sketches the context within which the strengths model evolved. I will first describe and critique the paradigm that has dominated mental health practice for the last century. We will then turn to ideas and conceptions that have been useful in developing a strengths perspective.

SOCIAL PROCESSES AND SENSITIZING VIEWPOINTS

People with severe mental illness continue to be oppressed by the society in which they live and reinforced by the practices of the professionals responsible for helping them. This is rarely done intentionally or with malevolence but, rather, is provoked by compassion and caring. Because the oppression is dressed up in the clothes of compassion, it is difficult to identify,

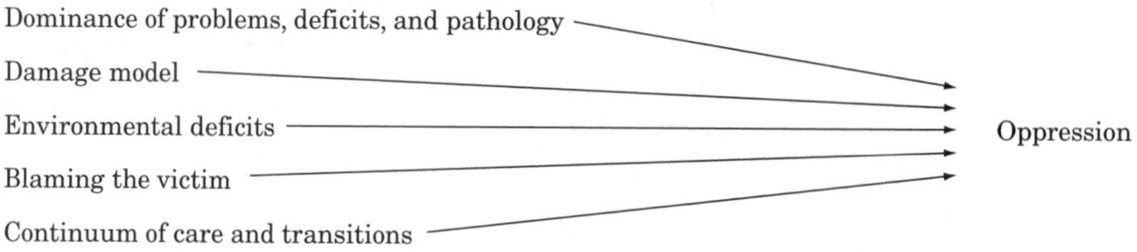

Dominance of problems, deficits, and pathology

Damage model

Environmental deficits   Oppression

Blaming the victim

Continuum of care and transitions

Figure 1.1. Social processes and practices contributing to oppression.

to understand its underlying dynamics, and to develop alternative approaches. This section seeks to describe those social processes and professional practices that contribute to the oppression. Figure 1.1 depicts the key elements of the current dominant paradigm.

THE DOMINANCE OF DEFICITS[1]

Dichotomies pervade human life. In trying to cope with complex realities, human societies have created stark divisions between the good and the bad, the safe and the unsafe, the friend and the enemy. It is a curious fact that greater attention invariably is paid to the negative poles of the dichotomy: to the bad, the unsafe, the enemy. This pull toward the negative aspects of life has given a peculiar shape to human endeavors and has, in the case of social work and other helping professions, created a profound tilt toward the pathological. Because of the subtle ways in which this bias is expressed, its contours and consequences must be examined to set the stage for a different perspective. The strengths perspective is an alternative to a preoccupation with negative aspects of people and society and is a more apt expression of some of the deepest values of social work.

Tracing the Roots

Social work is not unique in its focus on the pathological. Throughout history, cultures have been preoccupied with naming and conquering outsiders and waging battles against the enemy in people's souls. Judeo-Christian heritage has given rise to a clear sense of human frailty through its concept of sin and has used that concept to limit or punish those thought to transgress moral norms.

Social work's origins are in the concept of moral deficiency. The Age of Enlightenment created the philosophical backdrop against which to consider in a new way the plight of the less fortunate, but, given the economic environment in the late 1800s and the religious convictions of those in the Charity Organization Society, the strategy was one of moral conversion.

---

1. This section has been reprinted from Ann Weick, Charles A. Rapp, W. Patrick Sullivan, and Walter Kisthardt (1989), A strengths perspective for social work practice, *Social Work,* *89,* 350–52.

Poverty was attributed to drunkenness and other intemperance, ignorance, and lack of moral will (Axinn & Levin, 1975, pp. 89–94). Change was to come about not through provision of monetary assistance but through persuasion and friendly influence. The emphasis on human failings as the cause of difficulties established a conceptual thread whose strands are found in practice today.

The focus on moral frailty went through an evolution that both softened and disguised its presence. Soon after the turn of the century, social workers began calling for a more professional approach to the work of helping people (Leiby, 1978, p. 181). The adoption of the empirical method used in the natural sciences was the stimulus for the social sciences and for the emerging professions to define themselves not as crafts or philanthropic efforts but as organized, disciplined sciences (Leiby, 1978, p. 348). Mary Richmond was one of the earliest proponents of using a logical, evidence-based method for helping (Goldstein, 1943, p. 29). Through her and others' efforts, increasing attention was paid to defining the problems in people's lives so that a rational, rather than a moralistic, strategy of intervention could be pursued.

The development of this formulation of professional practice was intersected in the 1930s by increasing interest in psychoanalytic theory as the theoretical structure for defining individuals' problems (Smalley, 1967, pp. ix–x). But the cost of this affiliation with psychoanalytic theory and its derivatives was an evermore sophisticated connection with human weakness as the critical variable in understanding human problems.

These weaknesses became reified with the language of pathology. A complicated clinical nomenclature grew up as a descriptive edifice for these new psychological insights. The art of clinical diagnosis was born—an art far more complicated than Richmond's logical steps to assessment. In keeping with the scientific belief that a cause must be found before a result could be achieved, attention was paid to all individual behaviors that signified a diagnostic category. Once a diagnosis was established, treatment could proceed. In this process, every category of clinical diagnosis focuses on a human lack or weakness, ranging from the relatively benign to the severe.

Recent Directions

The profession has not been oblivious to the importance of recognizing individual strengths in practice encounters. Indeed, in 1958, the Commission on Social Work Practice included as a main objective of the field to "seek out, identify, and strengthen the maximum potential in individuals, groups, and communities" (Bartlett, 1958, p. 6). Current writers, such as Hepworth and Larsen (1986), Shulman (1979), and Germain and Gitterman (1980), have given attention to the danger of focusing narrowly on individual pathology while ignoring strengths.

However, a subtle and elusive focus on individual or environmental deficits and personal or social problems remains in recent frameworks. The "ecological perspective" of social work practice, a model developed by Germain and Gitterman (1980), illustrates this point.

Germain and Gitterman (1980) built on the social work tradition of focusing on the interface between person and environment, introduced ecological concepts such as adaptation, and suggested that attention should be focused on the transactions that occur between people and their environment. They contend that it is in these complex transactions between a person and the environment that "upsets in the usual adaptive balance or goodness-of-fit often emerge" (Germain & Gitterman, p. 7). These "upsets," from their point of view, often are the result of "the stress generated by discrepancies between needs and capacities on one hand and the environmental qualities on the other" (Germain & Gitterman, p. 7). In short, it is the characteristics either of the individual or of the environment that create a problem. Emphasis thus rests on the ability to assess adequately the nature of the problem. Although Germain and Gitterman acknowledge the importance of "engaging positive forces in the person and the environment," the goal is to reduce "negative transactional features" (Germain & Gitterman, p. 19). In a subtle way, negative aspects still dominate this view.

A focus on the adequate assessment and diagnosis of the "problem" has deep roots in the profession and remains a central tenet of modern practice tests. For example, Compton and Galaway (1984) see the focus of social work as "using a problem-solving focus to resolve problems in the person–situation interaction . . ." (p. 12). Hepworth and Larsen (1986), who devoted an admirable amount of attention to the identification and use of strengths, also considered the problem-solving process as essential to social work practice and promoted the importance of "assessing human problems and locating and developing or utilizing appropriate resource systems" (p. 23).

Problem-solving models are closely tied to the notion of intervention. As Compton and Galaway (1984) described it, "Intervention refers to deliberate, planned actions undertaken by the client and the worker to resolve a problem" (p. 11). Although writers such as Shulman (1979) sense the need to identify the strengths of both the individual and the environment, the focus of intervention is on the "blocks in the individual—social engagement" (p. 9). When read closely, these views all suggest that accurate diagnosis or assessment of a problem leads naturally to the selection of particular "interventions" that, it is to be hoped, disrupt the natural course of individual or social difficulty. The difficulty or problem is seen as the linchpin for assessment and action.

Charles Cowger (1992) claims that virtually all of our professional attention and assessment protocols are focused on deficits of the individual or environment. He developed a grid to group the approaches:

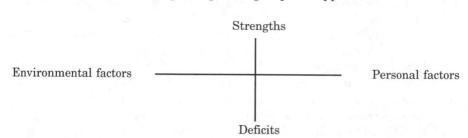

He opines, "A new theoretical interest in how environmental factors affect practice has been increasingly evident in the literature since the early 1970s. However, like renewed interest in client strengths, this interest has not been fully realized in actual practice because practice guidelines and specific practice knowledge have lagged" (pp. 142–43).

Maluccio (1979) found that social workers underestimated client strengths and had more negative perceptions of clients than clients had of themselves. "Social workers persist in formulating assessments that focus almost exclusively on the pathology and dysfunction of clients—despite the time honored social work platitude that social workers work with strengths, not weaknesses" (Hepworth & Larson, 1986, p. 167). As Cowger (1992) states, "a library search for assessment tools that include client strengths is a particularly unrewarding experience" (p. 140).

The Problem with Problem Focus

Attention to people's inability to cope is a central expression of the prevailing perspectives on helping. Approaches differ in the way the problem is defined, but virtually all schools of therapeutic thought rest on the belief that people need help because they have a problem—a problem that in some way sets them apart from others who are thought not to have that problem. The terminology "having a problem" suggests that problems belong to or inhere in people and, in some way, express an important fact about who they are. The existence of the problem provides the *raison d'être* for the existence of professional helpers. In an extreme form, it creates a view of professional helping that has a hidden logic and questionable results.

Concern about establishing the precise cause of a problem ensnares social workers in a strategy for dealing with the problem in those terms. If it is determined that a person's difficulties are linked to family dynamics in early childhood, then the approach "teaches" the person this view of the problem and justifies the attention given to understanding these formative relationships. If the cause of family problems is thought to be patterns of communication, then the approaches will train the family in new communication skills. No matter what the cause, there will be some strategy to teach the clients the nature of their problems and the particular route to recovery.

Using Gregory Bateson's work, Watzlawick, Weakland, and Fisch (1974, p. 39) analyzed this approach in relation to alcoholism. They showed that the view of the problem is carried into the solution. If alcoholism is defined as the disease of excessive alcohol consumption, then the therapeutic approach must be centered on abstinence. Getting an alcoholic to stop drinking is the first step in recovery. In this way, alcohol is both the center of the problem and the treatment. Even when someone is successfully sober for long periods of time, alcohol remains a central concern of his or her life. The image of the bottle is as prevalent in sobriety as in drunkenness.

When the cause of a problem is defined, the problem exists in a new way. The process of naming something heretofore unnamed creates it as a reality toward which therapeutic effort must be directed. Instead of the vague unease or intense discomfort a person in her or his situation experiences, the source of the difficulty is identified and feelings are focused on it. It is named—a process that carries with it a magical quality because it makes something comprehensible that has been puzzling, frightening, and mysterious. The sense of control that often comes with naming provides a sense of initial relief. The unknown has been categorized and labeled. By making the problem subject to rational processes, the person in the grip of the difficulty sees that it has some shape and can be contended with. The power of the professional comes from naming the problem and from having in mind a strategy for overcoming the difficulty.

This process of naming occurs in a language that belongs to the professional, not the client. Diagnostic categories establish classes of conditions with which a client is matched. To accomplish this match, a clinician must look for broad commonalities rather than idiosyncratic characteristics. The client's situation must be made to fit predetermined categories and those categories are not ones that the client would devise as an adequate description of his or her situation. To categorize someone as depressed provides only the most global assessment. It does not reveal the meaning of that person's struggle or the strengths that lie hidden in that person's story.

Problem-based assessments encourage individualistic rather than social-environmental explanations of human problems. Although it generally is understood that people live in complex social milieus that dramatically affect them, assessment rarely takes into account larger social variables. Even when conditions such as poverty are seen to limit severely people's ability to manage their lives, attention often is concentrated exclusively on efforts to change the behavior of those affected. The difficulty in changing social conditions deters helpers from keeping those factors in the picture and results in a view of people as the cause of their own problems.

The problem–deficit orientation sets up other barriers for clients. One manifestation occurs frequently in residential treatment programs. Deficiencies in behavioral skills are identified in the initial assessment, and a treatment plan is devised to teach these skills. When the person demonstrates these skills, the staff is inclined to count it as a successful intervention. However, success is marred by other "dysfunctional" behaviors that are observed and the strategy of correcting them is similarly programmed. This pattern may be repeated numerous times, turning what was expected to be a three-month stay into several years of treatment. The focus on problem behaviors develops a life of its own and, paradoxically, is reinforced by the residential environment itself creating "problematic" behavior. Although a focus on such behavior may temporarily alleviate its expression, there is no evidence that the results of such residential intervention will carry into the person's life after release from the program. Gearing treatment goals to problem behaviors ensures that there will be a never-ending requirement for continued intervention and little sense of success.

Finally, the activity of searching out the problem creates the illusion that there is an identifiable solution or remedy for it. Underlying the problem approach is the belief that an accurate naming of the problem will lead to an appropriate intervention. Although that belief may occasionally be justified, the daily practice experience is far less precise. Many professionals find that naming a situation provides no clues about how best to proceed—and that the real clues emerge from the continuing and ever-changing interaction with clients who are in the situation. In addition, the very act of diagnosing the problem may add a new layer of problem that complicates notions about a clear course of treatment.

The focus on the problem and the process of defining it established the contours of much of what is identified as helping. Three dynamics are clear: (1) the problem invariably is seen as a lack or an inability in the person affected, (2) the nature of the problem is defined by the professional, and (3) treatment is directed toward overcoming the deficiency at the heart of the problem. This triumvirate helps ensure that the helping encounter remains an emergency room, where wounded people come to be patched up.

The Damage Model

One manifestation of the deficit orientation is described by Wolin and Wolin (1993) as the damage model. Based on their work with "survivors of troubled families," they describe the damage model as resembling the germ theory of disease:

> Troubled families are seen as toxic agents, like bacteria or viruses, and the survivors are regarded as victims of their parents' poisonous secretions. Children, according to the Damage Model, are vulnerable, helpless, and locked into the family. The best survivors can do is to cope or contain the family's harmful influence at considerable cost to themselves. (p. 13)

It is easy to replace "troubled families" with "people with major mental illness" and see that the same dynamic currently dominates the care, treatment, and expectations of the people so afflicted.

The authors describe the damage model as "half of a treatment" that:

1. offers few cues about how survivors could build and maintain loving relationships with other adults, function as effective members of the community, raise children . . .

2. solidifies an image of themselves as helpless in the past, which then because the basis for fault-finding and continued helplessness in the present . . .

3. the premise that family troubles inevitably repeat themselves from one generation to the next, coupled with the model's omission of resilience, does as much to frighten survivors as it does to help them. (pp. 14–15)

Environmental Deficits

The preoccupation with deficits has also colored our view of environments and communities. We talk of needy, impoverished, and pathological communities. We lament the presence of stigma and discrimination. We complain that the community lacks the resources to build a good life for people with severe mental illness and that the service system lacks resources to provide care and treatment.

Rather than attributing the cause to individual deficits, deviancy is seen as a result of pathological subcultures or social forces. Therefore, the failure of people with severe mental illness to be employed is attributed to discrimination, local unemployment rates, failure by employers to make reasonable accommodations, or the nature of the capitalist economic system.

The toxicity of the environment has been a dominant theme in mental health. The growth of asylums in the nineteenth century was viewed as replacing the chaos of urban life and unhealthy social conditions with new therapeutic environments located in less stressful rural environments (Rothman, 1971). There was wide agreement among sociologists throughout the first half of the twentieth century that urban life was linked to mental illness (Faris & Dunham, 1939; Park, 1952; Wirth, 1964; Hollingshead & Redlich, 1958). As Burgess (1939) wrote "definitely and unmistakably the incidence of the chief psychoses are related to the organization of the city" (p. ix). The need for replacement environments was implicit in the growing stature of "therapeutic community" and "milieu therapy" in hospital programming during the 1940s and 1950s.

The community mental health movement and the failure of "deinstitutionalization" placed renewed focus on the poor social conditions these former hospital patients were now living in. The solution was to develop a network of new professionally operated community support services (Turner, 1977). Unfortunately, these new programs followed the blueprint of the state hospital system:

> By developing segregated housing programs, therapy, and recreational groups, and by relying on sheltered employment opportunities, the state hospital, in effect, has been replicated in the community. As a result, thousands of mentally ill individuals are living in prophylactic environments, systematically and silently excluded from natural community processes. (Sullivan, 1992, p. 152)

Social policies are viewed as societal responses to social problems (Chambers, 1993; Jansson, 1990; Chapin, 1995). One result has been that "low income urban neighborhoods are now environments of service where behaviors are affected because residents come to believe that their well-being depends on being a client" (Kretzmann & McKnight, 1993, p. 2). Services, at best, ensure survival but significant improvements in quality of life can only be achieved by exploiting community capacities (Kretzmann & McKnight, 1993).

Blaming the Victim

The preoccupation with deficits, needs, weaknesses, and pathology when viewing individuals or environments has led to "blaming the victim." In Ryan's (1971) words:

The formula for action becomes extraordinarily simple: Change the victim. All this happens so smoothly that it seems downright rational. First, identify a social problem. Second, study those affected by the problem and discover in what ways they are different from the rest of us as a consequence of deprivation and injustice. Third, define the difference as the cause of the social problem itself. Finally, of course, assign a government bureaucrat to invent a humanitarian action program to correct the differences. (p. 8)

The perniciousness is increased because this line of reasoning is always cloaked in humanitarian language. Of course, severe mental illness is a biologically based brain disease. It is not people's fault. But the solution is to train them, to protect them, to change them. The same solution occurs if the focus is on the uncaring or toxic community. As Rappaport (1977) writes, "The genetic and the environmental victim-blaming strategies are functionally equivalent" (p. 118).

A necessary component of victim blaming is labeling. Once differences between one group of people and the rest are specified, then a name is given to this "different group." Since the difference is always based on deviations from some norm, the label quickly assumes a negative connotation or meaning. An "outgroup" is thus created, people assigned a degraded social identity. At its full flowering, the members of the group not only are assigned a degraded social identity but become that social identity.

People with severe mental illness, although this is changing, have been referred to by their affliction, "He's a schizophrenic" or "borderline," or by their social service status, "She is a patient." The disease is only one part of the person's being yet the person's identity is seen as being best described and explained by the disease. Sue Estroff (1989) has documented how that "sick" identity then becomes the self-definition of the person. With it comes the baggage of helplessness and weakness.

Labeling has another detrimental effect. Labeling groups leads to a muting of perceived within-group differences and a highlighting of perceived between-group differences. As a consequence, programming becomes generic; everyone so labeled needs about the same amount of the same thing. The continuing tendency, for example, is to recommend social skill training for all people with severe mental illness, so many treatment plans continue to look alike. The deindividualization of people with severe mental illness not only reduces the effectiveness of interventions but dehumanizes these people.

Continuum of Care and Transition

The mental health system has long been based on a continuum-of-care perspective. This orientation avers that the ideal service system would have various services at varying levels of intensity available to clients who, depending on the severity of their illness or social dysfunction, would then receive the appropriate level of service. In this pure version, continuum of care may be a useful conception.

Unfortunately, this perspective has been used in ways that have been destructive to clients. The first way has been to view the continuum as the logical progression that *all* people with severe mental illness *must* go through. For example, a person who wants to live in his or her own apartment must first demonstrate success in living in a group home. A person who wants to work as an accountant must first complete vocational testing, prevocational skill classes, a job (janitorial or clerical) at the mental health center, etc.

> **Absurd but True:** A young man with severe mental illness was enrolled in two university classes and had a part-time job. The mental health center staff was concerned that this level of activity would prevent the person's participation in the partial hospital program and sought to convince (it bordered on coercion) the person to drop either the classes or the job. After many discussions, the case manager got the staff to say that the partial hospital activity that was most important that the client had not completed was "How to Get a Volunteer Position" class.

Transitions are difficult for all people: moving, divorce or dissolution of a relationship, someone dying, a new job, going from school to work, homemaker to outside work, childless to having children, etc. Even those transitions that are eagerly awaited and exciting have elements of anxiety, adjustment, and stress. Other transitions are painful and fearful. Despite the difficulty of transitions, the mental health system has increased the number of transitions that a person needs to traverse. These increase stress, can exacerbate symptoms, and actually lead to deterioration. For many clients, they never seem to be able to complete all the "necessary" steps after languishing in one status or recycling through repeated attempts.

A second consequence of the continuum-of-care and transition perspective is that limited funds are often allocated to the most intense level of services. Psychiatric hospitals still consume well over 50% of all mental health expenditures. Group homes, half-way houses, and nursing homes consume a large portion of limited funds. There are therefore few funds remaining for tenant-based assistance (rent subsidies), case management, or attendant care services that would allow people to live in apartments. Funding allocated to the array of prevocational and sheltered employment programs means that the funds are not available for working with employers to create and maintain competitive jobs. The result is that the needed supports for a "normal" life are not present, trapping clients within the mental health system.

Oppression

Deficit orientations toward individuals and environments, labeling, and blaming the victim are part of the social processes that have oppressed people with serious mental illness. To oppress is defined as "to crush, burden, or trample down by or as if by the abuse of power or authority" (Websters, 1976). Bulhan (1985) suggests that "All situations of oppression violate one's space, time, energy, mobility, bonding, and identity" (p. 124). His example:

> The male slave was allowed no physical space which he could call his own. The female slave had even less claim to space than the male slave. Even her body was someone else's property. Commonly ignored is how this expropriation of one's body entailed even more dire consequences for female slaves. The waking hours of the slave were also expropriated for life without his or her consent. The slave labored in the field and in the kitchen for the gain and comfort of the master. The slave's mobility was curbed and he or she was never permitted to venture beyond a designated perimeter without a "pass." The slave's bonding with others, even the natural relation between mother and child, was violated and eroded. The same violation of space, time, energy, mobility, bonding and identity prevails under apartheid, which, in effect, is a modern-day slavery. (p. 124)

Although perhaps not as blatant, the situation of people with severe mental illness has parallels. It is not difficult to view psychiatric hospitals as violating a person's space, time, energy, mobility, bonding, and identity. It is perhaps less obvious but no less true for the person living in the "community." Many people with severe mental illness have little space they can call their own. Those living in congregate facilities (e.g., group homes, residential treatment centers) have little of their own space and even that space is often invaded by other clients and staff. People living in apartments are better off but are still renting. Home ownership is rarely a possibility. Privacy and control of space are virtually impossible in day programs, which still dominate much of community care. The recent data concerning physical and sexual abuse of people with serious mental illness suggest that their lives, like that of the slave, contain histories of even their bodies being treated as someone else's property (Rose, Peabody, & Stratigeas, 1991; Bryer, Nelson, Miller, & Kroe, 1987; Jacobson & Richardson, 1987; Rose, 1991).

Time, like space, has been expropriated. The so-called need of people with serious mental illness for "structure" has led to treatment plans and services that dictate a person's use of time. Day treatment and partial hospital programs, in particular, contain hour-by-hour activities to which clients are assigned. Failure to follow this schedule is often interpreted as "resistance to therapy" by the involved professionals.

A person's energy is devoted, not to creating a better life, but to conforming to the dictates of professional staff and sometimes families. Many people with severe mental illness are stuck in that stage of oppression called "capitulation" by Bulhan (1985), where energy is spent assimilating into the culture.

Mobility is constrained by the rules of congregate facilities (the most obvious being the psychiatric hospital), lack of car ownership, inadequate public transportation, or reliance on mental health worker's transportation. State policies often place barriers to clients moving between service catchment areas or actually restrict choice of service providers.

Relationship, or what Bulhan (1985) calls "bonding," is also restricted. Since most of their time is spent in the company of other clients and staff, people with severe mental illness have their social world constricted. Staff need to keep "professional distance." Many living arrangements are single gender. Apartment roommates of different genders are usually discouraged. Strict rules of conduct in day programs discourage heterosexual displays of affection. The courts combined with the lack of supports provided by human service agencies often lead to children whose parents suffer from mental illness being removed from their custody. It was not too long ago that sterilization was considered a desirable alternative for women with mental illness.

As has been discussed earlier, oppression shapes the self-identity of the person. People internalize the negative images conveyed upon them by their oppressors. They lose their identity as persons, as women or men, as members of a racial or ethnic group, and become the schizophrenic, the client, the "damaged goods." Many develop a "victim complex" whereby all actions and communications are viewed as further assaults or indications of their victim status (Bulhan, 1985). As Estroff (1989) describes:

> Having schizophrenia includes not only the experience of profound cognitive and emotional upheaval, it results in a transformation of self as known inwardly, and of person or identity as known outwardly by others. Schizophrenia is, like epilepsy and hemophilia, an "I am illness," one that is joined with social identity, and perhaps inner self, in language and terms of reference. (p. 189)

One's identity is shaped by this interaction between the individual and the environment, the oppressors and the oppressed, which Crapanzano (1982) calls a "conspiracy of understanding" (p. 192). It is this conspiracy that defines who we are, what categories we belong to, what labels are given and received.

The two worlds, client and professional, created by the oppression is captured by Paul Carling's (1995) reflection of his early mental health experience:

> I found myself spending more and more time with ex-patients, trying to learn what having a psychiatric disability was about from their perspective. Almost immediately, I began hearing about civil rights and involuntary treatment; the learned helplessness that so many services seemed to induce; the violations of personal dignity and choice; and the profound pessimism about ever being accepted as an equal. These issues were very different from typical professional concerns, and in fact there was surprisingly little discussion of them within professional circles. Thus, at an early stage of my career, it became completely obvious that I had to learn about two worlds: the professional world and the client world. These worlds seemed to overlap only rarely, since the power differences between those who inhabited them were so great. In fact, what I seemed to be seeing was a pervasive charade in which clients often framed their responses to professionals—and even their own internal experiences—in the professionals' terms, in order to retain access to the resources that the professionals controlled. (p. 11)

People with severe mental illness continue to be oppressed. Their space, time, energy, mobility, bonding, and identity are constantly being violated and assaulted. Fanon (1968) states that the first thing the oppressed learn is to "stay in your place" (p. 52). Your world is constricted and your personhood is constricted. Do not go beyond the limits. Limit your dreams or relegate them to the hereafter.

USEFUL CONCEPTIONS FOR STRENGTHS-BASED PRACTICE

In the first part of this chapter, the social and professional processes that suppress the quality of life and oppress people with serious mental illness were described. We now turn to conceptions that offer a foundation for considering a strengths model as an alternative to the current dominant processes. Figure 1.2 summarizes these useful ideas.

Integration and Normalization

Integration is the "incorporation into society or an organization on the basis of common and equal membership of individuals differing in some group characteristic" (Websters Third New International Dictionary, 1976). Simply, people with severe mental illness should have equal membership or citizenship in the human collective. All people are different. The presence of a mental illness should not exclude such membership. There are four dimensions of "equal membership": resources, options and opportunity, choice, and location.

1. Equal membership requires equal access to societal or environmental resources.
2. Equal membership requires equal access to options and opportunities.
3. Equal membership requires the equal power of individuals to choose from the array of options and direct their own lives; they have the same rights as others.
4. Equal membership requires that the "location of life," where people live, work, play, and pray, is the same as where others do so.

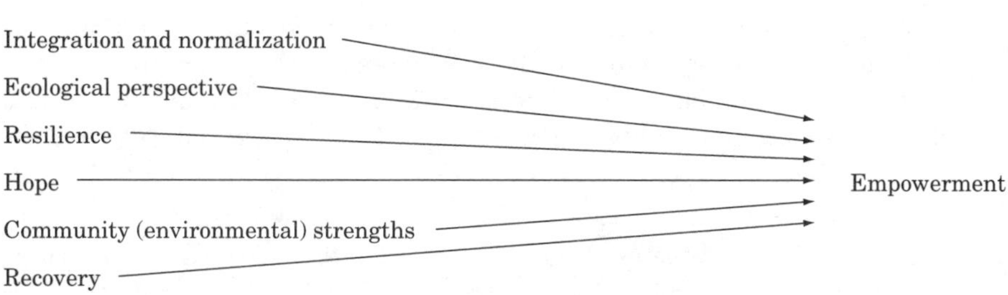

Figure 1.2. Conceptions contributing to empowerment and the strengths model.

It should be clear by now that integration is but a faint hope for the vast majority of people with severe mental illness. They are poor, their options for life are constricted, and their power to choose is constrained by society and professionals. The result is that much of their lives are lived in locations separated from the rest.

Charlene Syx (1995), a consumer who has achieved a high level of recovery, writes:

> For in a good faith effort to help, Archway and other mental health providers ensconce people in a protective bubble, shielding them from their community and ultimately from their future. Had I been encased in that bubble, I can't help but wonder if I, too, would now be trapped, working in the clerical unit or running for clubhouse president. (p. 83)

She urges a new system that replaces segregation with true community integration, that emphasizes change and movement not utilization, that uses resources as a means to access the real thing: "instead of purchasing buildings for people to gather in, we should help people make links in the community. Instead of buying vans, we should provide stipends for use of public transportation. And instead of being everything to everyone, we should help people develop real relationships" (p. 85).

Sullivan (1994b) has argued that higher recovery rates for people suffering from schizophrenia in Third World countries is partly a function of more accessible meaningful social roles (e.g., work, family) and niches provided by the societies. If we truly adhered to client self-determination, integration would be the norm not the exception.

As Patricia Deegan (1996) writes:

> The goal of recovery is not to get mainstreamed. We don't want to be mainstreamed. We say let the mainstream become a wide stream that has room for all of us and leaves no one stranded. (p. 92)

ECOLOGICAL PERSPECTIVE[2]

Ecology is the biological science that studies the relationship between organisms and their environment (Grinnell, 1917; Elton, 1927). Carel Germain (1991) used ecology as a metaphor to better understand the ways "people and environments influence, change, and sometimes shape each other" (p. 16).

Biologists define an "ecological niche" as "the environmental habitat of a population or species, including the resources it utilizes and its association with other organisms" (Strickberger, 1990, p. 518). By this definition, a niche exists as something in the environment. Its description requires de-

---

2. Much of this section is taken from James Taylor (1997), Niches and practice: Extending the ecological perspective. In D. Saleebey (Ed.), *The Strengths Perspective in Social Work Practice,* 2nd Ed. New York: Longman.

tails about the place and conditions where the species is found, the resources that allow a species population to maintain itself over time, and the relationships of that species with other species.

This biological definition needs revision if we are to describe niches in human social systems. One biological species inhabits, at most, a few niches over a lifetime, but we want a concept that allows us to describe an infinite variety of social niches filled by a single species, *Homo sapiens*. Unlike an ecosystem, a social system contains symbols and meanings and social forms. For these and other reasons, the biologist's "ecological niche" at best provides a framework, an analogue, for the concept needed by the helping professions.

The idea of "species" is central to the notion of ecological niche. Species inhabit a niche. Is there anything equivalent to "species" for "social niches"? In talking about niches in the social world it seems natural to refer to different categories of persons. Instead of bay-breasted warblers and myrtle warblers, we have niches filled by "welfare mothers" and "welders" and "college professors"—all with their own environmental habitats and their typical resources. Thus by analogy, we replace "species" with "social categories." "Species" of persons are commonly found in association with other categories of persons: students with teachers, physicians with patients, pimps with prostitutes, politicians with lobbyists, etc. Such associations help define the niche.

The idea of "habitat" includes the "place and conditions in which an organism normally lives" (Strickberger, 1990). Places are easily described: they include residences, stores, shopping malls, saloons, restaurants, etc. The term "community" captures some of this, as does the idea of "settings" in Roger Barker's (1968) ecological psychology.

The idea of "resource" is a bit more complicated. For an animal, a "resource" may be an optimal temperature range, the presence (or absence) of water, the availability of food or prey, the presence of soil suited for burrowing—the list can be long, but it generally will refer to tangible things. For humans, tangible resources are mainly acquired by money or barter, so for our culture and time we include "money" and access to sources of money (jobs, transfer payments, investments, etc.) as resources, and this has no analogue in the animal kingdom.

Other resources are also symbolic, since human beings are social and information-using animals, and they need such social and symbolic things as intimacy, specialized knowledge, a sense of direction and structure in life, conviviality, consensus on social reality, and reciprocal ties of mutual aid. These aspects of the human niche have no parallel in biological ecology.

Kelly and associates (Trickett, Kelly, & Todd, 1972; Mills & Kelly 1972) have suggested three principles of a human ecology model: First is the principle of interdependence whereby a change in one part of the ecosystem in turn alters the relationship among other elements. This suggests that interventions need not be limited to the individual level of analysis but, rather, efforts to change can be contemplated at family, small group, community or institutional levels.

Second is the principle of cycling resources, which refers to the distribution of resources within an ecosystem. This principle implies that intervention needs to include identification of resources and strengths and their redistribution on behalf of a client or client group.

Third is the principle of adaptation where environments and people change to accommodate each other. It places emphasis on different environments requiring different adaptive skills or behaviors than other environments. Intervention, therefore, can profitably be focused on "helping the client cope" (the dominant current strategy) or to find or create niches in which a client's current repertoire of skills, talents, and behavior are already valued by a particular environment.

In the next chapter, the application of this ecological perspective to the strengths model will be described (see section on "Niche").

Resilience

There is an increasing body of literature contradicting the dominant beliefs of developmental theories, the deficit orientations, and victim blaming. It is based on research that shows that most people (mainly children) who grew up under the most horrifying conditions have managed to become successful. This includes studies of children who were raised in harsh and punitive institutions (Goldstein, 1992), children of alcoholics (Wolin & Wolin, 1993), children who were abused (Kaufman & Zigler, 1987), children in poverty defined as "at risk" (Werner & Smith, 1982, 1992), and children with parents suffering from schizophrenia (Bleuler, 1978). The recent Vermont longitudinal research on people with severe mental illness indicates that most became woven into the fabric of community life (Harding, Brooks et al, 1987a, b; Harding, Zubin & Strauss, 1987). The evidence is that these people developed into fine human beings who worked well, played well, and loved well and that many thrived.

Wolin and Wolin (1993) identified seven resiliencies: insight, independence, relationships, initiative, creativity, humor, and morality. They indicate that it is these seven that develop from adversity and allow and explain a person's ability to overcome. Of particular importance to intervention is the relationship. As the authors describe:

> Relationships are intimate and fulfilling ties to other people. Proof that you can love and be loved, relationships are a direct compensation for the affirmation that troubled families deny their children. Early on, resilient children search out love by connecting or attracting the attention of available adults. Though the pleasures of connections are fleeting and often less than ideal, these early contacts seem enough to give resilient survivors a sense of their own appeal. Infused with confidence, they later branch out into active recruiting—enlisting a friend, neighbor, teacher, policeman, or minister as a parent substitute. Over time, recruiting rounds out to attaching, an ability to form and to keep mutually gratifying relationships. Attaching involves a balanced give

and take and a mature regard for the well-being of others as well as oneself. (p. 111)

Our professional relationships need to convey a sense of caring and respect. We need to act as "mirrors" reflecting our client's sense of worth, strengths, capacities, and attraction.

This literature suggests that most, if not all, humans have a capacity for overcoming the harshest of experiences and most actually do. For intervention, we must replace the imagery of deficits and pathology with the imagery of strengths and resilience. Assessment must include the uncovering and description of these for each individual. Given the importance of at least one key relationship, professionals and other helpers should seek to create and nurture such relationships between clients and others and between client and professional.

Hope

Snyder (1994) defines hope as "the sum of the mental willpower and waypower that you have for your goals" (p. 5). "Goals are the objects, experiences or outcomes that we imagine and desire in our minds . . . it is something we want to obtain or attain" (p. 5). "Mental willpower is the mental energy . . . the reservoir of determination and commitment that we can call on to help move us in the direction of the goal . . . it is made up of thoughts such as I can, I'll try, I'm ready to do this, and I've got what it takes" (p. 6). "Waypower reflects the mental plans or roadmaps that guide hopeful thought . . . a mental capacity we can call on to find one or more effective ways to reach our goals" (p. 8). In short, a hopeful person has goals, the desire or confidence, and the plan for achieving that goal. In contrast, the more prevalent experience of people with serious mental illness is described by Patricia Deegan (1996):

> Giving up was not a problem. It was a solution because it protected me from wanting anything: If I didn't want anything, then it couldn't be taken away. If I didn't try, then I wouldn't have to undergo another failure. If I didn't care, then nothing could hurt me again. My heart became hardened. (p. 93)

The research suggests that high-hope persons have "a greater number of goals, have more difficult goals, have more success at achieving their goals, have greater happiness and less distress, have superior coping skills, recover better from physical injury, and report less burnout at work . . . and this is true even when controlling for intelligence, optimism and other motives and emotions" (Snyder, 1994, p. 24).

Since hope seems to have much to do with achievement, its relevance for a strengths perspective and intervention is important. Intervention needs to be goal-oriented and help provided to set goals. Intervention should help build a person's mental willpower through confidence-building interactions and activities. Intervention should assist clients in developing step-by-step plans for achieving their goals.

Community (Environmental) Strengths

In contrast to the "deficit of the environment" perspective described earlier, a community of environmental strengths orientation is emerging. Most of the writing has derived from work with low-income and/or minority neighborhoods. Yet the precepts are relevant to the viewing of any geographic entity that we may term "community." As Kretzmann and McKnight (1993) state: ". . . wherever there are effective community development efforts, those efforts are based upon an understanding, or map, of the communities' assets, capabilities, and abilities" (p. 5).

The first precept is that each community possesses a unique configuration of capacities, skills, and assets. These strengths are embodied in the individuals, families or households, networks, and associations and institutions that comprise that community. The second precept is that all communities, no matter how poor or rich, how rural or urban, how racially or ethnically diverse, how old or young, have a wealth of strengths. The third precept is that once identified, these community strengths can be mobilized to build better life for our clients.

Rather than seeing the community as toxic or too demanding for people with severe mental illness, the environmental strengths position argues that each community is almost unlimited in the resources and opportunities available (Sullivan, 1992). In another article, Sullivan (1989) provides an example:

> Many urban areas hire recreational therapists to develop recreation programs and provide clients with a variety of opportunities to participate in active leisure-time activities. While recreation therapists clearly serve a valuable function in these programs, most rural programs do not have the luxury of hiring this type of staff person. Yet nearly every community has a gymnasium. In many small communities one can find exercise classes, and even aerobic instruction. Softball teams and leagues can be found everywhere. We must resist ideas that clients must engage in segregated activities. While the client may need help in making initial contacts and periodic support throughout the experience of engaging in community recreational activities, success is possible. Key personnel are also available to provide support for clients. High schools employ physical education instructors. Local athletes may be willing to help. All of these resources can be used to develop a good recreation program. (p. 22)

By placing a premium on the identification and use of community assets, the resources available to people with mental illness dramatically expands. At the same time, true community integration is fostered. Our attempts to "fix" individuals and communities have a dismal record. Perhaps, instead of fixing, we devoted ourselves to the exacerbation of strengths of individuals and communities. The questions and interventions become altered: "What resources exist and how can they be bolstered?" rather than "What is the deficit to fixed?"

First-Person Accounts of Recovery

The last 15 years have witnessed a dramatic increase in published first-person accounts of the experience of mental illness and recovery. Recovery refers to "a deeply personal, unique process of changing one's attitudes, values, feelings, goals, skills and/or roles. It is a way of living a satisfying, hopeful, and contributing life even with limitations caused by illness" (Anthony, 1994, pp. 559–60). Recovery does not mean that symptoms disappear but, rather, that despite the illness's symptoms life can go on. While the experience of mental illness and recovery is unique to each person, certain common elements can be discerned from the first-person accounts.

One critical element to recovery is that point when the person recognizes that they are afflicted with a mental illness and can perceive of it as only one part of them. It is that time when the "I am illness" (Estroff, 1989) becomes the "I have illness."

> The key for me to do this, I think, was to learn for the first time what schizophrenia was and what its different symptoms were; to develop a vocabulary to restructure the shattered jigsaw puzzle of my life. (Stanley, 1992, p. 25)

> In spite of biochemical disorders, consumers are still complete human beings, with emotional, psychological, social, intellectual, sexual and spiritual needs. All these characteristics must be addressed for real recovery to be possible. (Scheie-Lurie, 1992, p. 36)

> To my amazement, I discovered that I did have some strengths on which to build my future. (Leete, 1993, p. 121)

It seems that there is a correspondence between the separation of the illness and self, and increased attention to managing the illness (Strauss, 1989). Sullivan (1994a) reports that medication was viewed by 72% of the recovering consumers as critical to that recovery, and 63% noted that increased ability to self-monitor symptoms and make necessary adjustments was helpful.

A second theme is the need for personal control. The experience of mental illness is one of impotence in the face of the illness, its symptoms, and the social sequelae. People with mental illness feel "alienated and rejected, vulnerable and powerless, discounted and defeated" (Leete, 1993, p. 125).

> Recovery appears to be related to having control over one's life, having choices. . . . In contrast, involuntary treatment appears to leave individuals feeling hopeless, helpless, and believing they will never recover. (Blanch & Parrish, 1993)

> I needed to be in charge of my own changes. . . . I live alone and I have chosen pictures and colors and little touches that make it feel like my very own good, safe place. I work part time in a floral shop and I have acquired a relatively new car. I do my own laundry. Food is there if I cook it, and the house is as clean as I make it. I'm my own boss in other people's eyes. (Reilly, 1992, p. 20)

> Ultimately it is the consumer alone who decides what is helpful in over-coming the tremendous suffering of mental illness. (Scheie-Lurie, 1992, p. 36)

> To overcome these negative feelings and our resulting sense of impo-tence, empowerment is crucial, giving us the strength and confidence to individually and collectively make choices and control our own lives. . . . I find my vulnerability to stress, anxiety, and accompanying symptoms decreases as I gain more control over my own life. (Leete, 1989, p. 198)

As Anthony (1994) states: "Critical to recovery is regaining the belief that there are options from which one can choose—a belief perhaps even more important to recovery than the particular option one initially chooses" (p. 565).

A third element in the recovery matrix is hope. Pat Deegan's (1988) poignant reflections of her recovery places hope at its core. As she writes:

> When one lives without hope, (when one has given up), the willingness to "do" is paralyzed as well. (p. 13)

> Hope is crucial to recovery, for our despair disables us a more than our disease ever could. (Leete, 1993, p. 122)

> My mood changed—I was happy and hopeful once again. (Fergeson, 1992, p. 29)

> I find myself being a role model for other clients and am only a bit un-comfortable with this. For the first time, I begin to feel real hope. (Grim-mer, 1992, p. 28)

> Success will never be realized if it cannot be imagined. (Leete, 1993, p. 126)

A fourth critical ingredient seems to be purpose. The experience of men-tal illness is often one of: "I have nothing to live for, no drive but to just exist . . . Sometimes I sleep 12 to 14 hours because there's nothing else to do. No zest" (Stanley, 1992, p. 25).

> And so I took my dreams off the backburner and claimed as my personal goals, understanding, writing and doing something to help others who were afflicted. Doing so was neither grandiose or magnanimous. It was survival. (Keil, 1992, p. 6)

> One short term goal was to further myself educationally, and I took buses to get to college. (Reilly, 1992, p. 20)

> You can live through any kind of a situation, if you find a reason for liv-ing through it. We survivors were daily living through impossible situa-tions precisely by finding reasons for living. (Fergerson, 1992, p. 30)

> With Mark's death, I was snapped into a new awareness that resulted in my not only caring about others, but having a cause worth fighting for. (Risser, 1992, p. 39)

A fifth theme of recovery seems to be some early sense of achievement or assuming some responsible role. The experience of mental illness is often one of "I was a failure" (Fergeson, 1992, p. 29).

> I learned to find pleasure in the daily-ness of life. I looked with pride on the way my children were growing. I was working part-time, and I had learned so very much about the unexpected. (Keil, 1992, p. 6)

> It seems that I'm now in the role of helper and enabler—not client. (Glater, 1992, p. 22)

Another person who once described herself in mental illness or client terms wrote:

> I'm Donna Ferguson, 38 years old, and, for being betwixt and between emotional tides, I usually do very well. I'm currently going to school for an A.S. in Word Processing (I have an A.A. in Psychology, a Certificate as a Paraprofessional in Social Work, and am a Certified Respiratory Therapy Technician). I've worked about 8 years, and been on Social Security Disability before I worked and when I had to stop due to my illness. I go to school, see my friends, enjoy my job, and want to write a book, a personal account of living with Borderline Personality Disorder. I'm usually happy. (Fergeson, 1992, p. 30)

The most common types of achievement included in first-person accounts are helping others (often fellow consumers), work on vocational involvement, and hobbies or arts. Work, in particular, is commonly identified by consumers as both a goal and a force in recovery (Arns & Linney, 1993; Sullivan, 1994a).

A sixth element in recovery is the presence of (at least) one person. Although recovery is highly personal, most first-person accounts point to the presence of a friend, a professional, a family, a teacher, self-help groups, or at times the staff of a particular program that helps trigger and sustain the recovery process. This element parallels one of the seven resiliences, relationship, identified by Wolin and Wolin (1993). The experience of mental illness is one of "I was frightened and alone" (Glater, 1992, p. 22).

> Residents were accepted and always treated with respect, and thereby we clients gained in self-respect. (Leete, 1993, p. 120)

> . . . My expectations were of basket weaving and sheltered workshops. I'd had that dull stuff foisted on me before...a vocational counselor saw my potential and suggested that I look into music therapy as a career. (Glater, 1992, p. 22)

> At critical turns along the road, I was blessed with helpers (professional and others) who encouraged me to trust my own ability to make valid choices for my life and recovery. (Scheie-Lurie, 1992, p. 36)

> It is clear to me now that a supportive, accepting, and loving relationship with others—my interpersonal environment—has been the key element in my recovery from this major mental illness. (Leete, 1993, p. 114)

It is difficult to find a first-person account that does not attribute relationships as a critical ingredient to recovery (Sullivan, 1994a; Deegan, 1988;
Leete, 1988; Hatfield & Lefley, 1993). The characteristics of those relationships will be discussed in chapter 3.

The tapestry of recovery, according to people with severe mental illness
themselves, is comprised of a perception of the illness as only a part of them,
personal control, hope, purpose, achievement, and the presence of at least
one caring person who in part can mirror back to the afflicted person the
well-part of them.

· Empowerment

The last 20 years have witnessed considerable scholarly and practice activity focused on empowerment as a central construct of mental health and
social work. The concept is discussed both as a process and as an end or
goal or state. In the strengths model, empowerment is used as a state that
people aspire to and that clients and professionals collaborate in achieving.
The strengths model, itself, is a set of methods and perspectives that embodies the process. Therefore, empowerment will be described in terms of
a desired state. Despite the diversity of conceptions, theory, and methods,
options and power seem to be two prevalent elements. Each of these elements has an objective reality and a subjective reality that influence empowerment. The interplay of elements and the two realities help define the
components of empowerment:

	Objective Reality	**Subjective Reality**
Options	Choices or options	Perception of choices
Power	Authority	Confidence

To "be empowered," a person or group requires an environment that
provides options and ascribes authority to the person to choose. One can
hypothesize that the more options actually available to a person, the greater
the contribution to that person's empowerment. Authority refers to the person's actual power to select from the options. For example, many people
with severe mental illness do not have the authority to decide when they
will be discharged from the hospital or group home or nursing home. That
power has been granted to mental health personnel.

Empowerment is also affected by the subjective reality of the person. A
person could have many options, but their perception of the options is much
more limited. For example, a client who likes to dance may have a score of
options available but is aware of only one or two options. Most people are

not aware of all the options available. For people with severe mental illness whose lives have been sheltered and segregated, a limited view of options is even more pronounced.

Power is part authority and part confidence or perception of authority. A person can have the formal authority to make a choice or decision but may perceive they do not have that authority or they do not have the confidence to select. For example, in most mental health systems the client has the authority to decide where they will live and what services they will receive. The perception or subjective reality of many clients, however, is that the authority is vested in mental health personnel. Sometimes people lack the confidence to choose or to act on the options available. In these situations, a client may have the authority to choose and act (e.g., for apply and acquire a job) but, lacking in confidence, decides that is not an option and settles for a sheltered job at the mental health center.

The last element of empowerment is action. Most treatises on empowerment suggest that action by the person is indispensable. As Kieffer (1984) states, "empowerment is not a commodity to be acquired, but a transforming process constructed through action" (p. 27). As will be seen in the remainder of the book, the strengths model is designed to increase each of these components: choices or options, authority, perception of choices, and confidence, and facilitate action.

CHAPTER 2

A Beginning Theory
of Strengths

This chapter presents a formulation of the theory of strengths and reviews the research results on the model. This chapter acts as the backdrop to the practice methods.

The strengths model posits that all people have goals, talents, and confidence. That all environments contain resources, people, and opportunities. But that our usual perceptions of these are limited, modest, dysfunctional, barrier ridden, pathology ridden, and pale in comparison to the deficits. Both can be "objectively" true.

Theory is perceptual. By its very nature, theory seeks to explain a phenomenon by identifying the elements that contribute to the phenomenon and the interrelationship of these components parts. Theory, therefore, seeks to exclude parts of life that are judged to be of no importance or lesser importance. It's a perspective. A theory is at best a "slice of life" rather than life.

The strengths model then is about providing a new perception. It allows us to see possibilities rather than problems, options rather than constraints, wellness rather than sickness. And once seen, achievement can occur. As long as we stay in the muck and mire of deficits, we cannot achieve. Until we throw off the yoke of the "conspiracy of understanding" centered on deficits, we cannot effectively help. The stories of recovery powerfully resound with this kind of turning point.

A THEORY OF STRENGTHS

Desired Outcome

The theory of strengths is a practice theory that seeks to define those factors affecting a person's life and the methods by which these can be altered.

The theory must therefore begin at defining the relevant elements of a person's life; the desired outcomes (see Figure 2.1).

At the core, the desired outcomes are the achievements of clients based on the goals they set for themselves. While these are highly individualized, the goals do seem to group themselves into a decent place to live, employment and/or opportunity to contribute, education, and friends and recreation outlets. In other words, people with severe mental illness desire the same things that non-afflicted people want. In addition, because they are afflicted, they desire a lessening of their painful symptomatology and avoidance of psychiatric hospitalization. Like other people, they want choices and the power to decide among those options. Together, these outcomes comprise the quality of one's life.

These outcomes are achievement or growth oriented. Clients do not speak often of adaptation, coping, or compliance as desired outcomes. Neither do they often conceive of their aspirations as learning skills unless it concerns a specific technical skill affiliated with a particular job or task. Rather, they speak of jobs, degrees, friends, apartments, and fun. Skills may be an interim goal, but are rarely seen as an outcome in itself.

For the purposes of building a theory of strengths, reduced symptomatology poses some unique dilemmas. First person accounts of recovery suggest the following:

1. The nature of the illness is such that total elimination of symptoms is rarely possible.
2. People who are recovering experience a similar roller-coaster pattern of symptom exacerbation but the frequency, duration, and severity of the episodes is often reduced.
3. People who are symptomatic can often still work, play, and live.

Helping clients (who desire it) live healthy lives, identifying the proper medication regimen, and helping clients identify early warning signs of symptom exacerbation and strategies to attenuate their development are all worthwhile activities. Perhaps, the single most influential focus on reducing the pain of symptoms is to help people build a life that is satisfying and fulfilling.

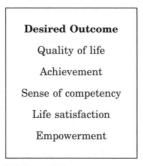

Desired Outcome

Quality of life

Achievement

Sense of competency

Life satisfaction

Empowerment

Figure 2.1.

NICHES

*Proposition: The quality of niches people inhabit determines
their achievement and quality of life.*

The quality of life, achievements, and the outcomes of a person's life
are determined by the qualities of the niches within which a person lives.
A niche is "the environmental habitat of a person or category of persons"
(Taylor, 1997). People live in a variety of habitats corresponding to different life domains: home or living arrangement, work, education, recreation,
spiritual, etc. (see Figure 2.2). Taylor (1997) goes on to describe the basic
feature of these habitats:

> The habitat conditions include the kinds of communities, settings, and
> domiciles in which these persons are usually found, the sources and lev-
> els of income available to these persons, the social resources and sup-
> ports typically used by those persons, and the other categories of people
> commonly found in association with those persons.

The concept of niche can be a unifying element in case management practice because it attends to both individual and environmental factors. As
Brower (1988) asserts, "It makes no sense to think of individuals separate
from their immediate environments, or to think of environments separate
from the individuals who inhabit them" (p. 413).

Figure 2.2.

There are two types of niches at the extreme: entrapping niches and enabling niches. Most niches, however, tend to lie somewhere between these two extremes and contain elements of both. Entrapping niches can be seen as having the following characteristics:[1]

- Entrapping niches are highly stigmatized; people caught in them are commonly treated as outcasts.

- People caught in an entrapping niche tend to "turn to their own kind" for association, so that their social world becomes restricted and limited.

- People caught in an entrapping niche are totally defined by their social category. The possibility that they may have aspirations and attributes apart from their category is not ordinarily considered. To outsiders, the person is "just" a bag lady, a junky, an ex-con, a schizophrenic . . . and nothing else.

- In the entrapping niche there are no graduations of reward and status. One cannot be certified as a Master Bag Lady, or work up to the position of Head Parolee. Thus there are few expectations of personal progress within such niches.

- In the entrapping niche there are few incentives to set realistic longer term goals, or to work toward such goals.

- In the entrapping niche there is little reality feedback; i.e., there are few natural processes which lead people to recognize and correct their own unrealistic perceptions or interpretations.

- In the entrapping niche there is little chance to learn the skills and expectations which would facilitate escape. Especially this is so when the entrapping niche is free from the usual norms of work and self discipline, and no demands arise for clear structuring of time and effort.

- In the entrapping niche economic resources are sparse. This in itself may lead to unproductive stress, and may cause some people to seek reinstitutionalization for economic reasons.

Entrapping niches are often reserved for those at the margins of social life, like people with mental illness. Once in such niches, the availability of resources or mechanisms for escape are scarce. In fact, social, political, and professional processes are in place which make escape virtually impossible.

"The net result is social isolation defined in this context as the lack of contact or of sustained interaction with individuals and institutions that represent mainstream society" (Wilson, 1987, p. 60). Wilson goes on to say that social isolation, not other factors, is the major determinant of unemployment and underemployment. The entrapped niche does not easily allow its walls to be penetrated.

---

1. The description of entrapping and enabling niches is from James Taylor (1997), Niches and Practice: Extending the Ecological Perspective. In D. Saleebey (Ed.), *The Strengths Perspective in Social Work Practice,* 2nd Ed. New York: Longman.

In contrast, enabling niches are more likely to produce the life benefits described earlier. Enabling niches have the following characteristics:

- People in enabling niches are not stigmatized, not treated as outcasts.
- People in enabling niches will tend to "turn to their own kind" for association, support, and self-validation. But often the niche gives them access to others who bring a different perspective, so that their social world becomes less restricted.
- People in enabling niches are not totally defined by their social category; they are accepted as having valid aspirations and attributes apart from their category. The person is not "just" a bag lady, a junky, an ex-con, a schizophrenic.
- In the enabling niche there are many incentives to set realistic longer term goals for oneself, and to work toward such goals.
- In the enabling niche there is good reality feedback; i.e., there are many natural processes that lead people to recognize and correct unrealistic perceptions or interpretations.
- The enabling niche provides opportunities to learn the skills and expectations that would aid movements to other niches. Especially is this so when the enabling niche pushes toward reasonable work habits and reasonable self-discipline, and expects that the use of time be clearly structured.
- In the enabling niche economic resources are adequate, and competence and quality are rewarded. This reduces economic stress, and creates strong motives for avoiding institutionalization.

The strengths model posits that creating enabling niches should be the major focus of work.

There is good reason to believe that the niches available to people with mental illness influence the recovery process and their quality of life. In fact, Sullivan (1994b) has argued that higher recovery rates for people with serious mental illness in developing nations is attributable to better access to enabling niches such as work. Sullivan (1994b) attempted to categorize niches for people with mental illness based on enabling or entrapping, and natural or created (Table 2.1). In the strengths model, most of the work occurs in the two enabling niche cells.

Enabling niches closely correspond to concepts such as normalization and community integration. Each of these concepts suggests that marginalized people would be "better off" to the degree to which they can be woven into the fabric of normal everyday life. As can be seen by Sullivan's matrix however, many of our attempts to assist people with serious mental illness have reinforced their segregation through sheltered workshops, group residences, and congregate day programs.

The concept of niches forces us to think beyond "social location" to "social relations" (Rose & Black, 1985). The history of mental health has been based on simplistic notions of "community" and "integration." The radical

TABLE 2.1
Natural and Created Niches

	Natural	Created
Entrapping Niche	Natural exclusionary processes	Institutionalization
	Stigma	Psychiatric hospitalization
	Labeling	Sheltered workshops
	Homelessness	Group/board and care homes
	Poverty	Partial hospitalization/day treatment
	Unemployment	
Enabling Niche	Natural inclusionary processes	Normalization
	Work opportunities	Supported employment
	Recreation opportunities	Supported housing
	Family involvement	Supported education
	Affiliation with community	Consumer programming self-help

downsizing of state psychiatric hospitals beginning in the mid-1950s was replaced by people moving to nursing homes or being discharged to urban ghettos. As Talbott (1979) stated: "The chronic mentally ill patient [has] had his locus of living and care transferred from a single lousy institution to multiple wretched ones" (p. 622). They lived in inadequate housing, did not work, and interacted with people similarly situated. They moved from one location to another; from one entrapping niche to another. Their quality of life, in many respects, was no better and perhaps worse than they had known in the hospital. Yet, they were said to be living in the "community."

There are many people with serious mental illness who live with others so afflicted, spend their days in day treatment programs, recreate with other clients, and if they work, do so in a sheltered enclave. Their lives are dominated by other clients and mental health professionals. They are in the community (social location) but still not of the community (social relations). In only the most nominal sense can they be thought of as achieving "community integration." This segregation reinforces stigma and discrimination and the devaluing of people with serious mental illness.

Entrapping niches created by society to care for people with severe mental illness reduce access to resources, valued social roles, and status and rewards. They tend to reduce individual choice and self-care and increase feelings of dependency (Rappaport, 1985). These created niches are based on compensating for the deficits, pathologies, and problems of people with severe mental illness. This then becomes a part of a person's self-definition. They themselves are their disease or problem rather than the disease being only one (small) part of them. Professionals often treat the person as a diagnosis. Failure to treat individuals as human beings with mutual respect has frequently resulted in the deterioration of their social behavior. Either because of this or in addition to this, programs like partial hospitalization/day treatment and sheltered workshops have failed to produce improved levels of client outcomes.

The factors that contribute to the quality of a person's niches emanate from two sources: the individual and the environment. We now turn to these factors.

INDIVIDUAL STRENGTH: ASPIRATIONS

Proposition: People who are successful in living have goals and dreams.

The strengths theory places a premium on human beings as "purposeful organisms." People have desires, goals, ambitions, hopes, and dreams. We have a driving motivation to be competent and to influence our world (White, 1959); we seek to achieve (McClelen, Atkinson, Clark, & Lowell, 1953). "Goals are any objects, experiences, or outcomes that we imagine and desire in our minds" (Snyder, 1994, p. 5). People who are successful in living, first and foremost, have goals of some consequence (see Figure 2.3).

For people with serious mental illness, their lives since the onset of their illness have been marked by pain and suffering, disappointment and

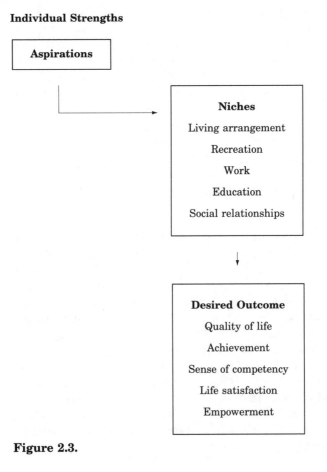

Individual Strengths

Aspirations

Niches

Living arrangement

Recreation

Work

Education

Social relationships

Desired Outcome

Quality of life

Achievement

Sense of competency

Life satisfaction

Empowerment

Figure 2.3.

failure, and overwhelming messages of what they cannot do. As with other oppressed people, their aspirations often are few, and non-specific. So many have lost their dreams or have diminished them to the most modest.

Professional helping often further restrains goal setting and achievement. For example, most professional helping methods begin with an exploration and definition of the client's problem (Cowger, 1992; Weick et al., 1989). The professional seeks to help the client solve that problem. Problems solved can be viewed as achievements but too often solving problems at best returns a person to their previous state of equilibrium. Social work in particular has emphasized "coping" which is defined as "to maintain a contest on even terms; to find necessary expedients to overcome problems" (*Webster's Third New International Dictionary*, 1976).

The outcomes of concern in the strengths model are quality of life, life satisfaction, achievement, etc. Solving problems is therefore seen as occasionally necessary steps toward these ends but not sufficient. Successful resolution of a problem is not an end in itself. The strengths model is more concerned with achievement than with solving problems; with thriving more than just surviving; with dreaming and hoping not just coping, with triumph not just trauma. For this to happen, people need goals, dreams, and aspirations.

INDIVIDUAL STRENGTH: COMPETENCIES

Proposition: People who are successful in living use their strengths to attain their aspirations.

Competencies include skills, abilities, aptitudes, proficiencies, knowledge, faculties, and talents (see Figure 2.4). "Continuing growth occurs through the recognition and development of strengths" (Weick et al., 1989, p. 353).

All people possess a wide range of talents, abilities, capacities, skills, resources, and aspirations. No matter how little or how much may be expressed at one time, a belief in human potential is tied to the notion that people have untapped, undetermined reservoirs of mental, physical, emotional, social, and spiritual abilities that can be expressed. The presence of this capacity for continued growth and heightened well-being means that people must be accorded the respect that this power deserves. This capacity acknowledges both the being and the becoming aspects of life.

In the midst of a recognition of capacity for growth is the simultaneous recognition that no person perfectly expresses this capacity on all or even most of the planes of development during his or her lifetime. A few rare individuals may show high levels of artistic, spiritual, or intellectual development, but for most people, the evidence of life shows far more modest results. In a strengths perspective, a conscious choice is made to attend exclusively to those aspects of a person's life that reflect the gains made, however modest they may be judged (Weick et al., 1989, 352–53).

Individual Strengths

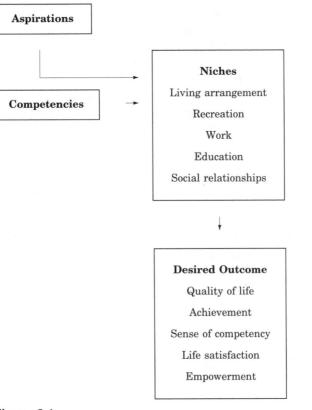

Figure 2.4.

For so many people with serious mental illness, their talents and abilities go unrecognized by themselves, acquaintances, family, and professionals. In fact, almost all helping methods are explicitly focused on uncovering the person's deficits, weaknesses, problems, and pathology. As Rose and Black (1985) have pointed out, many clients have developed their survival skills that are the opposite of the skills needed to achieve. For example, the skills and behaviors that make for a "good" patient or client often fall under the rubric of "compliance." Yet compliant behaviors are rarely associated with achievement or growth which often involve some risks.

One strength of all people is the capacity to determine what is best for them (Weick & Pope, 1988).

> This long-honored social work value recognizes that people have an inner wisdom about what they need and that ultimately, people make choices based on their own best sense of what will meet that need. Those who hold a strengths perspective assume that this inner wisdom can be brought into more conscious use by helping people recognize this capacity and the positive power it can have in their lives. (Weick et al., 1989, p. 353)

While most of our society, lay and professional, is mired in a deficit or problem orientation, there are interesting developments that further support a strengths orientation. The most notable is the work of Wolin and Wolin (1993) on resiliency and the development of the Challenge Model. They have found that the vast majority of children who grow up in abusive, troubled, and neglecting families not only survive but many thrive. These findings are echoed by the work of Goldstein (1992) and Werner and Smith (1982, 1992).

The challenge model disputes the assumption that only damage comes from a troubled family life which inevitably leads one to lifelong suffering. The Challenge Model validates the pain that occurs from a troubled childhood, while recognizing that resiliencies develop even against all odds. This framework for helping understands that trauma and triumph are forces that interplay with each other in managing an adverse childhood.

INDIVIDUAL STRENGTH: CONFIDENCE

Proposition: People who are successful in living have the confidence to take the next step toward their goal.

Related to the concept of confidence are power, influence, belief in oneself, and self-efficacy. A person's behavior is selected based on the desired end (goal) and abilities (competencies) but this is mediated by a person's perception of successfully behaving. There are many things people want to do and can do, but do not do because they lack the confidence (see Figure 2.5).

Confidence is of two levels. At the first level, confidence refers to the perceived ability of oneself to perform a certain task or set of behaviors. Can I cook lasagna? Can I interview for that job? This level is situation and task specific. A person can be confident in buying groceries but fearful of asking for a date. At a second level, confidence is a generalized sense of oneself that each person brings to different situations. Some people are just more confident when approaching any task while others perceive themselves as being generally inept. This second level has some similarity to "learned helplessness" (Peterson, Maier, & Seligman, 1993).

While it is wrong and dangerous to stereotype people with severe mental illness, two characteristics seem pervasive: they are poor and they are scared. Fear often dominates their lives. The niches they have been relegated to have not allowed them to achieve. Attribution of these "failures" often is directed to personal deficiencies of generalized and enduring nature: "I'm weak," "I'm sick," etc. Anxiety, dependency, depression, futility, and apathy result.

Professional services tend to reinforce these feelings of inadequacy. The focus is on what is wrong with a person and what they "have to" or "should" do differently. This blaming the victim (Ryan, 1971) message finds easy acceptance by people who already lack confidence and belief in one's self. Even if this were not true, just the coming for help is often perceived as admitting to the person's failure (Rappaport, 1985).

Individual Strengths

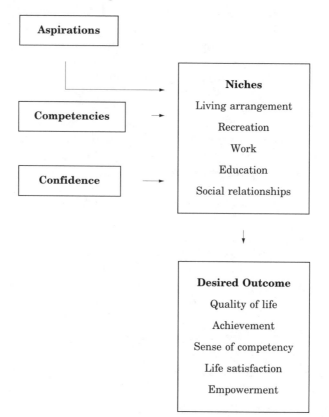

Figure 2.5.

INTERACTION OF THE ELEMENTS OF INDIVIDUAL STRENGTHS

Proposition: At any one point in time, people who are
successful in living have at least one goal, one relevant talent,
and confidence to take the next step.

The quality of a niche is determined by individual and environmental elements. Individual elements include aspirations, competencies, and confidence. The individual elements interact with each other. For example, a person with confidence is more likely to set ambitious goals. In contrast, it is difficult if not impossible for a person to dream if they live in fear. If you do not think much of yourself, it's hard to have a dream without that dream becoming a source of disappointment and pain rather than inspiration and energy. Similarly, people who are attuned to their competencies are more likely to set goals and have the confidence to pursue them.

Snyder's (1994) exploration of hope demonstrates other interactions. He defined hope as "the sum of the mental willpower and waypower that you have for your goals" (p. 5). Willpower refers to thoughts such as "I can, I'll try, I'm ready to do this, I've got what it takes" (p. 6). This corresponds to confidence in the strengths theory. Waypower is "the mental plans or roadmaps that guide hopeful thought" (p. 8). In the strengths model, the ability to formulate plans would be one of the competencies. The third part of the definition concerns goals which corresponds nicely to aspirations.

The research on hope suggests that hopeful people set more goals, set more difficult goals, and reach more goals. They also recover better from physical injury, report less burnout at work, and have superior coping skills. Most important, hopeful people report greater happiness and less distress.

People who are successful in living do not necessarily have large quantities of each element but they do have some of each. This can be stated mathematically:

$$\text{Aspiration} \times \text{Competency} \times \text{Confidence} = \text{promise and possibilities}$$

If any element is zero, then the product will be zero; no possibilities.

A case vignette may be illustrative. Sarah is 29 years old and suffers from paranoid schizophrenia. She has been in and out of the state hospital for the last ten years; nine times in the last five years. She wanted a full-time clerical job. Sarah had a work history limited to two attempts to work in fast-food businesses that lasted less than two weeks and a one-week clerical job eight years ago. She has limited typing skills (accurate but slow) and no skills using a computer. She requires quiet and few people around because the noise and activity increase her anxiety. Sarah is persistent. If given a task to do that she wants to do, she will stay with it until completion. In fact, her nickname in the program was "Bulldog." The other dilemma is that, despite a myriad of creative efforts by Sarah and her case manager, she seems incapable of getting out of bed before 11:00 A.M. Using the equation:

Aspiration	×	Competency	×	Confidence
full-time clerical job		accurate typist		willing to apply
		persistence		willing to interview
				willing to start work

With the case manager's assistance, Sarah got a job at the rural public library working from 1:00 P.M. to 9:00 P.M. From 1:00 to 6:00, she worked in the office typing card file entries, filing, doing the mail, etc. When the library closed at 6:00, Sarah shelved books in the library proper. The only people around at that time were the janitorial crew. For three years, Sarah has been working at the library and there has not been a return to the hospital.

It's probably obvious that at least on the surface, Sarah did not have an enormous reservoir of relevant competencies but she had something. Combined with her goal and confidence, it was sufficient for her to achieve; to find an enabling niche.

As can be seen by this example, the niche required certain ingredients from Sarah but also required environmental possibilities. It is to this side of the ledger that we now turn.

ENVIRONMENTAL STRENGTH: RESOURCES

*Proposition: People who are successful in living have access
to the resources needed to achieve their goals.*

Access to desired niches and the quality of those niches are influenced by the environmental resources available to a person (see Figure 2.6). Some resources are needed to make a niche accessible. Public transportation, a car, or carpooling are resources that would allow someone to accept a particular job. The proper clothing would allow others to accept a job. Other environmental resources affect the quality of the niche itself. A television, a cleaning service, or a Monet print could contribute the quality of one's home environment.

Environmental resources are those tangibles and services that the wealthy tend to purchase. Tangibles would include food, clothing, housing, appliances, furniture, a car, compact disc player, etc. Services are viewed as people who do for you what you cannot or prefer not to do for yourself. Examples would include travel agents, baby-sitters, maids, teachers, team organizers, repair people, public transportation, typists, etc.

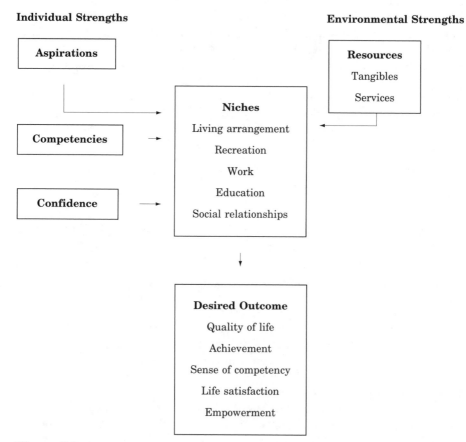

Figure 2.6.

Entrapped niches by definition tend to be resource poor and restrict access to resources outside of the niche. Of the people with severe mental illness who are poor, many are trying to eke out an existence on a $450-a-month Supplemental Security Income check. The services with which they are most familiar are those specialized mental health services.

Yet the environment can also be a rich source of resources. A client worked at a Pizza Hut in a small community. She loved her job and found satisfaction and confidence from working. Her hours were 3:00 to 10:00 P.M. The community she lived in had public transportation (bus) that ran throughout the day but ended at 7:00 P.M. She had a way to get to work but relied on friends and family to pick her up and take her home. After several weeks of this her friends and family were getting tired of this task. She was in jeopardy of losing her job because of lack of transportation at the end of her shift. The consumer elicited help from her case manager. The two of them sat down and brainstormed options and resources. The one that was used: Pizza Hut had an evening delivery service in the community at the end of the shift. The consumer would ride along with the delivery person and then be dropped off by her apartment.

ENVIRONMENTAL STRENGTH: SOCIAL RELATIONS

*Proposition: People who are successful in living have a
meaningful relationship with at least one person.*

Access to and the quality of a person's niches are influenced by the social relations that the person enjoys (see Figure 2.7). Social relations concern people and the benefits that accrue from these relationships. "People" would include family, friends, acquaintances, co-workers, church members, local grocer, etc. "Benefits" would include companionship, emotional support, caring, partnership, sexual relations, recreation, socialization, opportunities to give, etc.

In entrapped niches, social relations are constrained. Typically, a stigmatized group's interaction is dominated by intragroup relations. For many people with serious mental illness, their social contact is dominated by interaction with other clients and staff. While this is obvious in psychiatric hospitals, it is also true for that larger group of "deinstitutionalized" people. For many, their waking hours may be spent in day treatment or a psychosocial clubhouse, and their evenings in a group home or other form of group residence. Those who live in apartments may have another client as a roommate, and may spend evenings closeted in their apartments.

The dilemma is that this constricted social network denies opportunities. The interaction is with people who themselves lack resources and who are otherwise similarly situated. For example, it is not unusual for somebody to find a job possibility or a recreation opportunity (e.g., club or team to join) through "word of mouth" by friends. Yet if all your friends are job-

Individual Strengths   **Environmental Strengths**

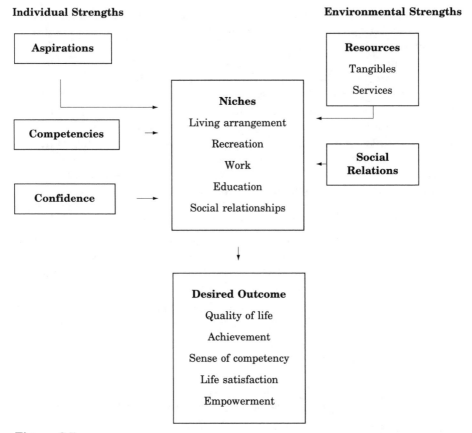

Figure 2.7.

less and only recreate at programs sponsored by mental health providers, the chances of such possibilities occurring are slight.

Yet every community is comprised of many people, all unique: people who care; people who would enjoy and benefit from relationships with people who happen to have severe mental illness. This is not to deny the presence of stigma, discrimination, labeling, etc., but rather to open our eyes to the good, if only we can see it. As Charles Kuralt said:

> The country I see on my television screens and on my newspaper front pages is not quite the country I see with my eyes and hear with my ears or feel in my bones.

ENVIRONMENTAL STRENGTH: OPPORTUNITIES

*Proposition: People who are successful in living have access
to opportunities relevant to their goals.*

The notion of niche conjures an image of a space waiting to be filled or, in other words, a vacuum. Our society and its communities contain a myriad of these vacuums that are potential opportunities for people with severe mental illness (see Figure 2.8). For example, in the previous vignette of Sarah, the vacuum was the library's need for clerical assistance. Other common examples include a vacant apartment, a team that needs another player, a junior college class that has room for another student, or an elderly person who needs companionship.

Despite the many opportunities available in communities, people with severe mental illness have rarely taken advantage of them. Inculcated with a deficit or problem-oriented viewpoint, mental health professionals rarely are able to perceive a client's strengths and the vacuums that would match those strengths. We tend to see not only the weaknesses in people but also weaknesses in communities and therefore have created a "protective bubble" around people. In fact, we have developed professional-sounding explanations, like "setting a client up to fail," to justify decisions not to pursue opportunities.

We need to develop a mind set that recognizes the community as the primary source of opportunities that are not formally constituted mental

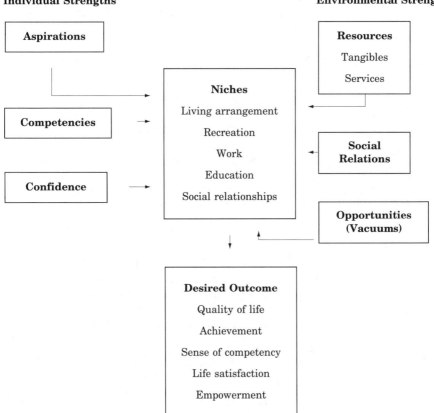

Figure 2.8.

health programs. Funding for specialized mental health programs has always been, is now, and will always be limited. Instead of bemoaning this situation, we need to see the naturally occurring resources and opportunities in our communities that are expandable, reusable, renewable, and almost infinite in possibilities.

INTERACTION OF THE ELEMENTS OF ENVIRONMENTAL STRENGTHS

Proposition: People who are successful in living have access to resources and opportunities and meaningful relationships.

As was the case with individual factors, the three environmental factors are interactive. For example, different people bring access to different resources and different opportunities. A friendship with an artist is more likely to lead to access to artistic decorations for an apartment than a relationship with an athlete who may allow access to sporting events or participation. Employment places a person within a certain web of people that another job would not.

A person's behavior is largely a function of setting and resources. People behave differently in church than they do at a pep rally or dance. For example:

> A student case manager had been working with a person with severe mental illness for three months. They would always meet in the community: at restaurants, parks, coffee shops, or the client's apartment. The case manager described the client as talkative, humorous, and energetic. At one meeting, the client noted that he had to go to the mental health center to pick up his medication. The case manager said she would drive him. As the client approached the entrance to the mental health center, he slouched his shoulders, shuffled his feet, and pointed his eyes toward the ground. He walked down the hall, received his medication, and shuffled back. Upon entering the car, he asked with great animation whether the case manager had time for a cup of coffee.

While the student was befuddled, the explanation was clear. The client had learned how to act the client or patient and knew when to do so. Similarly, the wealthy behave differently than others. They spend their time differently; they meet their responsibilities differently; they interact with different people who in turn have access to many resources.

This then places a premium on where life occurs and who is involved. Naturally occurring community resources are more likely to engender "correct behavior" and allow access to more people, more resources, and more opportunities. Examples:

- Art classes offered by a recreation department or by a private artist is preferable to those offered by a day treatment program.

- Daily living skills taught by a junior college home economics department on campus is preferable to a partial hospital program.
- A residence being an apartment is preferable to a group home.
- Membership on a bowling team is preferable to the weekly outing of clients in the van with the agency name on the side.

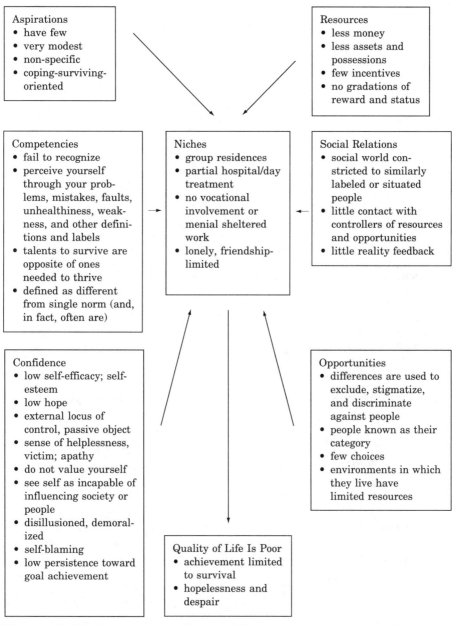

Figure 2.9. The theory of strengths and characteristics of the oppressed.

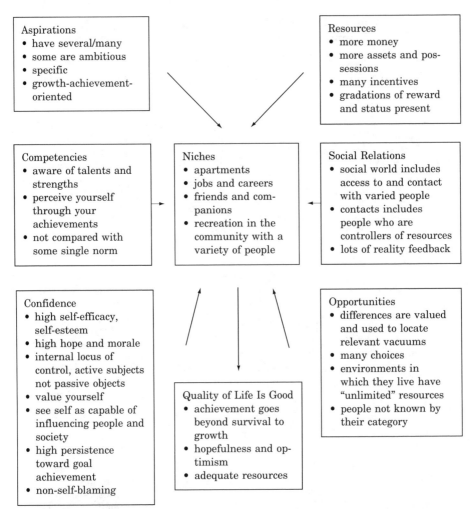

Figure 2.10. The theory of strengths and characteristics of the empowered.

Not only are natural resources preferable and more plentiful but it is possible to make them work on behalf of our clients.

SUMMARY OF STRENGTHS THEORY

The strengths theory posits that a person's quality of life, achievement, and life satisfaction are attributable in large part to the type and quality of niches that a person inhabits. These niches can be understood as paralleling a person's major life domains such as living arrangement, work, education, recreation, social relationships, etc. The quality of the niches for any individual is a function of that person's aspirations, competencies, confidence, and the environmental resources, opportunities, and people available to the person.

TABLE 2.2
Key Propositions of the Strengths Model

1. The quality of niches people inhabit determines their achievement, quality of life, and success in living.
2. People who are successful in living have goals and dreams.
3. People who are successful in living use their strengths to attain their aspirations.
4. People who are successful in living have the confidence to take the next step toward their goal.
5. At any one point in time, people who are successful in living have at least one goal, one relevant talent, and confidence to take the next step.
6. People who are successful in living have access to the resources needed to achieve their goals.
7. People who are successful in living have a meaningful relationship with at least one person.
8. People who are successful in living have access to opportunities relevant to their goals.
9. People who are successful in living have access to resources and opportunities and meaningful relationship.

This formulation helps explain the poor life circumstance of so many people with severe mental illness. Approximately 5.5 million Americans are disabled by severe mental illness. Other facts:

- One third of the estimated 600,000 homeless are believed to have a serious mental illness (Center for Mental Health Services, 1993).

- Twenty-five percent are hospitalized or living in some other psychiatric institution; only 10% live in their own housing; 60% live as adults with families (U.S. Department of Health and Human Services, 1983).

- Only 20% are employed (Dion & Anthony, 1987).

- At least 30,700 severely mentally ill are in jail and approximately twice that number are in prison (Friedrich, 1995).

- The majority live off Supplemental Security Income (SSI) of about $5,400 a year.

Even those living independently are often confined to low-income neighborhoods where substandard housing and high crime rates exist. For those who work, employment is dominated by entry-level, menial, and "dead-end" jobs (Carling, 1995). Figure 2.9 seeks to explain these life circumstances by placing the research (reviewed in this book) in the context of the elements of the strengths theory. It is these elements that the strengths model seeks to influence. Figure 2.10 provides a contrasting example of the factors that contribute to empowerment, achievement, growth, and good quality of life. A recap of the nine key propositions of the strengths theory can be found in Table 2.2.

CHAPTER 3

The Purpose, Principles, and Research Results of the Strengths Model

THE PURPOSE

The purpose of case management in the strengths model is to assist consumers in identifying, securing, and sustaining the range of resources—both environmental and personal—needed to live, play, and work in a normally interdependent way in the community. Furthermore, case management is individually tailored to the unique needs of each person who requests services: "A strengths model of case management helps people achieve the goals they set for themselves" (Rapp, 1993, p. 145).

The purpose is to assist another human being, not to treat a patient. The work and decisions are done with people in partnership, not to someone. As the theory would suggest, a case manager works to "identify, secure, and sustain" resources that are both external (i.e., social relations, opportunities, resources) and internal (i.e., aspirations, competencies, confidence) rather than a focus on just external resources (brokerage model of case management) or internal (psychotherapy or skills development). It is this dual focus that contributes to the creation of healthy and desirable niches, niches that provide impetus for achievement and life satisfaction.

It is common in mental health to express our ultimate goal for clients as "independence." In contrast, dependency is abhorred. It is common for professionals to express concerns about a client's dependency and to formulate decisions based on these considerations: "They must do it themselves"; "He is becoming too dependent on his therapist and case manager." This dichotomized thinking of "independence versus dependence" is overly simplistic and harmful to clients.

All people are interdependent. All people rely on resources, opportunities, and social relations, and contribute to these. People use travel agents, baby-sitters, dry cleaners. Are they dependent? Is this some form of universal pathology? The very wealthy, by this conception, are the most dependent people yet we not only do not think of their lives as pathological, but many aspire to their circumstance. It is ironic then that for people with serious mental illness a different standard is set, one that often acts as a professional excuse for not helping.

Most of life is interdependent. In the strengths model the purpose is to help a client establish mutually satisfying interdependence between landlords and clients, employers and clients, friends and clients, clergy and clients, teachers and clients, etc.

The following six principles are derived from the previously described theory. The principles are the transition between the theory which seeks to explain people succeeding in life and the specific methods for assisting people toward that end. The principles are the governing laws, or values, or tenets upon which the methods are based.

PRINCIPLE 1: THE FOCUS IS ON INDIVIDUAL STRENGTHS RATHER THAN PATHOLOGY

People tend to develop and grow based on their individual interests, aspirations, and strengths. We tend to spend time doing things that we do well, that we enjoy, and that have meaning. We tend to avoid things we do poorly or that we think we will do poorly. At best, solving problems returns us to an equilibrium, but exploiting strengths and opportunities promotes growth.

The work with clients therefore should not be directed at their symptomatology, psychosis, or, for that matter, problems, weaknesses, and deficits. Rather, the work should focus on what the client has achieved so far, what resources have been or are currently available to the client, what the client knows and talents possessed, and what aspirations and dreams the client may hold.

A focus on strengths should also enhance motivation. The typical assessment process, for example, subverts client motivation with its obsession with problems, weaknesses, and deficits; it is a process clients undergo every time they confront yet another mental health professional. If the client has not entered the encounter depressed, by the time she has completed the process, she is sure to be depressed and unmotivated. As Disraeli stated, "The greatest good you can do for another is not just to share your riches but to reveal to him his own."

The strengths model enhances the individualization of clients. The idea that we can help only once we comprehend the person as an individual has been a hallmark of psychology, social work, and mental health practice. It transcends specific methods and applies whether speaking of Freud, behavior modification (person-specific menu of reinforcers), or cognitive approaches (the person's specific thoughts and sentences). Despite this, current mental health practice with people suffering from severe mental illness is dominated by a generic imagery of "client."

The last decade has provided us at the University of Kansas the opportunity to witness the professional practice of thousands of mental health personnel in scores of agencies in over three dozen states. The development of case plans is central to virtually all efforts at helping and, despite great variations in formats, all case plans include as their centerpiece a delineation of goals. In the more typical program, one might conclude that there are only two or three clients being served in all these venues because the case plans and goals vary little or are all the same: They are generic. Ninety percent of the goals are included in this listing: (1) improve personal hygiene, (2) improve daily living skills, (3) improve socialization skills, (4) improve prevocational skills or work readiness, (5) take medication as prescribed, and (6) show up for appointments and follow through with treatment plan. While these case plans can often be criticized for lack of specificity and behavioral referents, inadequate specification of the actions to be taken to reach these goals, and the absence of time frames and client participation in their designation, the most abhorrent observation is that they reflect a form of practice that sees all clients as the same.

Our first reaction to the generality of case plans was that it reflected poor practice, poor supervision, and poor training. In other words, it was technical in nature. The prevalence of these plans, however, suggested that it may be less technical than conceptual. This explanation gained plausibility when we found that "generic brand" client case plans were found in some of the best agencies and written by otherwise exceptional professionals. We therefore believe that the problem or pathology model of practice promotes the homogenization of clients and prohibits individualization.

The lesson seems to be that human problems are finite and shared by many of us, although how we experience these problems is highly personal. On the other hand, our uniqueness as individuals seems to be more a function of strengths that are highly idiosyncratic, and the configuration of these strengths in a given individual is even more so.

To enhance and reveal the client as individual, then, assessment and case-planning methods need to be based on an exploration of a person's strengths. To do otherwise is to direct our minds and our practice toward "standardized" human beings and thereby do injustice to the cardinal value of social work and mental health, which places the individual, in all of his or her elegance and uniqueness, at the center of our concerns, and ultimately to reduce the effectiveness of our efforts.

The domination of the generic client idea can be experienced through talking with long-time clients. In the vocational domain, for example, women clients will often state their job interests as some form of domestic or secretary, despite one woman having a profound interest in art, another having a long-time gardening hobby, and still another being devoted to animals. But they have all been socialized to accept that the job for them is a maid at Holiday Inn at minimum wage. The irony is that these women are not necessarily even interested in keeping their apartments or room in a group home orderly and clean. Then we wonder why clients do not follow through on job opportunities or fail to keep jobs for more than the briefest time. They do not need more skill development or more medication to control their symptoms but jobs that they are interested in if not passionate about. And this kind of job can only be arranged by being fully apprised of a person's unique strengths.

We, as professionals, can sometimes deceive ourselves by thinking that we are using a strengths assessment perspective when we actually are reframing problems positively and thereby operating from a problem (or deficit) assessment perspective. For example, a professional who has assessed a client as being overly dependent on her parents may discuss with the client her enormous capacity for caring about others as exemplified by her relationship with her parents. This would represent a positive reframing of a problem to make it more palatable for the client to hear and therefore grapple with the problem. It is a problem focus leading to a set of case plans aimed at the parent–child relationship. A strengths assessment would identify and develop strengths that may have little to do with parent–child relationships and issues. The case plans for strengths development lead in an entirely different direction, and a result of developing strengths is usually greater autonomy. The diminution of the identified problem—reframed or not—occurs spontaneously in the process of human growth. The initial focus of the professional's work, not a reframing of that focus, is the determinant of whether the strengths or problem orientation is being employed.

A shift in paradigms from a pathology orientation to a strengths and resilience focus allows for a different way of thinking about clients. It provides a framework for helping that uncovers strengths and the power within clients. It is more than "add strengths and stir" to existing pathology paradigms. Instead, a shift in paradigms allows for new and creative ways to work with clients that honor their skills, competencies, and talents as opposed to their deficits.

PRINCIPLE 2: THE COMMUNITY IS VIEWED AS AN OASIS OF RESOURCES

This principle is the corollary of the first. The strengths model attends not just to the strengths of the individual but the strengths of the environment. While the community is not the source of severe mental illness, it is the community that is the source of mental health. It is the community that provides the opportunities: the people to care and support and the resources necessary. The presence of community-based services, their geographic and physical accessibility, and the establishment and enforcement of civil rights are insufficient to ensure community integration (McKnight, undated; Sullivan, 1992). In fact, the presence of community-based services can act as an obstacle to community integration (Sullivan, 1994b; Syx, 1995). A "needs-based strategy can guarantee only survival, and can never lead to serious change . . ." (Kretzman & McKnight, 1993, p. 5).

Two assumptions underlie this principle. First, a person's behavior and well-being is in large part determined by the resources available and the expectations of others toward the person. Second, clients have a right to the societal resources they need (Davidson & Rapp, 1976; Rappaport, 1977). The case manager's task is to create community collaborators; to become a catalyst for others in the community to care. Juxtapose this position with the more common stance of blaming the community for lack of employment, housing, and recreation opportunities. The community as scapegoat can be just as inimical to effective helping as blaming the clients. Both can lead to a sense of paralysis, frustration, and impotence.

The task of resource acquisition should emphasize normal or natural resources, not mental health services, because community integration can occur only apart from mental health and segregated services. The assumption, which has been largely confirmed in our experience, is that in any given population there are a sufficient number of caring and potentially helpful people available to assist and support clients. "Each community boasts a unique combination of assets upon which to build. A thorough map of those assets would include an inventory of the gifts, skills and capacities of community residents . . . associations . . . formal institutions like schools, banks, businesses" (Kretzman & McKnight, 1993, pp. 6–7). The burden of proof on case managers should be that to use a mental health service, it must be first demonstrated that, natural helpers, community services (e.g., recreation department) and social services (in that order) cannot be organized on behalf of the client. As depicted in Figure 3.1, the size of the ring reflects the size of the available resource pool. Also, as you move outward from the center, integration replaces segregation. *The identification and use of community strengths and assets are as critical as the identification and use of individual strengths.*

The case management research seems to bear this out. Common to the case management models with demonstrated effectiveness (assertive community treatment—ACT, rehabilitation, and strengths models) is that service delivery minimizes the use of formally constituted mental health services in favor of direct provision by case managers and use of natural community resources. For example, both ACT and strengths models target initially the provision of assistance with the basics of housing, income and entitlements, and medication and health. Except for medication, these domains involve work with landlords, social security, housing authorities, welfare, food pantries, etc., not mental health providers. As clients pursue vocational, socialization, living skills, etc., the two models encourage the case manager to do this rather than make referrals to specialized programs. For example, the case manager may work with employers to find and maintain employment rather than refer the client to vocational rehabilitation, teach the living skills rather than refer the client to a day treatment or partial hospital program, and arrange socialization opportunities rather than relying on mental health programs. The strengths model goes even further,

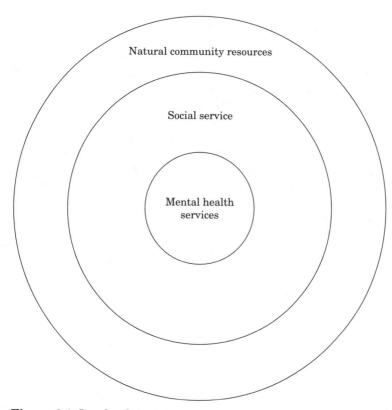

Figure 3.1. Levels of resources.

in explicitly requiring the exploration and use of non-mental-health and non-professionally driven resources prior to consideration of these formally organized services.

Research has found that:

1. Accelerated participation in in vivo–supported employment is more efficacious than transitioning through clubhouse prevocational activities that are generally viewed as effective (Bond & Dincin, 1986; Test, 1992).
2. Brokerage of services was the only variable negatively associated with client satisfaction (Huxley & Warner, 1992).
3. The treatment condition that fared best was that in which the case manager provided the most services directly and had "minimal contact with community based direct service providers other than for medication review" (Rydman, 1990, p. 233).

Referrals and community or environmental work do occur. While not precisely "a referral," the strengths model and one ACT project placed a premium on the use of available or natural community resources like families, volunteer opportunities, neighbors, junior colleges, sports leagues, YMCA's, art clubs, etc. The results of this approach have included lower rates of hospitalization and a high ratio of client goal achievements in most life domains (Santos et al., 1993; Rapp & Wintersteen, 1989).

The evidence strongly suggests that case managers who deliver the preponderance of service and use naturally occurring resources and avoid traditional mental health services (except medication) produce significantly better client outcomes and they do so over a wide range of outcomes (e.g., hospitalization, employment, independent living, client satisfaction, client goal achievement, etc.). In contrast, common to each of the brokerage model studies is the reliance on referral, with an emphasis on mental health services (Franklin, Solovitz, Mason, Clemons, & Miller, 1987; Hornstra, Bruce-Wolfe, Sagduyu, & Riffle, 1993; Curtis, Millman, & Struening, 1992). These studies uniformly found poor outcomes.

PRINCIPLE 3: INTERVENTIONS ARE BASED ON CLIENT SELF-DETERMINATION

A cornerstone of the strengths perspective of case management is the belief that it is a client's right to determine the form, direction, and substance of the case management help she is to receive. People with major mental illness are capable of this determination, and adhering to this principle contributes to the effectiveness of case management. Case managers should do nothing without the client's approval, involving clients in decisions regarding every step of the process. Opportunities to move each client closer to being the director of the case management scenario should be found, created, and exploited. One benefit of this stance is that it protects case managers from asking too much of clients or from asking the client to do something that would be the "wrong" thing for the client, both of which can contribute to symptom exacerbation. It also foreshortens tension between clients and case managers.

People often ask, "What do persons with major mental illness need?" The answer is, "What such people need is what they want. What they want is what any of us want: a decent place to live and adequate income, friends and opportunities to recreate, an opportunity to contribute (work, family, helping others), and recognition for that contribution." A study by Ewalt and Honeyfield (1981) found that hospitalized psychotic patients viewed the following as their needs in order to "make it" in the community: (1) money, (2) availability of health care, (3) a decent place to live, (4) transportation, (5) opportunities for socialization, (6) availability of help if needed. Thirty-three percent of those interviewed ($N = 253$) also stated the importance of the need to "be of help to others." These findings parallel the recent findings of successful programs (Gowdy & Rapp, 1989); that is, the programs that have produced the best results are those that conscientiously address these areas. In contrast, "Efforts at deinstitutionalization that rely primarily on professional judgments, at least in the mental health field, have failed miserably, with an overwhelming proportion of discharged long-term residents unable to maintain ongoing community tenure" (Ewalt & Honeyfield, 1981, p. 223).

Contrast the language, if not the substance, of the above list reflecting client perceptions with the following list generated by researchers and professionals at the Research Meeting on Community Support and Rehabilitation Services (1988). Outcomes included: (1) service integration, (2) access to mental health services, (3) service coordination, (4) brokerage, (5) service availability, (6) interagency cooperation, (7) systems level support, and (8) systems interface issues in relation to case management. Whether taken literally or metaphorically, selecting one language over another will inevitably lead one down a very different path. The position here is that if client self-determination is to be taken seriously, the client's desires must be given absolute primacy.

The tension between clients and workers is often obscured by the professional lexicon, including such phrases as "resistance to therapy" and "setting up the client to fail." The first phrase has the wonderful effect of camouflaging the conflict by explaining the behavior as a rather natural occurrence in the helping process and as a function of the client's personality. It is therefore neither upsetting nor remediable by the professional attempting to change the client's behavior. The second phrase is heard when a client suggests a goal or aspiration that the professional views as unrealistic and thinks giving permission to pursue it could lead to pain, suffering, exacerbation of symptoms, and regression. Its effect is to deprive the person of one of the most precious elements of humanness: the need for a dream. It further suggests a parent–child relationship of unequal knowledge, power, and protection, guarantees not of a partnership but of an adversarial relationship.

Believing and adhering to a strict code of client self-determination and the skillful assessing of strengths seem to facilitate a partnership between client and worker. The professional works on behalf of the client, and the client's goals and aspirations become the centerpiece of the work. Why do clients not follow through on medication regimens? Why does a client refuse to take a bath? Why doesn't this person show up for her group session and when she does, why is she disruptive? Clients' lack of compliance and lack of progress seem as much a function of their hostility toward a system that is irrelevant to their needs and hopes as it is a function of their personalities and their disability. In fact, failing to follow alien prescriptive demands is often the only way we allow clients to express their opinion and their sense of power.

Adherence to a strict code of client self-determination should not suggest that the case manager assume a passive posture in the helping relationship by becoming a servant to the client: If the client wants a donut, I will run and get him a donut. This is no more a partnership than when the professional dictates to the client. In almost all cases however, this exaggerated perspective comes from a sincere acceptance of client self-determination. It also assumes the client knows all rather than the client knows best—two very different ideas.

An alternative perspective is for the case manager to help the client explore new vistas. Guitar lessons can turn into getting paid for working in a music store, or giving lessons, or performing—ideas that the client may never have considered or may have discarded years earlier. This is not talking a client into something, but creating new possibilities by blending different strengths. In some cases it may be nothing more than "planting seeds" that can be regularly watered. It may mean visiting a music store, talking to musicians, attending performances, or scanning classified ads for "gigs." The client has the right to make the choices, but freedom may best be served by knowledge of the choices possible and the confidence that the person could successfully select from among these choices.

PRINCIPLE 4: THE CASE MANAGER–CLIENT RELATIONSHIP IS PRIMARY AND ESSENTIAL

Many case management programs ignore the importance of the case manager–client relationship or prohibit it. The brokerage model of case management is built with an assumption that the work can be done without a close relationship. Nationally, case management caseloads have often exceeded 80 to 1 and have even reached 200 to 1. A close collaborative relationship cannot be established with 80 people. In contrast, Richard Lamb (1980) advocates a therapist–case manager model for the central reason that a therapist is the one professional with a relationship of sufficient intensity and intimacy necessary to carry out case management.

As Deitchman (1980) stated:

> Economic survival is not successfully dealt with by referral; neither is psychological survival. For the chronic client to survive psychologically, he needs someone he can have a relationship with, someone he can confide in, someone he can depend on. The chronic client in the community needs a traveling companion, not a travel agent. The travel agent's only function is to make the client's reservation. The client has to get ready, get to the airport, and traverse foreign terrain by himself. The traveling companion, on the other hand, celebrates the fact that his friend was able to get seats on the plane, talks about his fear of flying, and then goes on the trip with him, sharing the joys and sorrows that occur during the venture. (p. 789)

It is the relationship that buffers the demands of the tough times, anxious times. It is the relationship that attenuates the stress and prevents or mitigates the exacerbation of symptoms. It is the relationship that supports the client's confidence in tackling the multiple requirements of the environment and other people.

A cooperative relationship often starts with playing basketball or doing the dishes or going shopping together as the client tests the worker's promises, interests, and sincerity. As confidence in the relationship replaces skepticism, the client becomes reaffirmed as a person with assets and valid aspirations, goals become more ambitious, communication more honest, and assistance more accessible.

PRINCIPLE 5: AGGRESSIVE OUTREACH IS THE PREFERRED MODE OF INTERVENTION

Given the above principles of client self-determination and the priority of naturally occurring resources, it should be clear that office-based involvement and interventions are contraindicated. A case manager cannot sit in the office and locate, arrange, and support an employer with a job the client desires. The work must occur in apartments, restaurants, businesses, parks, and community agencies. Office contact with clients should be limited to the few cases where the client prefers it (usually for psychological safety), and this is rare and usually time limited.

An outreach mode offers rich opportunities for assessment and intervention. Office-bound assessment limits the sources of data to what the client says, the case manager's observations of the client, and the 10-inch stack of paper referred to as a case file. This is simply not enough for a variety of reasons.

First, a client's behavior in a mental health program is often different from behavior in other settings. The "Thorazine shuffle" disappears in many cases once the individual leaves the mental health center and work on developing strengths begins. The opposite is also true. Many clients can and do cook, clean, and socialize while in structured day treatment or partial hospitalization programs, but fail to do so in their own apartments and neighborhoods. Skills learned inside agencies do not appear to generalize easily to more normalized settings (Gutride, Goldstein, & Hunter, 1973; Jaffe & Carlson, 1976; Liberman, Massel, Mosk, & Wong, 1985). Second, the client's perception of resources available is just that, a perception. Most people are unaware of the potential resources available. There have been many examples of this in the 12 years of our program. In one case, a client wanted to earn his GED certificate and attend classes to do so. The case manager helped the client arrange such classes only two blocks from the boardinghouse, but discovered that the client did not go to the first two sessions. The indication was that the client was scared. Because the case manager was doing the work in the community and more specifically in the boardinghouse, he came to know another resident (not suffering from mental illness) who was more than willing to walk the client to class. After three sessions, this was no longer needed and the client went on to earn his certificate. It was unlikely that successful resolution of this problem would have occurred if the work had been done in an office.

Finally, part of a case manager's job is to provide direction to clients, to model certain behaviors, and to teach others. Given the sometimes disorganized and jumbled cognitions of people suffering from major mental illness, each new encounter may produce new anxiety and an inability to use skills in their repertoire (Jaffe & Carlson, 1976; Liberman et al., 1985). As has been already suggested, teaching a client to cook spaghetti for 20 people in a day treatment program on a gas stove can be perceived as very different from cooking spaghetti for one on a hot plate. In vivo instruction removes many of the conditions that impede generalization.

The case management research supports this principle. The average retention rate of clients for at least a year is 84% across Assertive Community Treatment (ACT) studies which produces a highly significant (p,.001) difference with control subjects. The more than 80% retention rate for a year greatly exceeds traditional aftercare, where retention rates seldom exceed 50% for even 6 months (Bond, McGrew, & Fehete, 1995; Axelrod & Wetzler, 1989). This is no small achievement given the historical difficulty in engaging and retaining people with severe mental illness in service.

Another study found that a number of assertive outreach variables, including out-of-office visits, were correlated with client satisfaction with service accessibility (Huxley & Warner, 1992, p. 801). Bond (1991) commented that "one program using office visits because of a reluctance to make home visits had minimal success until it changed its treatment strategy" (p. 75). McGrew and Bond (1995) found nearly unanimous agreement of ACT experts on the importance of outreach and in vivo service delivery. The failure of the brokerage model of case management, which is largely office bound, and the positive results of the other models (ACT, strengths, rehabilitation) argue for the criticalness of an outreach mode of operation.

PRINCIPLE 6: PEOPLE SUFFERING FROM MAJOR MENTAL ILLNESS CAN CONTINUE TO LEARN, GROW, AND CHANGE

This principle overlays the entire perspective. The central belief of the strengths model is that these people are not schizophrenic or chronically mentally ill but that they are people with schizophrenia. It is only one part of their being. They, like us, have a history of pain as well as accomplishment, of talents and foibles, of dreams and aspirations. Interestingly, a recent study of effective programs in Kansas found that the most prevalent common denominator was the managerial and direct service staffs' holistic view of clients (Gowdy & Rapp, 1989).

In so many ways, the mental health system has institutionalized low expectations. In contrast, data from the 20-year follow-up study in Vermont more than suggests that most people suffering from major mental illness can eventually merge into the fabric of a community having jobs, families, friends, and homes (Harding et al., 1987a, 1987b; Harding, Zubin, & Strauss, 1987). What has to be built into any strengths perspective of social work practice is an absolute belief in individuals' capacity to better their lives. With a little help, they will do so. The practice perspective must reek of "can do" in every stage of the helping process.

STRENGTHS ORIENTATION FOSTERS EMPOWERMENT

Two of the most oppressed groups in mental health are clients and their case managers. While the oppression of clients has been well documented (Goffman, 1961; Szasz, 1970), that of case managers has not. Basically, they are the lowest paid, the lowest on the organizational hierarchy, and the least credentialed, yet have the most cases and have the most ambitious goals established for their work. They also have to complete the most paperwork, go to the same meetings as others, and are the most supervised members of the organization. They have the least control over their jobs and have the least influence over organizational or client matters.

The strengths orientation cannot address this body of factors. In some small way, however, it may provide some enhanced sense of power for both clients and case managers by: (1) replacing the mutual conflict with a partnership; (2) encouraging the vigilance needed to identify strengths, which forces the individual to look for the good rather than the bad and to enhance the positiveness of worker activities; (3) defining the community as oasis, allowing individuals to see possibilities where only limitations were seen before; (4) leading to improved client outcomes, so that both worker and client can see results and experience the satisfaction they can bring. In short, we have seen workers (and clients) with a new sense that they can make a difference.

One indicator of this perspective as an empowerer of clients is the consistent phenomenon of client achievements in areas not targeted or attended to by the case manager. Here is an example:

John R. is a 27-year-old man who has a diagnosis of Schizophrenia, Paranoid Type. In the absence of a group home bed or transitional apartment in the community, John was discharged from a three-month admission at the state hospital to his parents' home. Upon intake, the following problems were recorded for attention by the treatment team at the Community Support Program where he was referred for aftercare: (1) lacks motivation to engage in social activities; (2) displays poor judgment regarding how he manages his money; (3) needs to improve communication skills with peers; (4) needs to become more compliant with medication regimen and reduce abusing alcohol; and (5) needs to individuate effectively from family of origin. The chart also noted that John enjoyed sports, was in good physical health, and was assertive with staff in expressing his wants and needs. In order to achieve these treatment goals, John was scheduled to attend the partial hospitalization program, attend a medication clinic, and work with a case manager.

During the subsequent weeks, John's behavior began to concern the staff. His parents were reporting that he was staying up very late watching TV, drinking despite their protests, and not attending the partial program on a regular basis. The case manager made a home visit, and reluctantly John agreed to come downstairs to talk with her. At this meeting the case manager focused on identifying John's strengths (aspirations, confidence, competencies) and learned several things: He did not want to move into his own apartment at this time, and he did not want to go to the partial program and spend all day with "those crazy people." What he did want to do was to get his driver's license and save up enough money to buy a car. This information led to a discussion of cars.

John showed the case manager the many model cars he had put together, and they talked of how much he enjoyed the auto mechanics class he had taken in high school. They agreed to meet the following week at a local gas station, where the case manager knew the manager. The manager agreed to allow John to volunteer for two hours each day, doing odd jobs and going to pick up needed parts at the nearby parts dealership. During the next few weeks, John began to take his medication more regularly, and his attendance and participation at the partial program showed marked improvement. His parents also reported that he was no longer staying up late watching TV and that he was not abusing alcohol at home. After three months of volunteering at the gas station, John began to talk of trying to move to his own apartment with a roommate, a mechanic he had met at the station. The owner of the station was also considering hiring John as a part-time paid employee.

The observed pattern over the last eight years of our program is so strong as to demand an explanation: Regular trips to the library lead to working on grooming; working on joining a bowling league leads to better maintenance of an apartment; participation in the local theater group leads to work on weight loss and nutrition; work on moving to an apartment leads to better medication compliance. These secondary achievements occur without explicit attention by the case manager. Rather than appealing to some notion of "spontaneous recovery," it may be that success in one area breeds efforts and success in others; that success empowers clients to try areas where they lacked the confidence or willingness to try before.

RESEARCH ON THE STRENGTHS MODEL

There have been six studies testing the efficacy of the strengths model as delivered to people with severe mental illness. Three of the studies employed experimental or quasi-experimental designs and three used non-experimental methods (see Table 3.1 for a summary of each). This section reviews the client outcomes from this body of research. This review will exclude the companion qualitative study done by Kisthardt (1993) that sought to capture the client experience with the strengths model. These results will be reported in the following chapters.

Hospitalization

Four of the six studies include hospitalization as a dependent measure. In the three non-experimental studies, the incidence of hospitalization was 50% lower than the usual rate for that locale. In the Modrcin, Rapp, and

TABLE 3.1
Summary of Strengths Model Case Management Research

Study	Sample size	Character of sample	Design	Outcomes
Kansas Modrcin et al. (1988)	$N = 44$	Referrals to a CMHC mostly psychotic (schizophrenia or depressive)	Experimental	After 4 months A = 0, B = +, C = +, C1 = +, C2 = +, M = +
Colorado Ryan, Sherman, & Judd (1994)	$N = 382$	Psychotic diagnosis multiple hospital	3 group post hoc Correlational CSS, strengths, traditional	C = +
Logan, Utah Macias et al. (1994)	Experimental = 19 Control = 18	Seriously mentally ill	Experimental	A = +, C = +, D = +, J = 0, K = +
Lawrence, Kansas Rapp & Chamberlain (1985)	$N = 19$	Seriously mentally ill	Non- experimental	A = +, J = +
Kansas Rapp & Wintersteen (1989)	$N = 235$	Seriously mentally ill	Non-experimental	A = +, C1 = +, C2 = +, C3 = +
Kansas Kisthardt (1994)	$N = 66$	Seriously mentally ill	Non-experimental	C = +, C1 = +, C2 = +, E = +

Coding schema for outcomes
A = Hospitalizations, + = fewer, − = greater, 0 = no difference (n.d.)
B = Quality of life, + = increase, − = decrease, 0 = n.d.
C = Social functioning, + = increase, − = decrease, 0 = n.d.
D = Occupational/Vocational functioning, + = increase, − = decrease, 0 = n.d.
E = Leisure time activities, social isolation, + = increase or less isolation, − = decrease, greater isolation, 0 = n.d.
F = Independence of residential living, + = more time housed, more stable, less structured, improved, − = less time housed, less stable, more structured, 0 = n.d.
G = Behavior symptomatology, + = reduction, − = increase, 0 = n.d.
H = Social support networks, social support, + = improved, increased − = fewer, lesser, 0 = n.d.
I = Client satisfaction with treatment, + = high satisfaction, − = low, 0 = n.d.
J = Family burden, + = decrease, − = increase, 0 = n.d.
K = Amount of service contracts, + = increase, − = decrease, 0 = n.d.

Poertner (1988) experimental study, the 50% reduction in hospitalization was not statistically significant, owing perhaps to the small sample size. Macias, Kinney, Farley, Jackson, and Vos (1994) did find a statistically significant reduction in hospitalization incidences for the group receiving strengths model case management. In addition, they found that the frequency of contacts with the crisis center were dramatically reduced over time while the control subjects increased the number of crisis center contacts. The study by Ryan, Sherman, and Judd (1994) also suggests that clients receiving strengths model case management had fewer hospitalizations or emergency room visits.

Independence of Daily Living

Rapp and Wintersteen (1989) and Kisthardt (1993) found that people receiving strengths model case management set more goals in this life domain than any other. Of the 2,624 goals set in this area, 2215 were achieved (84%). Macias et al. (1994) found that clients receiving strengths model case management demonstrated statistically significant greater competence in daily living than the control group as rated by both consumers and case managers. Modrcin et al. (1988) found experimental clients to score higher on community living skills and appropriate community behaviors. Ryan's et al. (1994) research suggests stability of residence was enhanced by strengths model case management.

Vocational/Educational

The three non-experimental studies all found high rates of client goal setting and goal achievement in the vocational/educational life domain. Combining the Rapp and Wintersteen (1989) and Kisthardt (1993) results, clients achieved 1,541 of 1,998 goals set (77%). Modrcin et al. (1988) found a statistically significant difference in favor of the strengths model group in the number of clients involved in vocational training.

Leisure Time and Social Support

Again, all three non-experimental studies found high rates of goal setting and goal achievement in this life domain. Combining the Rapp and Wintersteen (1989) and Kisthardt (1993) results, clients achieved 2,225 of the 2,766 goals set (80%). Modrcin et al. (1988) found significant differences favoring the strengths model clients in the use of leisure time.

Financial/Legal

Two of the non-experimental studies (Rapp & Wintersteen, 1989; Kisthardt, 1993) found that clients receiving strengths model case management achieved 701 of 902 goals (78%) set in this life domain. Ryan et al. (1994) also found "a stable and secure income" to be associated with clients who received strengths model case management.

Health

Macias found the clients receiving strengths model case management showed statistically significant greater overall physical and mental health. Rapp & Wintersteen (1989) and Kisthardt (1993) found that clients achieved 85% of their goals in the health domain (1,834 of 2,157).

Symptomatology

Macias et al. (1994) found that clients receiving strengths model case management reported fewer problems with mood, fewer problems with thinking, and greater psychological well-being than the control group. Family members ratings of cognitive psychiatric symptomatology was significantly more positive than the control subjects as were ratings of anger and of paranoia. Similarly, professional staff assessed the strengths model group as less depressed in mood and more clear-thinking and rational than the control group. Modrcin et al. (1988) found clients who received strengths model case management showed statistically significant improvement in tolerance of stress over the control group. Ryan et al. (1994) suggest that strengths model case management was associated with compliance with medication regimes and being judged not to be a danger to self or others.

Family Burden

In the one strengths model study to measure family burden, Macias et al. (1994) found that family members of strengths model consumers reported feeling less burdened by their consumers' problems than family members of the control group. Furthermore,

> family members of case managed consumers reported being less depressed when around their consumer, less in need of help in dealing with the consumer, less trapped, less frustrated by an inability to plan ahead, and less strained by tension and conflict caused by the consumer. (p. 333)

Research Summary

The research on the strengths model of case management is suggestive of its efficacy (see Table 3.1). On the downside, the research is limited to two experimental, one quasi-experimental, and three non-experimental studies. The size of the samples in the two experimental studies was small. The measures used across studies varied and questions have been raised about most of them (Chamberlain & Rapp, 1991).

On the plus side, the strengths model research results have been remarkably resilient across studies. Even within studies, consistency is shown. Rapp and Wintersteen (1989), Kisthardt (1993), and Ryan et al. (1994) all used multiple sites with different case managers, different supervisors, and affiliations with a total of 15 different agencies. A second strength of the research has been the attention paid to monitoring the intervention as delivered. In each study, the fidelity of implementation of the strengths model was very high and therefore results, especially in the experimental studies, can be more confidently ascribed to the model itself.

With the caveats not withstanding, the research on the strengths model suggests that its application can reduce the use of psychiatric hospitalization and increase client achievement and well-being in a variety of life domains. There is also beginning evidence that the strengths model may also reduce symptomatology and family burden.

FUNCTIONS OF STRENGTHS MODEL CASE MANAGEMENT

Strengths model case management includes a practice theory, a set of principles, and a set of methods. These methods can be best organized into five functions:

1. *Engagement and relationship:* The initial meetings with a potential consumer, where the purpose is to begin the development of a collaborative helping partnership.

2. *Strengths assessment:* The process of gathering information regarding six "life domains" which appear to be directly related to successful community tenure. Information focuses on the current situation, what the consumer wants (may indicate a change or desire to sustain), and information regarding resources and activities that have been exploited in the past. The goal is to collect information on personal and environmental strengths as a basis for work together.

3. *Personal planning:* The creation of a mutual agenda for work between the client and case manager focused on achieving the goals that the client has set. Personal planning requires the client and case manager to discuss, negotiate, and agree on the long-term goal, short-term goals or tasks, assign responsibility to each task, and target dates for accomplishment. A primary activity is the generation of options from which a client can select. The strengths assessment is the primary source of information and guidance.

4. *Resource acquisition:* The purpose is to acquire the environmental resources desired by clients to achieve their goals and insure their rights, to increase each person's assets. A primary focus is to break down the walls separating clients from the community, to replace segregation with true community integration. To be successful, case managers require new perspectives concerning "community" and a wide variety of interpersonal and strategic skills.

5. *Collective, continuous collaboration and graduated disengagement:* Typically thought of as "monitoring," this concept addresses the multidimensional nature of ongoing modification and adaptation that takes place during the helping process, determining the extent to which consumers are able to engage in activities noted on the personal plan. In the strengths model, case managers are less concerned with assuring "patient compliance" with a treatment plan, and more concerned with a person's ability to creatively use their own strengths and community resources to cope from day to day in ways that promote self-efficacy and community integration. Graduated disengagement refers to the helping behavior that is consciously designed to replace case manager or program staff in something they are doing with or for a consumer.

A chapter will be devoted to each of the first four functions. "Collective, Continuous Collaboration and Graduated Disengagement" depicts the ongoing nature of strengths-based case management. The methods used are the same as those in the first four functions.

CHAPTER 4

Engagement and Relationship: A New Partnership

Purpose: To create a trusting and reciprocal relationship between case manager and client as a basis for working together.

Engagement is most frequently thought of as the initial coming together of clients and case manager. While there are a few considerations and methods unique to this stage, most apply across the helping process. In a sense, with each contact, the relationship becomes reengaged. So, before turning to engagement as a specific function, the importance and nature of the client–case manager relationship need attention.

NATURE OF THE RELATIONSHIP

The relationship between the client and professional is seen as a keystone in virtually all approaches to casework, psychotherapy, and counseling. Some approaches view the relationship as the crucial therapeutic ingredient (Rogers, 1959), while other approaches see it as the context for practice thereby enhancing the effectiveness of techniques (Fischer, 1978). Even newer empowerment models of practice underscore the importance of the relationship (Lee, 1994; Dodd & Gutierrez, 1990; Simon, 1994).

The relationship between the professional and the person with severe mental illness has been shaped by its context. Traditionally, mental health workers practiced within the confines of the state hospital, group residence, office, day treatment program, or sheltered work enclave. Contact with others was severely limited; the work was "private." Within these walls, the rules governing the relationship between worker and client were similarly

constrained. Each had roles to play and rules, professional and organizational, were established to maintain those roles. The quest was for "professional distance," with its lack of reciprocity, rules against self-disclosure,
and power differentials. While the relationship has always been viewed as
critical to helping, it was a very limited relationship that was of concern.
The brokerage model of case management places little emphasis on relationship; rather, it focuses on assessment and referral. "It stops short of
coaching the client or taking responsibility for making sure the client gets
the services" (Robinson & Bergman, 1989). This is the only case management model that has failed to demonstrate its efficacy (Rapp, 1995). The
ineffectiveness of these types of services with people suffering from severe
mental illness suggests that something else is needed.

Case management, when characterized by out-of-office/in-community
work, interaction with a variety of community actors, emphasis on relationship, etc., is a dramatic break from past modes of helping people with
serious mental illness. Case management, literally and figuratively,
breaches or extends the walls of mental health services. Many of the old
rules become irrelevant with the new context and methods of helping others need adaptation (Curtis & Hodge, 1994). The characteristics of this new
partnership are described below.

Purposeful

The relationship is best seen as a medium to achievement. For many clients,
the relationship with the case manager becomes a primary mechanism for
increasing confidence, identifying goals and risking dreaming, and recognizing talents and strengths. The relationship acts as a rocket booster and
a safety net. The stronger the relationship, the more powerful the rocket
booster and the stronger the safety net. Everything that the case manager
does in the interpersonal sphere should be done for the client's benefit. We
will return later to purpose when discussing boundary dilemmas.

Reciprocal

There is an inherent pull in the client–case manager relationship for it to
be one-sided: The case manager gives and helps, and the client is the recipient. After all, the case manager is being paid for this. As Curtis and
Hodge (1994) write:

> However, when staff are always the "givers" and consumers are always
> the "recipients," we perpetuate the idea that staff have what is most
> valuable and that staff hold the power to allocate or give based on their
> judgment. Very few of us would describe this as a normal adult–adult
> relationship. Most of us look for a kind of balance in our personal and
> professional relationships, and often this balance is based on mutuality
> and reciprocity. Refusing offers of reciprocity—whether it is an offer of
> a cup of coffee, a small gift, or of knitting lessons—may be as rejecting
> as outright stating to the person "You have nothing of value to offer this
> relationship." And it is downright unfriendly. (p. 348)

There is a Chinese proverb, "The greatest gift you can give someone is to allow them to give." Among people with severe mental illness, the desire to give and help is prevalent and strong. Too often we have shut off this opportunity.

A powerful frame of reference that helps avoid this temptation to the one-sided, is viewing the relationship as an experience in mutual learning. In fact, the best case managers and therapists also are the best learners. The client is learning about themselves, their environment, and ways to better achieve the goals they set. The worker has the opportunity to learn about that individual's highly personal experience of life. In particular, the case manager has a real-world classroom to teach them what it is like to live with a mental illness and the societal oppression that coexists. How does one survive? How does one recover? The case manager is in daily contact with the experts.

Rose and Black (1985), based on the work of Freire (1968), describe the process as one of dialogue. The case manager seeks to enter the reality of the clients by learning the objective conditions of their lives and their subjective experience of that reality. "The dialogue cannot be reduced to the act of one person's depositing ideas in another, nor can it become a simple exchange of ideas to be consumed by the discussants" (Freire, 1968, p. 77). Rather, it's a dialogue based on reflection, respect, and mutual learning.

Friendly

One can view relationships on a continuum from the stereotype of detached and limited psychoanalysis to intimate friendships. The case manager–client relationship would generally fall a little to right of normal friendship on this continuum. In other words, case managers are not paid friends. In fact, case managers should devote considerable effort to clients building "real" friendships with others. On the other hand, the relationship should be friendly. The relationship should be characterized by warmth, acceptance, caring, respect, and even fun. It should be uplifting for both parties.

Trusting

The relationship needs to be based on a high degree of trust. For most people with severe mental illness, their relationships have been limited and a source of frustration and pain. The messages have reinforced their sense of inadequacy.

Sometimes it is a strength for clients to not trust because of past circumstances that have created pain and discomfort. The professional needs to allow for the trust process to evolve naturally as opposed to jumping in and saying "you can trust me." Clients will set the pace of when they are able to trust; to be mistrustful is normal considering what most clients have gone through in their lives and with other helping professionals. Trust involves several dimensions. First, trust means honesty. There will be no lies or shading of the truth. Second, trust means that promises will be kept, or if doubt is present, promises will not be made. Rather, the case manager will promise "to try." When a case manager promises to do something, the client can "take it to the bank." This also means that limits must be set. "I'll be there for you" does not necessarily mean forever or within 10 minutes of a client's call in every situation. Third, trust is the assumption that the client is always doing the best they can given their understanding of the situation and themselves.

Trust for clients is the perception that "they can risk sharing thoughts, feelings, mistakes, and failure with the worker" (Schulman, 1992, p. 60). Mistrust is grounded in fear of imagined hurts, exploitation, rejection, criticism, punishment, and control by others. Given the past history of relationships, trust is given reluctantly by most clients. It is therefore built in small steps, with each encounter. Empathy, non-conditional acceptance of the client, and honesty are required (Hepworth & Larsen, 1986).

Empowering

Client–case manager relationships should be empowering; they should provide strength to the client. Given the discussion of empowerment in chapter 1, an empowering relationship would:

1. increase the client's abilities and perception of their abilities;
2. increase the client's options and perception of options;
3. increase the opportunities and confidence of the client to chose and to act on those choices.

Even allowing the client to choose where to meet begins to reflect a relationship that empowers.

METHODS

Core Conditions

The foundation for the client–case manager relationship is empathy, genuineness, and unconditional positive regard. Maluccio's study (1979) of clients' opinions of social workers included these three characteristics as among the most frequently mentioned.

Accurate empathy refers to the ability of the worker to perceive and communicate accurately and with sensitivity both the current feelings and perception of experiences of another person and their meaning and significance (Truax & Mitchell, 1971). "It is sometimes described as the ability to step into someone's shoes and see and feel life as that individual does" (Sheafor, Horejsi, & Horejsi, 1991, p. 84). The focus is often on feelings, whether they be frustration, pain, loss, anger, pride, happiness, or satisfaction. As the definition suggests, empathy must be communicated if it is to contribute to the relationship. The case manager shares understanding of the client's feelings and perceptions with the client. The job of the worker is to be sensitive to exposed and apparent feelings but also to go further and clarify and expand what may only be hinted at by voice, posture, and content cues (Truax & Mitchell, 1971).

Unconditional positive regard "refers to the worker's communication of respect, acceptance, liking, caring and concern for the client in a non-dominating way" (Fischer, 1978, p. 196). These feelings are not conditional on the production of thoughts, feelings, and actions by the client that are acceptable to the worker. This does not imply approval of all behavior and actions but, rather, even in the face of destructive or harmful behavior, the case manager can convey to the client that they continue to cherish the person and their inherent worth.

Genuineness refers to a worker being themselves in the moment rather than presenting a professional facade (Truax & Carkhuff, 1967). As Fischer (1978) states, "it would be difficult to conceive of the meaningful communication of empathy and warmth by someone who was not at least minimally 'real'" (p. 199). He goes on:

> Genuineness is not synonymous with being totally honest. Workers need not disclose their total selves . . . they do not employ [negative responses] in ways that will be destructive to their clients. (p. 199)

Mirroring

People develop their identity and perceptions of the world, in large part, based on the cumulative feedback they receive from others. In a sense, each of us acts as a mirror to other people. All mirrors are distorted to some degree; they mute some things and exaggerate others. As has been discussed in the first two chapters, the lives of people with severe mental illness have been dominated by weakness-oriented mirrors that have muted their strengths and exaggerated their deficits.

A strengths model case manager consciously uses themselves as a countervailing mirror. Where it has been concave, it now is convex. This new mirror is highly sensitive to the abilities and talents of clients. It is highly sensitive to the courage and resilience they have recurringly demonstrated. It is highly sensitive to their achievements, no matter how seemingly insignificant. The purpose is to allow clients to see this other side of themselves that is as real and present as the side of problems and deficits.

> I knew that Noreen's only way out was to suspend her pain, to see her past not only as a stumbling block but also as a challenge, and to recognize her own resilience. I also knew that she would resist. I remember the first time I suggested the idea to her. She was talking about her mother:
>
> My mother had a label for all of the kids. My sister had big breasts, so she was the "tramp." The babies—the twins—were "ugly"; my mother said she wanted to hang veils on their faces. I had something wrong with my eyes, and I had to wear a patch, so I was "defective." A lot of times I would fall or bump into things because I had an eye problem, and she would berate me for being clumsy and out of control. I wouldn't let myself cry. I would stare at her and think of something

else . . . like, "I'll know how to be a good mother. I'll do the opposite of everything she does, and my children will love me, and maybe then, I'll finally have a family."

Noreen related the incident for the same reason she had told other similar stories in the past: to let me know about her mother's verbal abuse, the total absence of support and love in her family, and her own suffering. Certainly all of this was present in her story. I knew the pain she was feeling, and I would never want to dismiss or minimize any of it. But from my outside perspective, I also recognized the affirmation that could be salvaged from her story, and I knew that she would benefit from seeing that side of her story too. I forged ahead and reframed the story to reveal its submerged themes.

"I find it remarkable," I ventured, "that under unbearable stress you could exercise terrific self-control, see your siblings' plight, and keep your hopes for yourself alive." (Wolin & Wolin, 1993, p. 57)

Most interactions with clients offer multiple opportunities to mirror the "good." But the effects on confidence, increased goal setting, and improved recognition of the client's competencies may take quite some time. The feelings of "damaged goods" are usually long-standing; very much a part of the client's identity. In some cases, it is likely to take "a lot of positive mirroring" before changes can be ascertained.

Contextualizing

People who are oppressed have a high degree of self-blame (Fanon, 1968). They perceive themselves as the major contributor to their unfortunate circumstances. This self-blame then translates into low self-worth, lack of confidence, and constricted life goals. There are two parts to people with severe mental illness: the illness itself and the social sequelae of the illness.

Clients need to have accurate information on the nature and cause of their illness. It is not, in any way, their fault that they have mental illness. Efforts should be made to transform the self-perception to one of "the illness is one and only one part of me."

The second part concerns the social sequelae of the illness. Known variously as conscience raising or contextualizing, it refers to the process by which a person becomes aware of the societal context for their situation and in this process becomes aware of others in similar predicaments. It allows a person to perceive forces other than themselves as contributing to the current situation. In fact, no one has ever oppressed themselves (Rose & Black, 1985).

Contextualizing, then, seeks to teach clients the factors that contribute to their poverty, unemployment and underemployment, social isolation, and lack of achievement including stigma and discrimination based on the illness, racism, sexism, ageism, distribution of resources, governmental and agency policies, the models by which professionals practice, etc. Contextualizing also involves demonstrating that others are similarly situated due to similar processes. In other words, they are not alone.

Care must be exercised in using this method so that self-blame does not transform into environmental blame which Rappaport, Davidson, Mitchell, & Wilson (1975) argue can be as inimical to achievement and helping as individual blaming. There are people who have involved themselves in consciousness-raising activities that get stuck in the stage of awareness and the anger that often results. Much like admitting that one has a severe mental illness yet it is only one part of me, the view is that "Yes, these social processes go on, they affect me profoundly, I am not to blame, but they are only one slice of the social world." That social world is also constructed of opportunities, resources, and caring people.

Self-Disclosure[1]

Similar to reciprocity, self-disclosure is a normal component of most relationships. The self-help movement is based on the idea that personal disclosure and reciprocal helping are both appropriate and healing. Conventional wisdom has been that workers should reveal little about their personal values, problems, fears, opinions, etc. (American Psychological Association, 1977; Hackney & Cormier, 1975; Wells & Masch, 1986). This stricture places a constraint on staff to act as if they had no problems, emotions, or experience with life. Such pressure is unrealistic and withholds one of the most powerful aspects of a helping relationship.

Ironically, consumers and ex-patients are often hired by mental health agencies with the expectation that they will disclose personal history and openly draw upon their experiences in their role as staff. Self-disclosure by workers can help to establish bonds of trust and understanding, to validate the normalcy of consumer feelings and concerns, to provide examples of how situations can be alternatively handled, and to demonstrate effective ways of expressing both positive and negative emotions.

The fundamental points for discussion in self-disclosure issues are "To what degree?" and "For what purpose?" It is important for staff to be clear that the purpose of self-disclosure in helping relationships is not to meet the needs of the worker, but those of the consumer. The relationship does not exist to work out the problems of the paid staff person. Staff disclosure of personal feelings, attitudes and values happens both deliberately and inadvertently through non-verbal cues. Like most people, consumers are sensitive to any lack of congruence between verbal and non-verbal messages. It is far better to convey this information explicitly in a way that is constructive to the relationship than to communicate mixed messages.

While self-disclosure is an intricate part of most relationships, the type and amount varies widely between individuals and relationships. Individual interests and experience are often most easily shared. Family configu-

---

1. Much of this section has been reprinted from L. C. Curtis & M. Hodge (1994), Old standards, new dilemmas: Ethics and boundaries in community support services. In the Publication Committee of IAPSRS (Eds.), *An Introduction to Psychiatric Rehabilitation*. Boston: The International Association of Psychosocial Rehabilitation Services.

rations and relations (e.g., "My brother is like that too") are usually next. Feelings are often the most difficult. Each case manager needs to determine the amount and nature of disclosure that is comfortable and use that level purposively with each client. Of particular importance is sharing with the client your positive feelings about them, the benefits you have enjoyed because of the case manager relationship with the client, and what the client has taught you. Maluccio (1979) found that one of the characteristics of social workers most cherished by clients was their ability "to share of himself or herself with the client" (p. 125).

Accompaniment

Walter Deitchman's (1980) wonderful metaphor of the travel companion (chapter 3) at times assumes a literal translation. Most people are scared or anxious when confronting a new task or situation. For people with severe mental illness, that fear and lack of confidence is acute and immobilizing. For some, even obviously simple and mundane tasks, can be a source of great anxiety.

Accompaniment refers to the case manager going with the client, in a sense "holding their hand," while the client does a task. Just the physical presence of a trusted person can often provide the emotional support and courage for the client. Accompaniment in this regard does not necessarily refer to doing part of the task for the client (although at times this can be another justification for accompaniment). Many times, a client's lack of followthrough on tasks they readily established as desirable is due not to "resistance" or lack of skills but, rather, to overwhelming fear.

> Joe was 46 years old and had spent the last 18 years in a Veterans Administration hospital for paranoid schizophrenia. Upon release, Joe needed to apply with Social Security for SSI. Joe readily wrote this goal on his personal plan but while working on defining the steps necessary (e.g., finding the address in the phone book, looking at a map, locating transportation, etc.), the case manager began noticing some hesitation. A week later, few of the tasks were accomplished. During the discussion, Joe admitted how fearful he was. The plan was changed. Over the next few days, the case manager drove Joe past the Social Security office several times. They then walked past it several times. They walked into the lobby and then returned to the street several times. Only then was Joe able, again with the case manager accompanying him, to apply for benefits. At no time did the case manager do any of the tasks. Joe got the appointment, completed the forms, talked to the receptionist, answered the eligibility worker's questions, etc. The case manager was just there.

For many professionals, this type of assistance raises the specter of dependency and is therefore contraindicated. The position here is that simplistic and unrealistic notions of "dependency" have undermined client achievement and at times have acted as professionally sounding excuses for *not* helping. No person is independent in any pure sense. Human beings are, rather, interdependent. We all exist and survive based on our interactions with others and the resources available to us. The most "dependent" people are the wealthy. They need not cook, clean, drive, or even raise their children. Yet we rarely describe the wealthy as dependent in some pathological sense.

The aim is not to do for a client what they can do for themselves, although at times this is necessary. This could undermine a client's sense of achievement and confidence. Rather, it is to provide the interpersonal support necessary for the client to do, to achieve.

Reinforcement and Celebration

Most satisfying relationships involve the regular if not frequent exchange of reinforcing comments (e.g., "That's great," "I'm proud of you for. . . ," "You really did a nice job on the . . ."). Reinforcing comments are usually contingent; they are based on the occurrence of something caused by a person's behavior. In this way, they are different from statements that communicate unconditional positive regard (e.g., "I really like you," "I am in awe of your courage").

Most people respond positively to praise. For maximum effect the praise should:

1. be for a specific behavior,
2. have immediacy—some time proximity between the behavior and the reward.

Praise is often warranted for the smallest achievements. Given the lack of confidence and the fear that dominate the lives of people with severe mental illness, even the accomplishment of some small and seemingly mundane task is worthy of recognition. In the previous case of Joe, walking past the Social Security office warrants a "pat on the back." It is as important for effort to be recognized as for a tangible achievement. In fact, one can argue that praising effort, possible learning, and the "little" accomplishments within a "failure" is more important than praising successes because successes inherently contain positive feedback where failures rarely do.

The reinforcement need not be limited to verbal communication. Writing notes or giving certificates of achievement can be used. One case manager used little stickers, affixing one next to each task the client achieved. For some clients, this would be demeaning, suggesting an adult–child relationship. But in this case it fit, it was meaningful within the specific case manager–client relationship. This same case manager used this technique with only this one client; discrimination is required.

This leads to another dimension: The nature of the reinforcement, its frequency, and its form need to be individually tailored. What is most meaningful for one person is not necessarily most meaningful for another. For example, telling another person of an accomplishment in front of the client may embarrass one client while for another their face beams with pride.

This is especially true of "celebrations." Celebrations are those events involving the case manager and the client, designed to recognize a specific and special achievement. In Joe's case, completing the application process could warrant a celebration. For another client, this would be demeaning. A celebration for one client who got a job may be a celebration for another client who stayed on the job for two weeks. The nature of the celebration needs to be similarly tailored to the individual, the relationship, and the achievement. Going to lunch or a ball game or an art exhibit would have differential meanings for clients.

The relationship between case manager and client should be infused with reinforcement. In this way, case managers help clients to feel competent and confident that they can achieve, often achieving what they could not achieve before. The goal is to make every client "feel like a winner." The old adage that "nothing succeeds like success" has some scientific basis:

> Researchers studying motivation find that the prime factor is simply the self-perception among motivated subjects that they are in fact doing well. Whether they are or not by any absolute standard doesn't seem to matter much. In one experiment, adults were given puzzles to solve. All ten were exactly the same for all subjects. They worked on them, turned them in, and were given the results at the end. Now, in fact, the results they were given were fictitious. Half of the exam takers were told that they had done well, seven out of ten correct. The other half were told they had done poorly, seven out of ten wrong. Then all were given another ten puzzles (the same for each person). The half who had been told that they had done well in the first round really did do better in the second, and the other half really did do worse. Mere association with past personal successes apparently leads to more persistence, higher motivation, or something that makes us do better. (Peters & Waterman, 1982, p. 58)

Positively reinforced behavior slowly comes to occupy a larger and larger share of time and attention and less desirable behavior begins to be dropped.

ENGAGEMENT

While engagement, in a sense, is a recurring theme throughout the relationship and even with each contact, engagement in the initial stages of helping has some unique properties and methods. In the strengths model, engagement is a separate function unlike most formulations that prescribe assessment as the initial stage (Levine & Fleming, undated; Kisthardt, 1992). Given the importance of the relationship as the bedrock of work, and the painful histories of a professional and interpersonal relationships experienced by people with severe mental illness, engagement is viewed as the indispensable and critical first step.

Some clients enter a new relationship with a case manager eagerly and easily, but for most the encounter is a reluctant one, characterized by suspicion. So many past relationships, professional and otherwise, have been a source of disappointment, pain, and messages of incompetence, damaged goods, and inadequacy. Many have had professional helpers before, if not case managers. So I am still sick, still poor, still lonely, etc. Given the nature of most professional practice, the professional held most of the power. "They told me what to do and how to do it. They committed me. They would not adjust the medication when I told them of my side effects. They made me work as a janitor and blamed me when I quit. They made me make Halloween masks in their program and criticized me for being disruptive."

The reluctance and sometimes downright rejection of a newly assigned case manager is understood not as a symptom of paranoia but as an understandable and logical response to the client's experience. On the other hand, reluctance is normal for most people as they confront an uncertain and somewhat invasive interpersonal situation. Most people experience some misgivings and doubt when asked to become involved in an endeavor that is new or that has not turned out well for them in the past. Most people are somewhat guarded and distrusting when being persuaded to become involved in a relationship of which they are unsure. We need to give that same consideration to clients as we reach out to them, without resorting to familiar labels which place this normal reaction in the context of paranoid ideations or other forms of symptomatology.

Given this situation, specific methods of engagement need to be added to methods identified for relationship. Some of the following methods have been lacking from other helping formulations or have been deemed unprofessional, unnecessary, or even harmful to clients. Therefore, those methods can be easily viewed as non-traditional.

Location of Engagement

The first meeting, as well as subsequent ones, should occur where and when the client specifies. Most clients will select a community location: their apartment, a coffee shop, a park. Some will assume, based on past experience, that it has to be at the mental health center or other agency. A few will actually prefer an agency office, usually based on familiarity or psychological safety. Whenever possible, the case manager should encourage a community location comfortable to the client (see "Rationale" in Chapter 3 in section on "Outreach"). At times, this may simply be a matter of the case manager asking the client where they would feel most comfortable meeting and if necessary proposing options. As one client stated:

> Sometimes we do it at the Pizza Hut, we both like to eat, I don't mind meeting with my therapist here at the center, but it's kind of nice to meet other places, it's just easier to talk about things when I'm out of here.

In many situations, just the offering of this choice of time and place can signal to the client that this may be different. Kisthardt (1993) reports that this is important to clients. As one consumer who, at the time, was not engaged in service reflected:

> When we first got together Kim (CM) would say things like "Let's get together and have some coffee and talk and get to know each other." She would let me pick out the places I wanted to go. This made me feel like she was respecting me, she was saying you make the decision and I'll go where you want to go. In other words, Kim was serving me and me not serving Kim [sic]. She accepted me for the way I am. I could feel it, she projected warm, caring feelings. (Kisthardt, 1993, p. 176)

A community location also enhances the likelihood of contact. It is less reliant on the client to necessarily get somewhere (and in the face of some suspicion) and more reliant on the case manager following through.

Engagement is often facilitated when an activity is used as a backdrop to conversation. It is often more relaxing. A conversation in a closed office heightens tension and pressure; all you have is conversation. Going for a walk, feeding pigeons, working, cooking, shooting baskets, or washing a car can make that set of initial meetings more comfortable. It also allows the client and case manager to early on "share" an event or experience. If the activity backdrop is unfamiliar to the case manager, shooting baskets for someone who has never picked up a basketball, it places the client in the position of competence, an expert, and perhaps a teacher.

Attempts should be made to contact consumers you will be working with prior to the first face-to-face meeting. This strategy appears to serve three purposes. First, it represents a non-threatening way to introduce yourself and the case management process to potential consumers. Also, it demonstrates a respect for the individual's right to privacy, as well as the right to be informed regarding decisions made by the treatment team. Usually, case managers attempt to reach consumers by phone if this is possible. They have also used correspondence and report that this seems to be valued by some consumers. The following example of such contact attempts to incorporate the philosophy of a strengths approach:

> Dear Mr. (Ms.) _____
>
> My name is _____ , and I am a case manager at (program's name). I wanted you to know that I have been assigned to contact you, to see if you would be interested in working with me. As a case manager, I might be able to help you with the things that you think are important for you in your life. I would like to meet you so that we can get to know each other, and answer any questions you might have. I can meet with you whenever, and wherever you like. If you want to call me to talk further about case management my number is _____. If I am not here please leave a message and I will call back. If I do not hear from you may I drop by your place on (day, date, and time)? I hope you'll consider working with me. I look forward to meeting you soon.
>
> Sincerely,
> (Case Manager's Name)
> (Kisthardt, 1992, p. 68)

Conversational

The focus of the first and early client–case manager encounters should be conversational. The flavor should be similar to that used when any two people are first meeting. As Kisthardt (1992) describes:

> During the initial meetings, case managers attempt to model the belief in mutuality and a helping partnership by engaging in a normative social dialogue rather than a more formal question and answer interview. These meetings involve a bilateral information exchange. In contrast to the traditional mental health intake interview, where the clinician typically asks most of the questions from which the diagnosis or psychosocial assessment will be generated, the engagement process encourages mutual sharing and self-disclosure on the part of the case manager. These relate to efforts to establish areas of common interest, such as music, sports, television, or other interpersonal common denominators, which serve to establish an emerging helping relationship. (p. 67)

It almost resembles "chatting," an informal process of getting to know another person, not a client. This is in direct contrast with the interrogation style often displayed by mental health professionals during intake and early encounters.

Interviews with consumers have tended to support specific helping strategies that may serve to increase the desire to engage in the case management process. When asked about the first meeting with case managers, consumers stated such things as "being easygoing and laid-back," "having a good sense of humor," "asking me about the things I wanted to do," "not asking me a lot of personal questions" (one consumer said that the case manager "did not impress him as a snoopervisor"), and "sharing things about themselves," as being important to them (Kisthardt, 1992, p. 166).

Doing the Concrete

In contrast with or, rather, in addition to chatting, engagement can be facilitated by doing a concrete case management task with the client. A person who has no food would rather receive help in getting food than waiting for a relationship to form before tangible tasks get pursued. People who work with homeless persons have learned that the provision of a cheese sandwich is more welcomed and can act as a basis for a yet-to-emerge relationship than some stranger who wants to talk. Seventy years ago, Mary Richmond (1922) discussed the power of helping another with a tangible task as a way of promoting a relationship.

Many clients are living in circumstances where basic needs are not being met and these are blatantly obvious. If the client desires, the case manager should seek to meet these needs immediately. Care must be exercised, however. For some clients, their definition of basic needs may be different from the case manager's and their desire for assistance may not be welcomed. Except in the most dire circumstances, where there is an immediate danger to themselves or others, the case manager needs to receive sanction for action from the client.

At times, the case manager may want to provide information to the client about services and rights. Steve Rose's (Rose & Black, 1985) program in Sayville, New York, gave each client at the first meeting with the case manager a packet of information containing:

CASE MANAGEMENT

Client Check List

1. Our agency's Community Support Systems Information packet. Describes case management program and day program, with names, addresses and telephone numbers included along with meeting times for day program.
2. Eligibility Form—a State Office of Mental Health form that we are required to fill out (copy given to client)
3. Office of Mental Health consent form, releasing state hospital to give dates of hospitalization to Community Support Systems agencies. Necessary for eligibility (copy given to client with information about our interpretation of confidentiality).
4. Information about how to get and use Medicaid transportation.
5. Bus routes along a map of the area.
6. Handicapped ID form and information packet (for use in getting reduced bus fares and for general identification purposes).
7. Adult Home or SRO legal rights/entitlements booklet (copy given to client).
8. Voter registration packet (given to client).
9. Rent rebate—State Income Tax Rebate form (copy given to client).

While clients have repeatedly expressed the importance of the relationship and there is some empirical evidence of its contribution to outcomes, some people do not desire a relationship that may be characterized by friendliness and intimacy. Some prefer a rather "business-like" relationship focused on getting tangible help with specific life tasks. Sometimes this will evolve into something more and sometimes it will not. In these situations, the case manger should not force intimacy but, rather, respect the client's desire and proceed to provide the assistance the client wants.

Role Induction

Strengths model case management is different from other mental health services and other models of case management. It entails a different and unfamiliar way of working for most clients. The expectations of clients and case managers are different. Role induction refers to the beginning efforts

TABLE 4.1
Engagement

Purpose: To create a trusting and reciprocal relationship between the case manager and consumer as a basis for working together.

Behavior

1. Schedules meetings with the consumer at a time and place (provides community choices) mutually agreed upon. (In most situations, minimum contact is one time per week.)
2. CM and consumer are involved in a leisurely activity as a backdrop for getting to know each other (e.g., cup of coffee, shooting baskets, walking).
3. CM engages consumer in a conversational manner, exploring interests and experiences in common.
4. CM uses empathy, reinforcing comments, both verbally and non-verbally.
5. CM discusses purpose of case management and mutual expectations. (Looks toward replacement of self, focusing on graduated disengagement.)
6. CM uses every opportunity to identify personal and environmental strengths.
7. CM reviews in group supervision (by presenting clear, concise consumer situation reviews to generate new ideas) if having difficulty engaging (after three "no's" with consumer).

to describe and manifest in behavior this new way of working together. The elements would include:

1. The purpose: to assist you to achieve the goals you set for yourself (goals can be to maintain things the way they are).
2. The client is the director of the helping. He or she decides the content, the pace, the location, the resources, the goals, etc.
3. The case manager will assist you to locate opportunities, options, resources desired by you.
4. The case manager will work with you to insure your rights are being enforced.
5. The case manager wants to know what is working well in your life despite the challenges you face each day.

Added to this list are any limitations on the work as directed by agency policy, personal preference, funding source, ethics, or resource constraints. A discussion of confidentiality and situations where the person is in immediate danger to themselves or others.

The most powerful way of conveying the differences, however, is based on action and consistency of action. Table 4.1 contains those core behaviors required for engagement in the strengths model.

CHAPTER 5
_____

Strengths Assessment: Amplifying the Well Part of the Individual

Purpose: To collect information on personal and environmental strengths as a basis for work together.

The compelling pull for society to the negative of life (Weick et al., 1989) is reflected in mental health and that of the relevant professional disciplines. The entire field is dominated by assessment protocols and devices that seek to identify all that is wrong, problematic, deficient, or pathological in the client and at times the environment. "The *Diagnostic and Statistical Manual of Mental Disorders IV* (DSM-IV), although only 7 years removed, has twice the volume of text on disorders as its forebear" (Saleebey, 1996). Although Axis V in this method evaluates a person's highest level of adaptive functioning, there is little evidence it is being used in practice, and serious questions have been raised about its reliability (Kirk & Kutchins, 1987). With some perplexity, Lois Barclay Murphy writes:

> It is something of a paradox that a nation which has exulted in its rapid expansion and its scientific-technological achievements, would have developed in its studies of childhood so vast a "problem" literature: a literature often expressing adjustment difficulties, social failures, blocked personalities, and defeat...! There are thousands of studies of maladjustment for each one that deals directly with ways of managing life's problems with personal strength and adequacy.

Taking a behavioral baseline on client deficits and examining the ability of social workers to correct these deficits have become the standard for evaluating the effectiveness of the profession (Kagle & Cowger, 1984). The same may be said of psychology (Rappaport, 1977) and psychiatry (Wolins

& Wolins, 1993). The skills orientation of much of psychiatric rehabilitation (Lieberman, 1992; Anthony, 1979) is focused on identifying skill deficits and then teaching those skills to clients.

A BRIEF CRITIQUE OF CURRENT APPROACHES

Regardless of method or orientation, the purpose of assessment is to collect information needed to establish the direction and means of intervention. In chapter 3, problem or deficit models were criticized as homogenizing clients and reducing motivation. Current deficit-oriented assessment protocols do this in part by amplifying the sick or weakness part of the individual. The message once again is one of ineptness. It is like "painting by numbers." Ask these questions and explore these areas and the portrait that emerges is of a weak and helpless client.

> In my psychiatric residency that followed medical school, I glibly applied the terminology of physical disease to the "disorders" of behavior and the mind. Eventually, I became so immersed in pathology that I no longer even used the word healthy. Instead, I conceived of health as the absence of illness and referred to people who were well as "asymptomatic," "nonclinical," "unhospitalized," or "having no severe disturbance." In retrospect, the worst offender was the term "unidentified," as if the only way I could know a person was by his or her sickness. (Wolin & Wolin, 1993, p. 13)

The result is that the professional must take charge and lead the way: They obviously know best.

Beyond the images created for the client and worker, assessment dictates—it seems inevitably—the nature of the intervention. Skill deficits lead to skill training. High expressed emotion leads to efforts to reduce it. Seeing current problems as rooted in historical family dysfunction leads to efforts to understand that history. Provoked by the assessment, therefore, the entire helping relationship and process are contoured.

Another ramification of the dominant approaches to assessment is the dearth of content related to the environment. At best, some attention will be devoted to family but again it usually reflects problems and conflicts. There are a few exceptions. Good vocational rehabilitation practice would involve a detailed description of desirable characteristics of the workplace and subsequent efforts to make "reasonable accommodations." Such an approach is suggested here for all life domains and niches.

While other professions have little in their evolution suggesting a consideration of strengths, social work is different. Since its earliest days, social work has acknowledged the criticalness of people's strengths as a basis for helping. "Actually, social work has been long on philosophy and theory that flaunts a client strengths perspective, but short on practice directions, guidelines, and 'know how' for incorporating strengths into practice" (Cowger, 1989). As Hepworth and Larsen (1986) state: "Social workers persist in formulating assessments that focus almost exclusively on the pathology and dysfunction of clients, despite the time honored social work platitude that social workers work with strengths, not weaknesses" (p. 167). As Beisser (1990) states:

> If we scrutinize a person selectively to discover his [sic] weaknesses, his faults, or the ways in which he is deficient, we can always find some, although in varying degrees of obviousness. If, on the other hand, we look to ways in which that person is whole or healthy, we will also discover many things. So it will appear that the point of reference determine the characteristics we will find. Seek and ye shall find. (p. 181)

If we are to help throw off the yoke of oppression, enhance a client's sense of empowerment, and help them achieve that which is important to them, we must remove the pathological imagery that our current assessment methods engender. As Rappaport (1990) states:

> To work within an empowering ideology requires us to identify (for ourselves, for others, and for the people with whom we work) the abilities they possess which may not be obvious, even to themselves. . . . It is always easier to see what is wrong, and what people lack. Empowering research [and practice] attempts to identify what is right with people, and what resources are already available, so as to encourage their use and expansion under the control of the people of concern. (p. 12)

Table 5.1 portrays one depiction of contrasts between a strengths assessment and a problems assessment.

STRENGTHS ASSESSMENT: CONTENT

Maluccio (1981) refers not to assessment but chooses the term "competence clarification." De Shazer (1988), in discussing his "clues" to brief therapy, remarks that one task incumbent on the therapist is to "note what sort of things the clients do that is good, useful, and effective" (p. 98). Strengths assessment is therefore a process by which a client's personal and environmental assets are identified. These assets are organized into six life domains:

> Daily Living Situation—includes the client's residence and specific features like roommates, furnishings, location, condition, access to resources such as food store, laundry, etc.
>
> Financial—focuses on the sources and amount of income, debts and loans, financial and possession assets (e.g., car, owns own home), sources of emergency funds.
>
> Vocational/Educational—pertains to employment and its features, formal and informal education activities, specialized training, credentials, etc.
>
> Social and Spiritual Supports—includes family, friends, co-workers, neighbors, and the nature of the relationships as well as the role of spiritual matters of relevance and formal religion.

TABLE 5.1

Strengths assessment	Problems assessment
What the person wants, desires, aspires to, dreams of. Information gathered about persons talents, skills, and knowledge. A holistic portrait.	Defines diagnosis as the problem. Questions are pursued related to problems. Needs, deficits, symptoms.
Gathers information from the standpoint of the consumer's view of their situation. Ethnographic.	The problem assessment searches for the nature of patient/client's problem from the perspective of a professional. Analytical.
Is conversational and purposive.	Is an interrogative interview.
The focus is on the here and now, leading to a discussion of the future/past—asking how they have survived so far.	The focus is on diagnosis assessment procedures to determine the level of functioning.
Persons are viewed as unique human beings who will determine their wants within self and environment.	The client/patient is viewed as lacking insight egarding behavior or in denial regarding scope of problem or illness.
Is ongoing and never complete with the relationship primary to the process. Encouragement, coaching, and validation is essential to the process.	Done at a set time (often at in-take) and largely viewed as completed at that time.
Strengths assessment is specific and detailed, individualizes person.	The intent of the problem assessment is to place the person in diagnostic or problem category. Often written with generic, homogenous language.
In conducting a SA, behavior is considered a desire to communicate.	In a PA behavior is seen as symptamology, attributed to disorder.
Consumer authority and ownership.	Is controlled by the professional.

Health—involves the status and resources relevant to physical and dental illness and health promotion (diet, exercise) as well as the mental illness (medications, doctor, side effects, awareness of early warning signs of symptom exacerbation).

Leisure/Recreational—focuses on the sources and circumstance of enjoyment and fun—the where, what, who of their leisure time.

These life domains correspond to those life areas that clients are most concerned about. They also reflect the major niches that people occupy. The focus is on actual life activities that reflect successful community functioning of the person and the resources, personal and environmental, that are and have been employed. Tied to the theory of strengths, the case manager is seeking information reflective of the person's talents, aspirations, and confidence, and the opportunities, resources, and social relations from the environment.

Each individual's behavior is influenced by the confluence of their own personal history, their present social context, and their visions of what they would like to achieve (Kisthardt & Rapp, 1992). Each life domain is therefore divided into three temporal categories:

1. Current status
2. Desires and aspirations
3. History

Current status includes the personal competencies and environmental resources being used in the client's present life circumstances. Moore-Kirkland (1981) has added that by "identifying what the client persistently and recurrently is engaging in will help the worker understand what motivations are important in the clients life" (p. 46). Desires and aspiration refer to the future. What does the client want? How would the client like to configure their lives?

Finally, there is an attempt to learn what kinds of resources the person has used in the past. The importance of this category is twofold. First, it is important for helpers and clients to recall that there are many histories embedded in their lives. Competence is a cumulative history of involvements with the environment. In most cases there have been periods, sometimes lengthy, of productivity or more successful community functioning. This helps both the worker and the client avoid the creation of artificial ceilings on expectations. Secondly, these past involvements may provide clues for additional client goals or may represent resources or involvements that the clients may wish to reestablish. Two examples:

> Ed Matthews is 56 years old and recently discharged from the state hospital. Ed has been hospitalized six times over the past 14 years. Ed admits having difficulty managing idle time which usually results in increased drinking and subsequent hospitalization. In completing the strengths assessment, the case manager learned of the long involvement of Ed's family in the restaurant business. Ed discussed his involvement with several of the restaurants. Ultimately the case manager helped Ed find a volunteer job at the local soup kitchen. Ed gained great satisfaction from this work and was able to successfully remain out of this hospital and began doing more outside the home with friends.

> Ms. G. stated her wish to stay in hospital, fill her days with basket work, and stop taking her medication. The Practitioner knew that the hospital was to close, that if she gave up basketwork she would start doing other more risky but exciting things, and that every time she cut her medication in the past it had been a disaster for her. As far as the Practitioner was concerned Ms. G. needed to face up to moving out, she needed to take her medication, and she would benefit from trying other activities. Saying such things to Ms. G. would result in instant rejection. Instead the Practitioner got to know what Ms. G. used to like doing and how she used to live. By discovering, and reminding Ms. G. of, the small positive things she used to manage, they began to talk theoretically about what sort of life she would like to lead. They visited some old haunts and Ms. G. began to talk about making some changes, and acknowledged that, since the hospital was going to have to close, she might think about moving out. In order to achieve her ideal, she was even willing to talk about how not taking her medication might ruin what she wanted. (Bleach & Ryan, 1995, p. 173)

There are three additional sections at the end of the strengths assessment instrument. First, there is a space for the case manager and/or the client to record positive personal attributes as perceived. This would include comments such as "good sense of humor," "persistent," "resilient," "energetic," "personable and friendly," etc. Second, there is space for the client to identify their priorities. At this point, what are those desires that are most important to the client? Third, there is a place for the client and case manager to sign the document symbolizing that it was a joint effort and accurately reflects the information that was shared. It does not symbolize that the identification and recording of strengths has been completed. As will be seen later, strengths assessment is a continuous process.

A blank strengths assessment instrument can be found in Figure 5.1.

STRENGTHS ASSESSMENT: PROCESS

The strengths assessment instrument does not resemble other assessment instruments. The process of strengths assessment also has differential protocols and guidelines. This section will describe the process in three areas: recording, style, and questioning.

Recording

The strengths assessment instrument requires brief narrative statements that are descriptive, not inferential. As such, the recording must be specific. For example, it should be recorded that a client says he likes to play basketball. It should also include information on where (e.g., park, YMCA, backyard), format (e.g., organized team in league play, pick-up games, just shooting), how often, and perhaps with whom. This information would be recorded in the leisure time category in each of the three temporal columns (e.g., currently, desired future, past). The specific information will likely be different in each column, although "playing basketball" would be in each.

A second recording guideline is: Do not obsess over the cell in which to place a piece of information. Life domains do not exist apart from other domains; overlap regularly occurs. For example, a client is sharing information about friends with the case manager. John is considered the client's best friend and the client goes on about their relationship and the activities they share. It does not matter if the case manager places those activities under social supports or leisure time activities. The important thing is get the information somewhere. Since there are no "right" or "wrong" places to record information, the consumer can be asked where it fits best for them. (See Figure 5.2 for two examples of filled-in strengths assessments.)

All assessment protocols require the professional to record the information. This is sensible given that the worker is most familiar with the device and knows what is required, and since it is largely for the worker's benefit, the worker can tailor it for their purposes. As Pincus and Minhan, (1973) describe:

> The purpose of the worker's assessment is to help him understand and individualize the relevant factors in a particular situation. Based on this

Manager's Name		Consumer's Name

Current status: What's going on today? What's available now?	Individual's desires, aspirations: What do I want?	Resources, personal social: What have I used in the past?
	Life domain Daily living situation	
	Financial/insurance	
	Vocational/educational	
	Social supports	

	Health	
	Leisure/recreational supports	

What are my priorities?

1.

2.

3.

4.

Case manager's comments:	Consumer's comments:
_____	_____
Case manager's signature	Case manager's signature
_____	_____
Date	Date

Figure 5.1. Case management; consumer strengths assessment.

Manager's Name		Consumer's Name
Harry Miller		Dan Fox

Current status: What's going on today? What's available now?	Individual's desires, aspirations: What do I want?	Resources, personal social: What have I used in the past?
	Life domain Daily living situation	
- currently living in a 2-bedroom apartment at Autumn Woods w/roommate (Jim) - has Section 8/IGR - has own stereo - has own TV - has 3 electric guitars - has telephone	- continue living in Section 8 apartment - would like to own his own house someday	- prior to living at Autumn Woods, lived at 2 bedroom apt in Olathe-Northwest apts. w/roommate for 1-1/2 yr. (Nov. 93 to Mar. 95) - lived w/parents (3 yr.) (1980–1983) - lived in an apt in Lawrence w/roommate 1 yr. - lived w/roommate in N. Lawrence for 8 months - lived at Breakthrough Group Home - at Tanners in Topeka (halfway house) - owned own cars (2) in past
	Financial/insurance	
- receives SSDI-$560 - currently has a guardian/payee - has Medicare (part A&B) - currently on spend down - good participant in CSS $ management program - receives weekly spending $20 - earns extra $ working CSS janitorial and mowing crew	- would like to get drivers license - would like to own a car	- received food stamps in the past - has Medicaid care once meets spenddown - earned extra $ doing odd jobs in past
	Vocational/educational	
- has high school diploma-1974 - recently complete VR assessment at JCCC-Community College - applied for Pell grant - completed Pass plan applications - currently working CSS janitorial crew, housekeeping and mowing crews	- would like to take courses at JCCC—this summer and fall - would like to be a research scientist (environmental scientist)	- completed 9 hr. of college classes at KU in 1976–1977 - worked as a dishwasher - worked as a gas station attendant - worked grounds attendant/landscaping/maintenance at KU - worked w/tree service in Lawrence-1 yr. - enjoys working outdoors

- janitorial sup. (Jim H.) - CSS staff/case manager - James (guardian) - family-parents/sister Sue - roommates parents (Mary & Abe) - girlfriends (Debbie & Sherry)	Social supports - would like to date more often! - would like to go to church more often	- family has always been supportive - Breakthrough-house manager Paul-1970's - peers at Fox Hollow/ Turning Point—client-run drop in center - Staff (Sally) at Residential Care Facility - Dr. Douglas (Topeka State) - Visits a family regularly
- Dr. Ericson - takes Clozaill - currently sets up weekly med. box w/assistance from CM - taking meds on own at this time - in excellent physical shape - smokes 1 pack/day	Health - would like to be more mentally and spiritually aware - exercise my mind more often - would like to quit smoking - get teeth fixed - get HIV tested	- has been on med. drops in the past - used Menninger's, Topeka State, KUMC for support in the past - was in Larned for 1 year - Yoga has been source of support - Family doctor-Dr. James
- plays guitar - spends time w/girlfriends - enjoys spending time at coffee house-Totos - enjoys reading (Buddhism, Philosophy, Yoga) - enjoys listening to music stereo/tapes/records (60's 70's Rock) - enjoy playing checkers - enjoys public TV-(KEPT))	Leisure/recreational supports - wants to take karate lessons - would like to form a band - would like to go target shooting - would like to go swimming	- read comic books - played backgammon - smoked dope and took saunas - used to go four wheel driving - drives out to the country - traveled (mostly U.S.) - has enjoyed playing guitar since he was 14 yr. old

What are my priorities?

1. Form a band.

2. Take courses at community college.

3.

4.

Case manager's comments:	Consumer's comments:
Upbeat, positive guy—likes people, very spiritual, *hard worker*!!! Bright & Articulate—a Lady's Man—Charming	I'm at 70% of my peak performance. If I continue my meditations and yoga and find a new girlfriend, I'll be at 90%.
Case manager's signature	Case manager's signature
Date	Date

Manager's Name

Marla Locke

Consumer's Name

Dennis Smith

Current status: What's going on today? What's available now?	Individual's desires, aspirations: What do I want?	Resources, personal social: What have I used in the past?
	Life domain Daily living situation	
- Currently living in Section 8 apartment at Whispering Falls - Lives alone-one bedroom-has a Buddha temple in living room-always smells of incense. - NO TV! (Doesn't like TV!) - Prays to Buddha 3 times a day. - Near grocery store and shopping center	- Wants to stay in the apartment-even if he has money someday so it will be easy to move. - Wants to live in a city someday: LA, New York or Washington DC	- Lived in Olathe for 3 or 4 years (alone) (1990–94) - Lived in Utah 7 years (apt, alone) (83–90) - Kentucky-first place he livedin US-with some bad people who cheated him (1970's) - Vietnam-Japan-Germany - France & Austria-moved frequently while working for Pan Am and the military.
- has had Social Security for 1 year-supported self working at restaurant for $2,000 a month (12 hr/day, 6 day/wk) before that at BoLings.	Financial/insurance - wants a job-a well paying one - wants to get new social security card and green card - wants to go to college - wants to improve his English - wants to win at Powerball	

- had some highly skilled jobs in the past in the service. - studies English everyday—3 hours a day. - seeking employment—checks want ads and works with Melinda-Vocational Staff - taking English as a Second Language as of 4/1/95	Vocational/educational - wants job and college - wants to be in the air force or to be a doctor someday - wants to be an electrician or air conditioning man for now.	- worked in restaurant (BoLings) 4 years - electrician in the air force in Vietnam (approx. 5 years-1960's) - Pan Am (5 years) 1960's
- Has many friends in his apartment complex and the community (Joe, Terry, Garret) - Buddhists - Asst. CM Bob, CM Beth - Friends are all over the world (from Vietnam) - Mother in Japan	Social supports - wants friends that are "good people" (no lying, keep secrets, honest, pray to God) no cheat anyone, don't hurt anyone, don't kill anyone, etc.) - Buddha will decide when it is time for him to get married.	- had a lot of friends in Vietnam
- good physical health - takes (Prolyxin) shots and pills, states that they help nothing - Dr. Ericson is his psychiatrist. - says the meds affect his vision negatively and cause dry mouth - hearing loss - feels weak due to weight loss	Health - says he wants to keep everything the same regarding his health - wants to gain weight: 220 lb. is his goal! - wants to get his teeth fixed!	- lost too much weight 6 months ago used to weigh 220—down to 180 now - no major illnesses or injuries—says Buddha protected him during the war.
- likes to cook - likes music-from China, Japan and all over the world - likes to talk and joke around with people - likes to eat out! Favorite Restaurant-China Royale - enjoys reading (fiction and Electronic magazines) - enjoys playing Powerball	Leisure/recreational supports - wants to go out to eat with some friends from his apartment complex	- used to like to play tennis - eating - parties - children and family - play with dog and duck - use to swim in lake and feed the ducks

What are my priorities?

1. Wants to improve his English

2. Wants to go to college.

3. Wants to gain weight.

4.

Case manager's comments:	Consumer's comments:
Friendly, Smiles a lot! Always helps others. Great at getting around town. Highly Intelligent, Educated	I need to live in peace and harmony.
_____ Case manager's signature	_____ Case manager's signature
_____ Date	_____ Date

Figure 5.2. Consumer strengths assessment.

> understanding he will make decisions on which aspects of the situation
> he will deal with, goals for the change effort, and means of achieving
> these goals. (p. 102)

In addition, some assessments require inferences and conclusions by the
worker that are to be kept secret from the client.

For a strengths assessment, either the client or the case manager or
both can be the recorder. Some clients recoil from seeing another form being "whipped out." Sometimes this reaction is in part due to paranoid elements of their illness and for some it is simply the recollection of another
instance of "unhelpful helping." As one client reflected:

> The strengths assessment just kept getting pushed back and I decided
> I didn't want to do it. Maybe I didn't want to be that positive. I didn't
> feel like I had any strengths then, but I do now.

After some discussion, if the client still is uneasy, the worker should gather
the information and shortly thereafter (preferably in their car) place the
information on the device.

Some clients are reluctant to discuss the details of their lives. For some
clients, asking them to identify their strengths and recount their achievements is so dissonant with their past experience that it engenders dis-

comfort. In some cases, the case manager has left a copy of a blank strengths instrument with the client, briefly described it, and asked if the client would write their ideas before the next visit. Occasionally, the actual form is dispensed with and the client is asked just to write down some talents or achievements or resources. The case manager may want to do a parallel recording; then at the next contact, the two documents are compared.

In most situations, the strengths assessment is placed between the client and case manager and described, and a choice is given to the client of whether the client or case manager should act as recorder. If the client selects the case manager, whenever possible the form should be easily viewed by the client. Sitting next to each other, rather than across a table, facilitates this. The case manager should also find frequent opportunities to tell the client what is being written (and checking its accuracy with the client).

Style

The style of assessing strengths should continue the friendly, two-way, conversational style described in the engagement chapter. *It should never resemble a one-sided interrogation!* Rather, the case manager should maintain as much eye contact as recording will allow. Demonstrate attentiveness with head nodding or changing facial expressions. Go at the client's pace. Remember the strengths assessment is never completed, its continuous, so there is no specific time by which it has to be done. As in any conversation, however, this does not mean that the case manager allows the client to ramble or overelaborate. In these situations, a case manager may say, "That's very interesting! I'd like to hear more about it but I'd also like to know more about . . ."

The assessment of strengths should be done in the client's natural environment whether apartment, cafe, or park. Not only does this facilitate the client's comfort but it provides rich possibilities for strengths assessment. A client may never mention a love for art and Claude Monet when sitting in an office. A case manager noticing two Monet posters in a client's living room may lead to information in an unyet mentioned area. The case manager can also meet neighbors, friends, family, and coworkers who are within the client's sphere.

> Susan James is 47 years old and suffers from schizophrenia. She has been married for 14 years. Her husband, Art, also has had bouts with mental illness that have resulted in hospitalization. Both are unemployed surviving on SSI benefits. Susan has been hospitalized nine times in the past year for what she terms anxiety. While she was interested in the services of a case manager, she was reluctant to leave her home. In completing the strengths assessment the case manager learned that Susan enjoyed soap operas. They agreed to spend some time together watching soap operas over the next several weeks. During this time, the case manager learned that Susan and her husband were formerly very interested in playing cards. The case manager came to meet other tenants of the apartment building and through chatting found out that there

was a weekly card game among the neighbors. The case manager helped Susan, and eventually her husband, join the group. Ultimately this led to increased activities outside the home and even a vacation in a neighboring state. Susan has not been hospitalized for the past two years.

Without the outreach mode, it was unlikely this environmental opportunity and resources, literally next door, would have been uncovered.

Questioning

The guidelines for questioning during strengths assessments include some that are common to most approaches and a few that are different.

1. Use open-ended questions because they have the potential for facilitating more and enriched information. For example, if you are interested in a person's leisure time activities, do not ask, "Do you like to garden?" Rather, ask, "Do you have any hobbies or activities you like doing?" or "What kind of activities make you happy?"

2. Use questions that are reflective of behavior as well as opinion. In addition to or instead of asking, "Do you have any hobbies or activities you like doing?" ask, "What do you do for fun?" or "What is a typical day for you?" or "Could you describe yesterday for me?" or "What did you do last week that you enjoyed the most?"

3. Probe until you have specifics and an understanding of what is being reported. If the client answers the last question above, "I went to movies and saw *Mrs. Doubtfire*," the case manager could ask questions about "Who went with you?" "How often do you go to movies?" "What are your favorite movies or types of movies?" "When do you like to go?" "What kind of snacks do you get?" "Which is your favorite theater?" "Which movie roles or actors are your favorite?" "How often would you like to go to the movies?" "Do you ever rent movies?" You get the idea!

4. Go where the client takes you. Since the strengths assessment is to be done conversationally, adhering to a row or column on the forms is contraindicated. For example, a mention that the client went to the movies with two friends from church suggests a focus on the friendships or social and spiritual domains. Reflective of a conversational style is a strengths assessment with information scattered across cells (i.e., life domains and temporally) and others possibly blank (for now). In contrast, a form with some rows filled in and others blank strongly suggests that it was done in a non-conversational and perhaps in an interrogatory style.

5. Reflect and self-disclose. As a client shows a piece of themselves, the case manager is encouraged to share a piece of themselves or a reaction: "I loved *Mrs. Doubtfire*, too. In fact, I love almost everything Robin Williams is in!" or "For some reason I have never felt comfortable going to a movie alone as you do. Sometimes I wish I did." These kind of responses help develop a personal bond between people and demonstrates that the case manager is listening.

6. Demonstrate empathy and the hearing of feelings. Most of the guidelines have related most directly to the content of the conversation. The case manager must also be able to hear the emotional content. Do the client's statements suggest sorrow, fear, disappointment, frustration, anger, inadequacy, anxiety, confusion, rejection, loneliness, guilt, or embarrassment? Or do they suggest joy, fulfillment, happiness, caring, love, satisfaction, competence, strength? The case manager must then communicate the feelings heard back to the client. "I sense you are feeling frightened"; "You seem to have received great satisfaction from . . ." (readers are referred to *Direct Social Work Practice* by Hepworth and Larson, 1986, for a fuller discussion of this topic).

7. Help clients see the well part of themselves. A client's life and the experience with the mental health and other systems is such that many clients have difficulty seeing their lives as one of strengths, talents, and achievements. A client who says, "I only completed one year of college and then I had to drop out," is conveying that self-identity as a failure. On the other hand, the case manager might respond, "So you have a high school diploma and one year of college under your belt." The case manager may also go on to check out the emotional content, "It sounds as if this is of some disappointment in not going further in college. Is that true?" Case managers should exploit every opportunity to feed back to clients that while their lives contain pain and disappointment, like others it also contains a history of achievement (e.g., "This is a strength I've noticed about you"). As one client reflected:

> We work on things each week, like goals and stuff. I remember her doing the strengths assessment. I think she saw a lot more in me than I saw in myself. It felt better talking about me as a person rather than as a manic-depressive.

8. In addressing areas that may be awkward or embarrassing, maintain a matter-of-fact composure. It is more likely to be received that way.

STRENGTHS ASSESSMENT IS CONTINUOUS

The gathering of strengths-oriented information begins at the first contact with the client and continues to occur throughout the service. It is not often that a case manager will use the strengths assessment device during the first meeting. A piece of paper for recording information is often awkward during the initial attempt at engagement. It is not unusual for several meetings to go by before introducing the instrument. With every meeting, however, the case manager is gathering information about interests, talents, goals, and resources. These are to be recorded on the strengths assessment instrument.

There usually comes a time when the client and case manager focus on filling in the strengths assessment. This can take from one to three meetings. Subsequent to these sessions, the case manager and client will continue to identify client strengths. Life is continually evolving. The client will experience new people in different situations. As the client's life story evolves, new achievements and resiliencies will be identified. Each of these pieces of data warrants inclusion on the strengths assessment and, perhaps more important, to be verbally fed back to the client.

CLIENT OWNERSHIP

The strengths assessment should not be something done to someone. It is desirable for the process to have the flavor of mutuality, of dialogue. It is also desirable for the client to feel some ownership of the assessment and the process. The strengths assessment can be viewed as a developing "portrait of the well-side of the individual." Like any art, it should be a portrait that brings some pleasure and insight to the viewer.

Client involvement is important. Having the client be the recorder, placing the device between you, and asking the client how to best phrase some item may help increase their involvement. Many agencies now use NCR paper so that a copy can be torn off and given to the client. The client may choose to start their own strengths assessment between meetings. The case manager can have the strengths assessment on a clipboard and have the client record strengths information while the case manager is driving.

THE EXPERIENCE OF STRENGTHS ASSESSMENT

There are several conclusions that have been drawn based on 13 years of experimentation and implementation of the strengths assessment process. For professionals, there is great difficulty in moving from an interrogation mode to a conversational mode. The tendency is to fire questions at the client. Despite the less rigid format of the instrument and the attendant protocols, new case managers tend to rigidly pursue their questions by sticking to one life domain until "completed." A second difficulty is to develop the skills needed to be specific, to get the details of a strength.

For clients, there is considerable difficulty at times in their willingness and ability to engage in the strengths assessment process. For some, it remains just another instance of some professional "nosing around" in my life. Their easily understood skepticism can be exacerbated when insufficient time has been devoted to engagement. For other clients, reflecting on strengths is a totally unique experience and, as with most new experiences, it can be difficult. Some have never been asked for their talents and dreams before. Others have used their illness and deficit identity as a shield to more pain and disappointment.

Despite the difficulties, the benefits of strengths assessment are clear. Clients tend to experience the assessment process as comfortable and energizing in and of itself (Kisthardt, 1993). As one consumer stated:

TABLE 5.2
Strengths Assessment

Purpose: To collect information on personal and environmental strengths as a basis for work together.
Behavior

1. Information is gathered conversationally (not interview or interrogation).
2. Assessment process occurs over time in a variety of community settings to look for consumer strengths in the natural environment.
3. Information is specific, detailed, individualized (can tell who it is by looking at it) and in the consumer's voice.
4. CM points out, brings up, and records consumer's skills, talents, accomplishments, abilities, what they know about, care about, have a passion for in each life domain.
5. Consumer interests, wants, desires, and aspirations are recorded in each life domain (including desires to sustain the current circumstance).
6. Past and present attempts to use community resources are identified in each life domain in a manner that suggests successful coping rather than lack of success or failure?
7. A variety of ways are used to increase consumer ownership of the SA process (e.g., consumer writes their own, consumer gets a copy, consumer asked what cell to record information).
8. Reflects cultural, ethnic, racial information that holds meaning for consumer.
9. CM uses SA in group supervision to develop stronger plans.

> The strengths assessment helped me to integrate the different parts of my life. There's so much to keep straight, so many areas to think about, it really helped to make sense of it. It kind of helped me to see that where I am today is O.K. (p. 177)

Many other clients found the process motivating: "I have done things"; "I'm not such a bad person"; "This is a side of me I forgot." Kaplan and Girard (1994) write:

> People are more motivated to change when their strengths are supported. Instead of asking family members what their problems are, a worker can ask what strengths they bring to the family and what they think are the strengths of other family members. Through this process the worker helps the family discover its capabilities and formulate a new way to think about themselves. . . . The worker creates a language of strength, hope and movement. . . . (p. 49)

This suggests that motivation is a transactional phenomenon that results from the interaction of the person and the environment rather than the usual perspective that motivation is a quality processed or not processed by people subject to assessment (Moore-Kirkland, 1981). The strengths assessment process is one instance of a motivating transaction. The process itself is often enjoyable. It is rather common for laughter to accompany the discussion. (How often does laughter occur during intake interviews or other assessments?)

The strengths assessment process often begins the process of building a more complete picture of a client. Experience with the strengths assessment suggests that in recounting and remembering past involvements, interests have been restimulated, past successes long forgotten are relived, and ultimately the self-perception of the life history has shifted.

The strengths assessment process does produce the information needed to develop effective interventions. Cowger (1989) opines, "Basically, client strengths are all we have to work with" (p. 4). If this is correct, the process detailed here gathers this information better than any other process we know of. Table 5.2 is a listing of key behaviors required to do a strengths assessment with fidelity.

CHAPTER 6

Personal Planning: Creating the Achievement Agenda

Purpose: To create a mutual agenda for work between the client and case manager focused on achieving the goals that the client has set.

Personal planning is analogous to case planning and treatment planning but it is different in many ways. In the strengths model, personal planning is viewed as establishing the mutual agenda of work between the client and the case manager at any one point in time. Personal planning requires the client and case manager to discuss, negotiate, and agree on the long-term goal, short-term goals or tasks, who is responsible for each task, and target dates for accomplishment. A personal planning form is located in Figure 6.1. Each of these will be discussed in this chapter.

THE IMPORTANCE OF GOALS

Humans are purposeful organisms; we do things for a reason. Sometimes the reason is not evident, leading to mystification and casual pseudo-explanations of "irrationality." Lionel Aldridge, consumer activist, speaker, and former professional football player explained his and other consumers' suicidal behavior as often a reasoned response to the pain experienced from the mental illness. For some, it is the accumulation of a failed life, but for others, causing physical pain can temporarily replace the intolerable "mind pain" with something else. Similarly, mental health professionals have come to believe that self-imposed social isolation is uniformly a detrimental situation in the lives of people with severe mental illness. Yet Kisthardt and Rapp (1996) identified seven rationales or logical reasons for social isola-

For: _____ Case manager: _____ Date: _____

Planned frequency of contact: _____

Life domain focused upon:

   Daily living situation   Vocational/educational

   Social supports   Leisure/recreational supports

   Financial/insurance   Health

Consumer's long-term goal				
Measurable short-term goals toward achievement	Responsibility	Date to be accomplished	Date accomplished	Comments

_____   _____

Consumer's signature Date   Case manager signature Date

_____   _____

Psychiatrist signature Date   Collateral/signature   Date

Figure 6.1. Case management personal plan.

tion, some of which can be growth enhancing like convalescence, opportunities to create, sense of personal power, autonomy, and control.

Goals are inherent to hope and indispensable precursors to achievement. First-person accounts of recovery place having a purpose squarely in the center of that process. In the strengths theory, aspirations and goals occupy a cell to themselves underscoring the importance. As Locke, Shaw, Saari, and Latham (1981) state: "The beneficial effect of goal setting on task performance is one of the most robust and replicable findings in the psychological literature" (p. 145).

HOW GOALS FAIL

The protocols for personal planning in the strengths model have been designed to facilitate the achievement of client goals. It is instructive to first understand how goals fail. Based on the assumption of human purposefulness, the strengths model does not accept that people, including people with mental illness, have no goals. Our experience also suggests that the reasons goals are not achieved by clients are rarely due to the mental illness. Rather, client goals fail for the same reasons that all people may fail to achieve. As you read this section, you may want to reflect on goals that you did not achieve and the reasons. While in most cases, the reasons goals fail for clients are the same reasons that goals fail for all people, traditional or typical mental health practice can exacerbate or reflect these factors. Using the strengths theory as a framework, the reasons goals fail are organized by aspiration, competencies, confidence, and environmental factors.

Aspirations

The nature of the goal itself has much to do with its probability of attainment. Goals that are not a person's or not owned by the person are rarely achieved. We have all experienced goals being set for us by parents, teachers, friends, and bosses. Is your current career that which your parents wished for you? Has a boss ever set an improvement goal for you that you did not share?

A goal may be too ambitious to be met given time or resources. Sometimes people establish too many goals at the same time, leading to diffusion of effort and thereby rendering some or all of the goals unattainable. Conversely, if goals are set too low, feelings of personal excitement and interest may be insufficient to fuel efforts designed to achieve the goal.

Goals may be vague, lacking a clear and concrete set of behavioral referents. For example, goals related to "feeling better about myself," "having meaning in my life," "feeling more connected," or "getting a job that makes me happy" may exist in an amorphous manner with little feelings of progress toward achievement.

Failure to achieve goals can be due to goals being conflicting or producing fear. Conflicting goals are experienced by anyone who seeks simultaneously to achieve high levels of achievement as parents, spouses, and professionals. At times, visions of goal achievements can produce fear. The client who wants a job can become fearful that benefits will be reduced or eliminated: "What if I cannot do it?"

Mental Health Practices   Many times the identified goal was never really the client's but someone else's. This situation typically occurs in programs that have a predetermined list of treatment goals that apply generally to all clients. Case managers report that clients frequently agree with the goals as stated by the program only to "sabotage" them by acting out in some way or by not following through on designated short-term goals. This situation may reflect more on the clients' lack of a sense of ownership of the goal than on identified pathology such as resistance to treatment or denial of what it is they need to do.

Since expectations of people with severe mental illness have been typically low, goals are often mundane or irrelevant. A person with an engineering degree does not necessarily want to be on a "janitorial crew." A person who wants their own apartment will not be motivated to "earn" the privilege by first staying in a group home. Professionals sometimes justify their setting of less ambitious goals in terms of "not setting them up to fail."

For many professionals, there is a logical progression of goals that they impose on clients despite the clients' desire. For example, a first goal should be stabilizing or reducing symptomatology and taking medications as prescribed before pursuing employment. Clients should achieve the goal of taking a daily shower before seeking companionship.

Another impediment to an effective use of systematic goal setting is the tendency of practitioners and clients to set goals that are far too global in scope, thereby asking clients to do too much. It is important to recognize that while many clients have led successful lives before becoming ill, the process of integrating and reintegrating into the community involves learning and relearning skills. Thus, many of the kinds of activities that others take for granted represent significant steps or obstacles for clients.

Consider, for a moment, the number of steps and skills it takes to take a bus from point to point. First of all, one must become aware of the bus schedule in some fashion. This may require calling the bus station (if one has access to a telephone) or securing a schedule from the station. Then one must learn where the bus stops and where one would be best advised to depart. If a transfer is involved, there are special behaviors involved in this procedure such as securing a transfer pass. Not insignificant is the need to learn the fare for the ride and to determine if exact change is necessary. Once on the bus there are a variety of spoken and unspoken rules and norms to bus travel that one must learn such as how to signal for the bus to stop and general rules for bus behavior.

When considered in this fashion, it becomes quickly apparent that riding the bus, a seemingly uncomplicated procedure, is very complex. The list of tasks presented could have been extended and decomposed to a greater degree. Such a breakdown does not even account for the potential for fear and anxiety associated with bus transportation that many face. Added up, it becomes increasingly clear that there are many potential avenues for a person to fail in an attempt to navigate the bus system successfully.

What is most problematic about this example is that few case plans even go so far as to suggest learning the bus system as a case goal. Instead, riding the bus is embedded in an even larger goal such as applying for a job, keeping a medical appointment, or attending therapy. The transportation is considered only a means to another, more important, end. Thus, the inability to understand the client's most basic struggles is lost. Inevitably, of course, the job application is never made and the two appointments are missed. In the end, the client is viewed as disorganized, unmotivated, and/or resistive and is continually viewed as unable to attack larger and more ambitious goals.

Often goals are written in professional language. For example, "to increase socialization skills" is a commonly recorded goal. No client has ever asked for "improved socialization skills," but many have said they would like more friends or do more with their sibling. Sometimes workers take responsibility for task accomplishment, and at other times clients are expected to do it all with little help.

The mental health system can powerfully constrain achievement-oriented goal setting. In some systems there is a tendency to focus only on the ongoing problems facing clients in their lives. This problem is particularly salient when case management case loads have climbed to unreasonable numbers (here defined as above 20). Crisis is a predominate feature of many clients' lives. These crises may come in the form of interpersonal trauma, strained family relationships, financial problems, and so on. There is always a pressing crisis for the practitioner to turn to. This often clouds the attempt to establish client goals which are, by nature, future oriented.

When attention is focused exclusively on client crisis little developmental work necessary to enhanced community capacity is possible. The consistent crisis focus also represents poor modeling on the part of the practitioner. While there are clearly times in the lives of all people where personal trauma makes it nearly impossible to function, case managers must convey to clients the importance of continuing to function in a variety of life domains regardless of difficulty in one aspect of life. This is not to suggest that legitimate crises should be ignored. It is suggested, however, that neglecting to address future-oriented goals is ultimately a great disservice to clients. It is important to always remember that a case manager is not likely to spend 10 to 15 years working with one client and therefore should always strive to project how today's activities will benefit the client throughout his or her lifetime.

Competencies

At times goals fail because there is a mismatch between the goal and needed information or skills. For example, a person whose goal is to acquire financial aid for college may resort to a loan in lieu of information on the myriad of scholarships and grants-in-aid available. An example of goal–skill mismatch could be the desire to fix a leaking faucet but not knowing how or how to organize goal-directed activities.

Goals fail when practitioners do not have a complete picture of client talents or underestimate those abilities. This leads to not pursuing some goals because they are "unrealistic" or placing numerous steps in the way of the client. A client who wants to be a hairdresser, for example, is asked to complete a prevocational program, vocational testing, vocational school, an apprenticeship, etc. The first two steps, at least, are often undesirable to clients and unnecessary.

Confidence

Many times goals fail because people lack the confidence to take the first step. How many dates have not occurred simply because one person did not have the confidence to ask? Doing something new is often scary. Recollections of past failures can undermine a person's willingness to try, to do.

Another aspect concerns goal-setting situations in which people experience feelings of powerlessness and fatigue. Powerlessness refers to feelings of anger, frustration, and dependency as efforts to make decisions and engage in behaviors to change circumstances fail to yield desired results. The constant emotional energy that is expended in this process may serve to decrease the level of energy needed to sustain goal-oriented efforts.

Practices in mental health systems can deflate one's confidence or at least not support it. The focus on what people cannot do versus what they can do places a pall on helping. Goals established without the identification of small incremental steps to accomplishment deny people opportunities for a sense of achievement and movement. Undermining client self-determination sends a message of incompetence.

Environment

Successful goal attainment is frequently the product of a complimentary match between the goal and the environment. Goal attainment may fail if the necessary resources are not available, accessible, or accommodating. If my goal is to go to the movie on Saturday night, the failure of the baby-sitter to show up means I stay at home unless some emergency child care resources (e.g., grandparents) are available. In our society, lack of money is the single most prevalent resource deficit affecting goal attainment.

Sometimes goals fail because of the lack of social relations or lack of useful feedback. Sustained efforts toward goal achievement often require the support and affirmation of others they trust and who are "right there with them." As was seen earlier, our social networks help determine access to resources, other social relations, and opportunities. Entrapped niches constrain these.

Goal achievement is affected by feedback from the environment, especially from people. Locke et al. (1981) in their review of the literature stated that "both goals and feedback are necessary to improve performance" (p. 136). People's opinions of us are important. Goal failure is enhanced when there is a lack of encouragement, reinforcement for accomplishments and efforts, and information suggesting progress.

Goal achievement is also affected by the opportunities available in the environment. A goal of making the basketball team or being cast in a play is limited to a few slots, vacuums, or opportunities. Economic opportunities within inner cities are severely constricted.

Mental health practice often reflects a limited view of the environment and its role in goal achievement. Resources, social relations, and opportunities are often perceived as those present in the formal mental health service system. Learning daily living skills means a partial hospital or day treatment program. Leisure time pursuits means groups of clients going bowling or making ceramics. Friendship means pairing a person with another person with mental illness. Work means jobs at the mental health center. Completion of tasks on case plans are dominated by the case manager and the client. Rarely do responsibilities suggest roles for other people in the client's social network.

Too often environmental factors are taken as given or fixed and therefore the options offered to clients are narrow. The lack of options is de facto disempowering. In contrast, the assumption that the environment is susceptible to change leads to creativity and increased environmental support for client goal attainment. For example, one program director negotiated effectively with the local transportation authority to include in the bus route the street where a number of clients were residing in transitional apartments. Another created a network of retired school teachers in her rural community who served as mentors for clients engaged in getting their General Equivalency Degree (GED). Another case manager, who was working with a client on the goal of getting her hair done, talked with beauty shop operators in the community until she found one who was willing to accommodate the special need of a highly anxious client. The client, who was scheduled as the last appointment, was allowed to smoke; she was reassured that if she needed to get up and go outside it would be acceptable and that if she left before the hairdresser was finished with her, she would not be charged.

Please see Figure 6.2 for a summary of how goals fail.

THE METHODS OF PERSONAL PLANNING

Personal planning and goal setting are considered normal and routine aspects of case management practice in the strengths model. This suggests that goal setting is not something one does apart from normal activities but should be woven into the daily routine with clients. The case manager should always have goal sheets handy, referring to them, writing new goals, and discussing them with clients. Like the assessment process, goals can often be deciphered and created in a conversational style. For neophyte case managers the goal-writing procedure often seems unnatural and mechanical. It is important, however, to learn to incorporate this into the normal flow of activities.

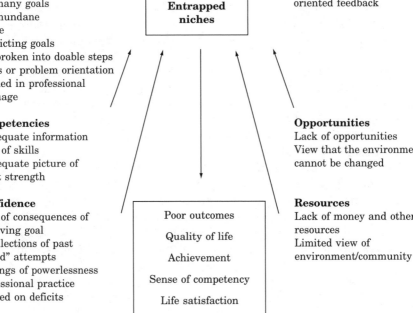

Individual

Aspirations and nature of goals

Not the client's goal
Too ambitious given time
and resources
Too many goals
Too mundane
Vague
Conflicting goals
Not broken into doable steps
Crisis or problem orientation
Framed in professional
language

Competencies
Inadequate information
Lack of skills
Inadequate picture of
client strength

Confidence
Fear of consequences of
achieving goal
Recollections of past
"failed" attempts
Feelings of powerlessness
Professional practice
focused on deficits

Environment

Social relations

Lack of accompaniment
Lack of encouragement
Lack of achievement-
oriented feedback

Opportunities
Lack of opportunities
View that the environment
cannot be changed

Resources
Lack of money and other
resources
Limited view of
environment/community

Entrapped
niches

Poor outcomes

Quality of life

Achievement

Sense of competency

Life satisfaction

Figure 6.2. How goals fail.

Client Involvement

It is required that if the client is to be the director of the helping experience and client self-determination is to be taken seriously, the personal plan should be created by the client. This would include the setting of goals, steps to the goals, strategies to be used, responsibility, and time lines. Increased goal attainment occurs when the person is committed to that goal (Naylor & Ilgen, 1984). Consumers who have been in a dependent position for some time, where their preferences have not mattered, have often lost sight of their own preferences, are seemingly unmotivated, and are reluctant to make decisions (Carling, 1995). This is not sufficient reason for case managers to jump in and prescribe goals, etc. It is rather the case manager's task to be "continually encouraging choices, no matter how small, and then supporting successively more important life choices" (Carling, 1995, p. 288).

Locke et al. (1981) suggested that participation leads to more ambitious goals, increased commitment, and acceptance of goals. Goals set by others reduce motivation (Naylor & Ilgen, 1984). The importance in using client-directed goals lies not only with the improved performance that results but also in potential long-term benefits. Moore-Kirkland (1981), for example, views collaborative goal setting as an important aspect of promoting competence in clients.

> By being involved in the setting of goals, the client sees them as coming largely from him/her and more easily incorporates them. As a result chances for success are enhanced since the problem is one he [or she] has helped define rather than one that has been thrust upon him. Equally important is the feeling of competence resulting from satisfaction demonstrates to the client that change is possible and rewarding, and it lays the groundwork for subsequent success instilling hope. (p. 46)

> Mr. A. was referred whilst in imminent danger of losing his hostel place and becoming homeless, or being admitted to hospital because of his lack of compliance to his medication regime. Initially, he would not accept taking his medication as part of his plans, since he clearly hated taking it. He was adamant that he did not wish to stay in a hostel where the rules insisted that he should take it. He was unwilling to accept that homelessness was a worse option than staying in the hostel. However, one of his aims was eventually to get a flat of his own, and in the short term, he expressed a preference not to be admitted to hospital. Initially, his prime aim was recorded as wanting to find his own flat. When he was assisted in exploring this, he came to the conclusion that he would be unlikely to be accepted into any of the potential options unless he could demonstrate a greater stability and stay out of hospital for longer than he had in the past. He and his Practitioner then agreed that a priority was to demonstrate this stability through a very public return to a limited but acceptable level of medication which would enable him to gain the endorsement of his psychiatrist and the head of the hostel. (Bleach & Ryan, 1995)

The core of empowerment is returning to consumers the responsibility for choices about their lives and their lifestyles" (Carling, 1995, p. 287).

Based on the work of Berg and Miller (1992), DeJong and Miller state that the first characteristic of well-formed goals is:

> Goals are important to the client. Goals are well formed when they belong to the client and are expressed in the client's language; they are not well formed when, first of all, they are thought appropriate by the worker and are expressed in the worker's categories. This characteristic constitutes a practice principle that rests on the belief that clients whose goals are respected are more motivated than those whose goals are over-looked. The principle is not compromised except in cases where the worker, after exploring for client strengths and coping capacities, is convinced that the client is overwhelmed or a danger to self or others. (DeJong & Miller, 1995, p. 730)

Goal Setting

What is a goal? A goal is a statement of a desired state or something that a person wants to achieve. Therefore, every person has multiple levels of goals corresponding to the goals' complexity and ambitiousness and the time and effort necessary for achievement. For example:

1. Earning a B.A. degree
2. Completing 24 hours of the freshman year
3. Completing 12 hours of first semester
4. Attending each class next week
5. Completing homework for biology by Tuesday

In the strengths model, these levels have been reduced to two levels: a long-term goal and short-term goals.

The long-term goal refers to a desire held by the client as the client states it. Typical examples would be:

1. Get a job as a social worker
2. Have more friends
3. Feel better
4. Get my teeth fixed
5. Get a car
6. Move to an apartment
7. Stay out of the hospital

Other clients may state their goals as "get my hair done" or "get a medical card." Most often, the "long-term goal" is derived from the priority list on the strengths assessment. The case manager may probe to develop a more specific picture of the goal (see the following two sections). These goal statements are written in the section labeled "Consumer's Long-Term Goal." As you can see, there is no precise definition of "long-term." The client's unique perspective and language dictate what is recorded.

In the strengths model, the long-term goal is rarely a subject of negotiation. These goals are not rejected by the case manager as "unrealistic" but, rather, are treated as sincere aspirations of the person.

> Mrs. J. was due to be discharged into the community after several years of hospital residence. When faced with her compulsory discharge, she was considerably panicked. She stated her wants in terms of residence in a nursing home with no responsibility plus daily day care activities. Everyone agreed that her likely self-care skills and anxiety levels seemed to indicate that this would be the best plan. Once a trusting relationship had been established, Mrs. J. divulged that she hated the idea of living in a home and going to day centers, and that she really wanted to be the Queen. She challenged the Practitioner to work toward that aim. Without promising too much, the Practitioner began to work out with Mrs. J. what she felt the Queen did that was worth aiming for. It emerged that Mrs. J. believed that the Queen did not have financial or administrative worries, she always knew where she was going to live,

people respected her because she helped them, and most importantly, she had "companions" and "ladies in waiting" who helped her and kept her company. The subsequent assessment stated that Mrs. J. needed a strong sense of financial security and the guarantee of help with day-to-day organization, she needed to move to one location and be promised that she need never move again, she needed to feel she was helping people and feel respected for it, and she needed some "old-fashioned" companionship. Mrs J eventually began considering sharing a house with another person being discharged who was already a firm friend and an effective organizer both of good works and administration. (Bleach & Ryan, 1995, p. 175)

Similarly, this statement should never be reframed into professional language. A client goal of "having more friends" should not be translated as "improve socialization skills."

Short-term goals are both means to the end (long-term goal) and ends in and of themselves; they are tasks *and* goals. As tasks, short-term goals have a logical link to the long-term goal. They are the steps taken to accomplish the goal. For example, "getting a job as a mechanic" would typically entail reading the classifieds, completing applications, interviewing, requesting references, etc.

Each of these can in turn be viewed as goals (i.e., something a person wants to achieve). For some people suffering from mental illness, "just" buying a newspaper, reading the classified, and circling possibilities is something they have never done before. It can be confusing or discomforting or can provoke memories of failed job experiences in the past. Therefore, a client who completes these has achieved something important in their own right.

Standards for Short-Term Goal Statements

1. Goals should be concrete, specific, and behavioral. It should be unambiguous as to whether a goal was accomplished or not. For example, "Ralph will do more things with friends" would be replaced with "Ralph will go to the movies with Terry next week." Two guidelines are helpful. First, avoid adjectives and adverbs (e.g., "Tom will wear a shirt to his support group meeting" rather than "Tom will dress appropriately"). Most adjectives and adverbs seek to capture qualitative differences that are usually open to wide interpretation (e.g., "appropriately," "successfully," "diligently," "regularly"). Second, each goal should set a single behavioral standard. The desired outcome should be explicit. For example, "Fred will work 10 hours this week" rather than "Fred will increase his hours of work." In the latter situation, is 1 hour enough? Is 5 hours enough?

2. Goals should be stated positively. The goal should identify what a client is expected to do, rather than what a client is expected to stop doing. For example, "Harriet will work until 5:30" rather than "Harriet will not leave work early." Goals seek presence rather than absence (Berg &

Miller, 1992). "Practice outcomes are improved when clients are helped to express their goals as the presence of something—for example, 'taking walks,' rather than the absence of something" (DeJong & Miller, 1995, p. 730) like "not being bored." Another example, "Sara will exercise at the YWCA on Monday and Wednesday" rather than "Sara will decrease stress," although the latter may be sufficient as a long-term goal.

3. Goals are broken down into discrete tasks with a high probability of success: "Mere association with past personal success apparently leads to more persistence, higher motivation, or something that makes us better" (Peters & Waterman, 1982). Successful achievement of goals for people, not just people with severe mental illness, is dependent on being able to identify specific behaviors or steps toward its achievements. For people with mental illness, failure to do so makes goals overwhelming and increases the likelihood that symptomatology (e.g., hallucinations) will interfere. For example, "Martha will lease an apartment" can be broken down into a myriad of steps that might begin with "select areas of the city that would be desirable" or "buy a newspaper." Any goal or task can be further subdivided. The author has seen the task of folding a piece of paper in half divided into 23 separate steps.

Breaking down a goal is a principal mechanism for building realism into the process. A client goal of being an airplane pilot could start with enrolling in junior college. Getting a girlfriend could start with brushing teeth and practicing asking for a date with the case manager.

How far to break down a goal is a judgment made based on the client, the goal, and the current situation. The standard is achieveability. For some clients, "doing wash on Wednesday" is adequate. For others, this would be asking too much. Perhaps it could be divided into the following tasks:

1. Sort clothes into a pile of darks and a pile of lights
2. Place one pile in laundry basket
3. Place detergent and apartment keys in basket
4. Carry basket down to laundry room
5. Place clothes in washer with one cup of detergent
6. Set dial to "REG" and push button

Breaking down a task like doing laundry this finely not only is not needed for some clients but would be insulting. But for others, each of these tasks can be seen as a challenging goal in and of itself and worthy of compliments.

Helping Clients Set Goals

Anytime a client begins a discussion about possible activities, the goal-planning process can concretize these activities. Case managers have found it useful to make copies of the goal-planning forms for clients to refer to. This helps them recall the plans that have been agreed upon and provides an example of the way one proceeds to achieve and to acquire resources.

Many clients have goals and can articulate them quite well. Other clients have great difficulty in doing so. Goals can be vague. Clients often state goals that they have been socialized to believe that the mental health professional wants to hear them choose. Others state that they have no goals and do not want anything. Sometimes a client does not want what all the previous mental health professionals were offering and assumes that the strengths-based case manager will "follow suit." Others believe that the goals they do have will be discounted and ignored. Still others are fearful of embarrassment over their goals as being too mundane, too childish, too ambitious. Refusal to express goals is a protective device. If one assumes that human beings are purposeful organisms, then it is impossible not to have goals although they may be quite different from those commonly thought of as typical.

At times a client's stated desires seem bizarre, grandiose (see the case example of the woman who wanted to be queen), or irresponsible. The typical professional response would be to discount these statements. However, often behind these stated desires are "sensible" reasons. The following client situation from England demonstrates this and ways to address it.

Mr. H. had increasing physical health problems. These problems were greatly exacerbated by his frequently not having enough money to pay for his heating and so on. If the situation were allowed to deteriorate further, he would probably have had to be taken into a nursing home at great expense, even though, once there, he would probably recover simply as a result of receiving proper care. As far as the Practitioner and everyone else (except Mr. H.) was concerned, he needed to be helped budget properly so he could heat the house, avoid a physical deterioration and thus being taken into care.

Mr. H. actually preferred to spend his money on gambling. As far as he was concerned, he wanted to feel he was earning his money, and he needed all the money to make enough winnings to be able to make his life easier by going to the pub a lot. He was not concerned about his ill health as long as he could keep meeting his friends in the pub and the betting shop. Since Mr. H. did not feel that he needed to reorganize his financial approach to budget for heating, it would not truly be part of a User-led plan if the Practitioner were to record this as a need. There might be a temptation to nag Mr. H. ("for his own good") into agreeing to put "don't gamble and drink less in order to save money for heating" in his plan. At this point it would not be Mr. H.'s plan but someone else's—no matter how sensible it might be. It would be less likely to succeed than a plan truly based on what he wanted, and intended, to do. The chances are that he would cheat and show signs of low motivation and try and return to the behavior he was actually motivated to do.

Mr. H. was helped to make the connection between his damp house and the likelihood that he would become so ill that he could not carry on his preferred pattern of life. It was pointed out that he would probably have to go to a nursing home some miles away, and would lose contact with his friends. He began to accept that he needed to reconsider his priorities to avoid losing everything. His idea was to work out how much money was needed to be sure that just enough heating was paid for. He would then save half the necessary money and bet the rest on safer "dead certainties" to earn more money. Whilst this was not the Practitioner's original idea of what needed to be done, Mr. H. had at least accepted that he needed to do something. His solution still gave him the opportunity to meet his other social needs and provided motivational challenges whilst taking on board his, and everyone else's, wish to keep him out of a nursing home. (Bleach & Ryan, 1995, p. 174)

How successful would the outcome have been if the case manager had ignored, denounced, or sought to deny the client his statement of goals? The professional fear is that by accepting client goals will lead to inappropriate goals, and unreal expectations must be replaced with acceptance of the goals and probing of the underlying desires.

A well-done strengths assessment with attention paid to how the client spends the day and the cues provided by possessions or other environmental factors can often suggest goals that have gone unstated. For example:

A case manager was assigned to work with a client who agreed to meet with the case manager in the client's home. When the case manager was invited into the home, he noticed right away a large bookcase in the living room that had hunks of dried mud and rocks on every shelf. As the engagement process unfolded the case manager asked the consumer, "Jim," to tell him about the items on the bookcase. Jim explained he enjoyed going to the river and finding rocks and fossils. The case manager listened and learned about Jim's interest while observing that Jim became more animated as he talked about the rocks and fossils. This was noted on the strengths assessment. The case manager asked Jim how he knew so much about the subject. Jim replied he'd picked it up by spending time at the river and remembering what he had learned in a high school science class. The case manager asked Jim if he would be interested in finding out more about this interest. Jim replied, "Yes." The community Jim lived in had a university. The case manager assisted Jim in securing a scholarship to take a geology class. Jim enjoyed the class immensely and signed up for more classes on geology. Eventually Jim was hired by the university to classify rocks and minerals.

This was less likely to have happened if the case manager didn't employ assertive outreach and look for clues in the consumer's environment based on the interest, abilities, and strengths of the consumer.

Sometimes the case manager should not use the language of goals but talk in terms of "what do you want to do today?" When appropriate, the case manager could record these on the personal plan and note their achievement. Another method is for the case manager to say something like, "Sometimes my only goal is cook lunch for myself" or "Getting through the day is sometimes the most I can handle and when I do I feel pretty good about it."

Some clients only want to discuss "what's wrong" with their lives, relating a history of problems and obstacles. It is important for the worker to listen, to respond empathically, to use these opportunities to convey that the client is not alone, and to reflect back the resiliencies imbedded in the story. The case manager should be attentive to opportunities to reframe problems into statements of aspirations or goals. One technique, the miracle question, has been proposed by DeJong and Miller (1995; Table 6.1).

With some clients who have had difficulty getting comfortable with the personal planning process, case managers have left forms with them to fill out on their own. In addition, case managers and clients have sometimes found it helpful to fill out personal plans retroactively in those cases where clients have taken significant strides in a manner not previously discussed.

> Marshall had talked of locating some old friends ever since he had left the hospital. While he talked about how good it would be to see these acquaintances, he did not actively seek them out. During the early phase of the case management process, Marshall found a volunteer job that he liked a great deal. Later he decided to buy a used car with some savings he had accumulated. Soon afterward the case manager was surprised to learn that Marshall had recontacted two old friends, one of whom lived in the same neighborhood. Now Marshall had an alternative to spending his leisure time watching TV.

While retroactively recording client accomplishments can be overdone and not reflect the true impact of case management, the opposite is also

TABLE 6.1
"Miracle Question"

The "miracle" question is often a good way to stimulate thinking about aspirations:
Suppose while you are sleeping tonight a miracle happens. The miracle is that the problem that has you here talking to me is somehow solved. Only you don't know that because you are asleep. What will you notice different tomorrow morning that will tell you that a miracle has happened?

This question is the starting point for a whole series of satellite questions designed to take the client's attention away from difficulties and to focus it on imagining a future when the problem is solved. The following satellite questions might be used:

- What is the very first thing you will notice after the miracle happens?
- What might your husband (child, friend) notice about you that would give him the idea that things are better for you?
- When he notices that, what might he do differently?
- When he does that, what would you do?
- And when you do that, what will be different around your house?

The intent of these questions is to help the client formulate, in detail, what will be "different" in his or her life when the miracle happens. As the client struggles to describe these differences, the client also often develops both an expectation of change and a growing sense of the goals toward which to direct effort.
The satellite questions mirror the characteristics of well-formed goals. Thus, when a client responds to the miracle question, "I'd have a sense of peace," the worker might ask, "What might your husband notice different about you that would tell him that you are beginning to 'have a sense of peace'?" With this question, the worker is attempting to help the client develop more concrete goals that are more the beginning of something rather than the end and that respect the client's language. Or, to give another example, when a client responds to the miracle question with, "I'd cry less," the worker would ask, "What would be there instead of the crying?" recognizing that well-formed goals are the presence of something rather than the absence. (DeJong & Miller, 1995, p 731).

---

true. It is important to measure as precisely as we can the range of activities that clients embark upon after becoming involved in case management.

Resource Options

A centerpiece of strengths model practice is the generation of alternative paths to goal attainment.

> More often than not people rise to the occasion when they are given positive options. People typically strive to set their lives straight, and given time, usually succeed. (Peele & Brodsky, 1991)

An inherent element in empowerment is the presence and perception of options among which to choose. It is the case manager's job to help the client generate the various resources and pathways available. By doing so, the case manager will inevitably emphasize naturally occurring community resources, because in most cases it is the community, not the mental health system, that contains most options.

Long-Term Goal: To be healthier
To attend aerobics classes at least twice a week
Alternatives:

1. Aerobics class offered through the partial hospital program
2. Classes offered by the town's park and recreation department
3. Classes held by the local YWCA
4. Classes offered by "Body Boutique" (a private fitness center)
5. Start a consumer-run aerobics class at the drop-in center
6. Start an aerobic class at the church after Bible study
7. Buy a video tape and do it alone in your living room
8. Buy a video tape and do it with a friend or family member
9. Do aerobics as a volunteer
10. Lead an aerobics class for senior citizens
11. Be an aide to an aerobics teacher
12. Get a job teaching aerobics

To maximize options, the case manager requires a broad-based knowledge of the community and knowledge of the client's strengths. For example, a strengths assessment that has church or religious involvement as a prominent area of importance in the client's life would stimulate option 6 where for others the idea of a church-sponsored aerobics class could be dumb. Similarly, a client who has talent and experience in aerobics, even if in the past, suggests consideration of options 10 and 11, but for a novice, this would be premature and probably frightening. The presence of a sibling could make option 8 viable. There is simply no shortcut to effective case plans without being apprised of the client's unique configuration of strengths.

Knowledge of the community is as much about perspective as about detailed information on all possibilities. Our experience is that a case manager who asks the question, "Where do adults in Springfield, U.S.A., do aerobics?" will find a way of finding an answer. Be clear! The question is not "where do mentally ill adults do aerobics?" nor "where do most adults do aerobics?" although the latter question is a good starting place. Rather, the case manager is asking the millions of people in the U.S.A. who do aerobics and the hundreds who do it in Springfield, what is the range of options used?

The first short-term goal or task is often finding information about options through the yellow pages, asking around, talking about it with the case manager supervisor or the team, and making phone calls. Again, the client should do as much of this work as possible.

With options generated, the case manager assists the client in choosing which ones are most desirable and worth pursuing. Each option is unique and its features need to be discussed. Relevant features in the previous example could be location, cost, schedule, type of people enrolled in the class, etc. Clients often rule out some options immediately. Selection from the shortened list often takes more discussion. Sometimes more information is needed or the client would like to visit and preview the different options. Sometimes the desired option, aerobics class offered by Body Boutique, for example, requires money, so the initial short-term goals would focus on getting sufficient money or aquiring a "scholarship" from the fitness center.

Fear of losing supports can affect a client's selection among options. As Carling (1995) writes:

> Often consumers will choose from a very narrow range of options (e.g., a group home or a boarding home) because of their past experience of only being offered support in a very narrow range of settings. A powerful strategy for increasing choice is to offer consumers support wherever they choose to live, work, or learn, and to assume that working out the complexities of offering services in this way is the service provider's responsibility, not an obstacle that should be used to force consumers to choose only from among those places where services are traditionally available. At times, this offer of support may be met with skepticism by family members or even by consumers themselves, given past experiences. In this case, it is the task of the service provider to build trust that the supports will be there, and to be diligent about providing them. (pp. 288–89)

Assigning Responsibility

There is a hierarchy of desirableness in assigning responsibility. It is most desirable for the client to be responsible for goal/task completion. The next level of desirableness is that the client with assistance from the natural support network (e.g., family, friend, neighbors) complete it. The third level is when the client and case manager do the task. The least desirable level is when the case manager does it for the client. The more a client can achieve independently or in a normally interdependent way, the greater the sense of achievement and empowerment, and the greater the likelihood of subsequent goal-directed efforts being exerted. It also frees the case manager from tasks.

The client should be the primary decision maker. If the case manager did a good job of role induction including defining mutual expectations, the client will know that tasks whenever possible should be done by the client and that the case manager's aid has limits; the case manager is a helper not a slave. Beyond this, the case manager helps the client configure the tasks so that the client has the ability and confidence to accomplish it. If the task is set by the client, therefore it is important to them, and they have the ability (competency) and confidence to do it, the task will have a high probability of achievement.

The case manager facilitates this process of assigning responsibility by not only helping the client to break down goals but also by providing options. A well-done strengths assessment will have identified a client's social network. Each of the members could be considered for accompanying the client in performing tasks. The case manager helps the client evaluate the possibilities for each person. Often the selection of a person leads to new tasks like "Jenny will call sister," "Jenny will ask sister if she would go grocery shopping with her on Tuesday," "Jenny will set a time with her sister," "If Jenny's sister cannot, Jenny will call the case manager." Even if Jenny's sister could not, Jenny had completed four tasks that she would not have done in the past and this deserves some celebration. Perhaps Jenny is too scared to call her sister; it is too big a step. In this case, the case manager can offer to be with Jenny when she calls (accompaniment) and Jenny could decide if she desires this.

There are situations when the case manager involvement and responsibility are warranted. The following client situation from England is a case in point:

> A plan is agreed whereby a service User intends to improve their prospects of getting work by increasing their literacy and then attending evening classes. It is clearly appropriate for the Practitioner to seek the services of an adult literacy trainer and to arrange for the service User to meet the trainer and begin to attend local literacy classes. The trainer is familiar with such situations, and is able skillfully to engage the service User and make them feel comfortable. Very little additional support is required of the Practitioner. At the end of the literacy classes, the service User wishes to attend a relatively unambitious but sensible evening class. However, the trainer of this evening class has no experience of, and no time to cope with, someone such as the service User. There is a clear need for the service User to be accompanied by a befriender. The course will start very soon and if the service User misses the beginning they will be even more of an outsider. From past experience, the Practitioner knows that the service User will be very suspicious of the Practitioner's motives in introducing someone else and that as a result it will take longer and use more time for the Practitioner to enable an adequate relationship between the User and a befriender than it would do for the Practitioner to take the service User along to the evening class and undertake all the integration work directly. (Bleach & Ryan, 1995, p. 124)

The most frequent reason for case managers to do for a client is time. Picking up an application for a loan, for example, takes less time for the case manager to do it on the way home than to pick up the client, take them to the office and return them. Sometimes the client's level of anxiety is so troublesome that it is just easier for the case manager to do it. On other occasions, the task is so complex (e.g., understanding low-income housing loans) that the case manager again may choose to do it alone rather than the client or the client with the case manager. In real-life agency practice, time is precious and it does affect decisions. The case manager needs to be acutely aware, however, that a fuller opportunity for empowerment and learning by the client has been sacrificed.

Establishing Target Dates

For each goal/task, a target date for achievement should be set. A target date further structures and directs the goal achievement process and enhances the likelihood of its completion. Most frequently, target dates are set for tasks that are to be accomplished between client–case manager visits so that the next visit can be used to review these tasks and set new ones.

A common practice in mental health is to write "ongoing" as the target date for some tasks such as "take medications as prescribed," or "shower daily," or "attend groups each day." This form of practice is contraindicated for several reasons. First, for many clients, if it was this simple to do they are probably already doing it. If they are not doing it, a simple statement to do it with "on-going" probably will not work. Second, it deprives the client (and case manager) of a tangible benchmark for success and the feelings success engenders. Therefore, in most cases, the task of "showering daily" would have seven target dates for the week. With each one, the client would mark its completion. Each shower taken would therefore be seen as the achievement it is for this particular client.

A Note on Pacing

For some clients time is measured in days, if not hours and minutes. One source of goal failure is the presence of too many goals (both long-term and short-term) during any one point in time. For clients this can lead to confusion, diffusion of effort, and feelings of anxiety and being overwhelmed. Clients and case managers both can be the instigator of too many goals. When this derives primarily from the client, the case manager may suggest directly that the focus be on a few areas for this week. The case manager could also share information on the deleterious effects of too many goals. Another response could be:

> This seems like a lot. It feels a little overwhelming. I know when this happens to me, I am less likely to accomplish anything. Have you ever felt like this? What about just focusing on your number one priority?

The client has the final say, but the client would be best served by having the information needed to make the best decision.

In other situations, the case manager is the major force in setting too many goals. As Kisthardt (1992) describes:

> Do not attempt to generate a comprehensive plan that includes a wide range of goals during the first planning meetings. Sometimes, in their enthusiasm to implement the personal planning function, case managers generate a lengthy list of goals, but soon discover that they have proceeded too quickly. Consumers may become overwhelmed if they feel that they have agreed to a plan where they are over-extended. The following example illustrates this point: During a goal planning meeting a case manager recorded thirteen short-term goals with a consumer after having been working with her for only three weeks. (This session was videotaped for evaluation purposes.) During the meeting it was evident that the case manager was strongly directing the development of the plans by making suggestions regarding what the consumer could do. The consumer was agreeing, but her facial expression and body language indicated that she was becoming increasingly anxious as the case manager recorded each goal. The case manager, enthusiastically writing the goals on the form, missed these very important cues. That evening the consumer, feeling overwhelmed and fearful that she would "let the case manager down," called the crisis line. She received the reassurance she needed, and the plans were scaled down at the next meeting with the case manager. (p. 76)

The following excerpts of a letter to the author best captures the subtlety of pacing:

> I know my work with Stuart began with assertive outreach. He was historically withdrawn and isolative. His parents frequently expressed their concern about his inability to initiate and to connect with others. It was their fear that he would be forgotten about because he rarely expressed any needs. When Stuart and I began working together, we would go to lunch. Stuart enjoyed eating out and from his viewpoint, this was an exciting part of his day.
>
> As case manager, I felt pressure to address his parents concerns—especially around Stuart's need for dental care. During our weekly lunches Stuart and I would talk about a number of things—he appeared most energized when talking about his past life in Arizona and going to college; he appeared most apprehensive when I brought up the dentist, so I would back off.
>
> Stuart expressed interest in going back to Arizona to complete his degree in Geology. His dream was to be a copper miner. We talked over lunch—week after week—about pros and cons and started looking at options. Stuart was aware he had been out of school for many years and that having his parents' support was important. We went to an area community college to explore the possibility of his volunteering in the geology department. And to make a long story short, Stuart became increasingly excited about his life and possibilities—he had me taking him to the library so he could get the address of the University of Arizona and send for his transcript. We went to Johnson County Community College and he wanted to take a chemistry class for audit to see how he

would do in school again. He had also agreed to go to a Dental Fears Clinic just to talk about his anxiety about going to a dentist (we had just driven by the clinic weeks prior to help him feel more at ease). In the end, Stuart chose to see a dentist and got new dentures (I really praised his wonderful smile!). He also decided to go to KU after successfully completing his chemistry class and moved to Lawrence!

The work with Stuart was paced by him and I remember wondering what was so productive about eating lunch once a week. Looking back, I can see how instrumental our lunches were because it sustained contact. Stuart was not being forgotten. It was part of being assertive and reaching out. By doing so, I was able to tap into those window opportunities and support Stuart in reaching his goals. It was fascinating to see a man who had seemingly little going for him come alive when he realized he could, in fact, do what he has always loved most—be a student. . . . It was impossible for me to know when Stuart's time for change was—I did know that I was going to be there when it happened.

Related to pacing is that sometimes no plan is the best plan. Sometimes a client need is so important (e.g., food, clothes) and the client desires it that there is no need to pull out the personal plan and strengths assessment before acting. Just do it! With some clients, doing something immediate and concrete can be the best way to establish trust and caring early in a relationship. Recording the set of goal-directed activities on the personal plan later may be useful to meet documentation requirements, to show the client how the personal plan works, and/or to provide an initial sense of accomplishment.

Reviewing Personal Plans

A centerpiece of client and case manager interactions is the personal plan. After all, it is the basic agenda for work together. Review of personal plans occurs at each contact. This entails a review of short-term goals to be achieved since the last meeting. Dates of accomplishment would be filled in if not already filled in by client or case manager. Achievements warrant compliments if not celebration.

Short-term goals that were not achieved usually require some discussion to locate the obstacles that were confronted. Listening carefully to the client's story in a non-judgmental, accepting fashion is necessary. A case manager is well served by being familiar with why goals fail. This can allow the case manager to "diagnose" what may have gone wrong and thereby better assist the client in setting achievable goals.

The comments section allows the case manager or client to make any further remarks about the status of the goal. It is a place where the case manager might wish to reinforce the client further by noting exemplary performance. It is also a place to note any obstacles or change that might have occurred or to note the help of a friend or resource. The important aspect of this column is that it continues to direct attention to goals that have been set rather than allowing them simply to fade away unattended.

FROM STRENGTHS ASSESSMENT TO PERSONAL PLANNING

The purpose of assessment is to gather information necessary for a personal plan and its implementation to occur. We have found the strengths assessment as described in chapter 5 to be the best method of gathering helpful information. We have all reviewed assessments that seem to have no or only superficial relevance to the case plan. This same phenomenon can occur in strengths-based practice as well. But in the hands of a skillful practitioner, the link is unambiguous. The strengths assessment seeks information on the individual and involvements with environmental resources in the past and the present and desired in the future across life domains or niches.

Goal Setting

The strengths assessment views the presence of aspirations as a strength. The column labeled "Individual's Desire/Aspiration: What Do I Want?" is the first place where possible goals are located. The client's list of priorities is usually a direct source of goal statements although often the priorities need to be made more congruent with the standards for goals (e.g., specific).

The strengths assessment often contains other information suggestive of goals. Past activities or involvements may be long-buried in the client's mind or relegated to "well, that was then." Sometimes these can be rekindled by gaining confidence or being presented with new options. For example, in the Fossil Vignette, the client had no desire to work until he reinvolved himself in this area of interest and became aware that you could get paid for it. The strengths assessment provides a variety of clues for activities and interests that can be combined to generate goals. Thus, an interest in swimming can lead to volunteer employment at the city pool or simply an activity worth pursuing in leisure time.

Options

The aerobics example highlighted the use of a strengths assessment to generate alternative resources and pathways. To recap:

1. Considerable skill in aerobics suggests the option of leading a class, not just participating.
2. Past successful involvement in aerobics classes suggests group options. In contrast, if group options were associated with pain and failure, more individual options need to be generated.
3. The presence of a VCR suggests the possibility of in-home aerobics. Similarly, owning a car makes other options available.
4. Involvement with a consumer organization or the consumer-run drop-in center suggests a consumer-run class.
5. The presence of a friend, a sibling or other relative, a neighbor suggests an in-home pairing arrangement.

6. Knowing that Jane Fonda is one of the client's favorite movie stars provides leads to which video to select.

7. Knowing that the client is gregarious or desires friends suggests a group option.

It was mentioned in the assessment chapter that interests that appear inconsequential may be the key to a success. Consider the following case example:

> Martha claimed that the only thing that she liked to do was to drink coffee and smoke cigarettes. Rather than ignoring this, the case manager listed it as a personal interest on the strengths assessment. Eventually the case manager, working with the strength, talked with Martha about meeting at a nearby restaurant for coffee. This constituted Martha's first trip into the public for over a year. After several trips to the restaurant, Martha asked the case manager if they could go shopping together someday.

A strengths assessment that contains detailed information on the social relations and supports of the client can provoke a variety of creative options. A client situation from England is illustrative:

> Mrs. C. was being considered for discharge into residential care at the reluctant application of her husband who was concerned for her safety because of bouts of disorientation particularly when he had to work on nightshifts. The Practitioner established that Mr. C. had considerable support from neighbors and family but felt that he would be overloading them and was at risk of losing his job if he was absent from too many nightshifts as a result of his wife's "bad days." With their permission, the Practitioner negotiated with the potential carer network that Mrs. C. would be "looked in on" or could stay elsewhere when required, providing that this was convenient to all concerned. The Practitioner also arranged to be responsible for ensuring access to local respite care if the support network could not provide it. Both Mrs. and Mr. C. were pleased to be able to avoid the breakup of the household and the other carers felt much happier about not always being obliged to put Mrs. C.'s needs before their own. (Bleach & Ryan, 1995, p. 187)

Short-Term Goals/Tasks

One of the most difficult skills for practitioners to develop is using strengths to configure strategies toward goal achievement. Many personal plans, even otherwise good ones, lack the presence of client strengths in the short-term goals. Perhaps an extended example can help demonstrate the methods. This is a client with a long history of erratic medication compliance due largely to memory and confusion (he forgets) rather than lack of motivation. The following was the case plan:

> Goal: To stay out of the hospital and continue living in my apartment.
>   To take medications as prescribed and see Dr. Holly.

Short-Term Goal:

1. John will take his meds as prescribed for two weeks.
2. John will buy a five-day pill box for his medication by 7/26.
3. John's case manager will call him two times a day for a week to remind him to take his medication.
4. John will see Dr. Holly one time this month for scheduled appointment on 8/6.

This is a typical goal plan for many people with serious mental illness in many agencies. After using this goal plan, John has not been able to remember to take his medication. What is missing in this goal plan? Now look at John's strengths assessment (Figure 6.3). By using the strengths and resources from the assessment, these other options are generated:

1. John's neighbors (Roger and Amy) will check on John two times a day to help remind him to take his medications for one week.
2. John's mother, June, will call John in the morning of 8/6 to remind John to go to his doctor's appointment.
3. John's mother will call him two times a day to remind John to take his medication for one week.
4. John will take a bus to his doctor's appointment on 8/6.
5. John will call his old friend Pete to ask him if he would work with him to make a buzzing medication box that will remind him to take his medication.
6. John will take his medication when he feeds Muffy for one week.
7. Scott will take John to his doctor's appointment on 8/6.
8. John and April will walk to John's doctor's appointment on 8/6.

John wanted to pursue option 5 involving his old friend Pete. Figure 6.4 contains the personal plan that was developed.

This example highlights three points:

1. People have a multitude of strengths and resources they can use to get what they want.
2. Options increase as you explore and use the strengths and resources people already have.
3. The strengths assessment and goal plan are connected in such a way that you must use them in combination for highest effectiveness.

In terms of John, this personal plan allows him to reconnect with a friend and to engage in an activity he enjoys, and because of this investment it has a heightened chance of working. By using the strengths assessment, John's personal plan will be unique, that is, tailored to him.

Since spirituality is an often neglected aspect of assessments, another case vignette may be helpful in demonstrating the critical connection between the strengths assessment and personal plan:

> A case manager was working with a woman who recently displayed multiple symptoms of her mental illness. She was off her medication and was on the verge of losing her apartment and her job in the community which she did not want to do. The consumer, despite her illness, never missed a day in church and this was recorded in the strengths assessment. When the case manager asked why she wasn't taking her medications, the consumer stated that she was worried that they were "evil and could be poisoned." What the case manager did was simple . . . yet showed creativity and innovation. The case manager asked the consumer, "Would you be willing to take your medicine if the priest blessed it first?" The consumer agreed and the case manager went to the priest with the request. The priest was happy to help. The consumer has taken her meds ever since. The case manager learning about her interest in spirituality made a significant difference.

Responsibility

The client should do as many of the short-term goals/tasks as he or she is willing to do. By breaking goals down to manageable pieces, expressions of confidence by the case manager and client ownership of the goal as meaningful to them enhance the likelihood of achievement. When the client is uncomfortable in performing, other alternatives need to be considered.

The strengths assessment provides possibilities beyond the case manager. In particular, people currently or formerly involved in the client's life can be considered in the personal plan. These social relations are a strength on which to build. The sister who attends church with the client can be the sister who goes to the movies with the client. The friend with whom the client plays cards can be the friend who goes grocery shopping with the client. The co-worker can be the person who takes the client to work and back. A landlord or apartment superintendent could be a source of companionship or reminders. A coach many years ago may use influence to get a client on a basketball team.

Most times a client has the competency and skill to perform a task. The chaos of the mind, the disorder of their lives, and the lack of resources interferes with its accomplishment. For others, it is fear and lack of confidence. Mobilizing social supports for prompting (reminding the client) and accompaniment are critical. Just the presence of another person can make a task doable and enjoyable.

THE CLIENT EXPERIENCE WITH PERSONAL (GOAL) PLANNING[1]

The personal planning methods described in this chapter are believed to mightily contribute to the positive client outcomes found in strengths model

---

1. This section is based on Walter Kisthardt's doctoral dissertation *A Consumers Evaluation of Strengths Model Case Management* for the University of Kansas School of Social Welfare, 1995.

Current status: What's going on today? What's available now?	Individual's desires, aspirations: What do I want?	Resources, personal social: What have I used in the past?
	Life domain	
	Daily living situation	
- Lives alone in 1 bdrm Apt (2yrs) - Has Cut—Muffy - Apt. is on bus route - friend April cleans his Apt 1×per week - goes out to eat a lot - Apt. has pool & laundry facility - has sec. 8 apt. - has a fish aquarium	- Keep my apartment - Get a car - Own my own home someday	- lived in a group home for 3 yrs.—liked Fred who also lived there - enjoyed sharing meals - lived with his parents for 5 years and enjoyed helping with yardwork - had a dog "Jake" growing up
	Financial/Insurance	
- SSI $442/month - Has Medicaid - Has Medicare - $200 per month spenddown - Sec. 8 Apt - Foodstamps $20/month - Parents give him extra $ occasionally	- Wants to earn money working and get off social security	- Was on parents insurance until 1988 - "I used to live off of $3 a week when I lived at the group home"
	Vocational/Educational	
- Helps father in his job as Real Estate Appraiser (volunteer)-goes out with him 2–3×/month - Loves electronics - Types - Beginning to learn to use a computer at dad's	- Wants to work full time at Radio Shack	- McDonalds (3 months in 1986) - Dishwasher (2 months in 1988) - MHC prevocational library unit in 1990 - High School graduate 1985 - Has looked into electronics program at DeVry Institute
	Social Supports	
- Mom & Dad-June and Brett - Friends-Scott and April - Neighbors-Roger and Amy - Case Manager-Mary - AA sponsor-Bob	- Wants more friends to do to things with - Wants a girlfriend	- Best friend in high school—Gary—who is an electronics graduate - Past girlfriend—Kerry - Friends from state hospital—Jeff, Eldon, Ray, Sue - Church Youth Group (Lutheran Church)
	Health	
- Meds—Haldol, Cogentin - Psychiatrist—Dr. Holly - Physician—Dr. Rayton - Walks a lot	- Stay out of the hospital and keep my apartment - Wants to pump iron at a gym	- Used to do a lot of active sports for exercise—basketball and tennis in high school

- Substance free for 3 years - AA meetings—2× per week	- Wants to quit smoking	- Hospitalized 3× at Os. State Hospital—usually for 3 months to 1 year - Had a therapist 1987–1989—says it was not helpful
- Loves music—listening to rock - Likes electronics "messing with machines" - Board games (chess) - Attends movie and bowling 1×per week with day program - Smoking and drinking coffee with friends - Watches sports on TV - Plays with cat—Muffy	Leisure/Recreational Supports - Wants to do more fun things	- Played basketball in high school - Used to read a lot of science fiction - Was on the debate team in high school - Used to go to rock concerts—loved them!!

What are my priorities?
1.

2.

3.

4.

Case manager's comments: - John is fuuny and likes to tell jokes - He is friendly and outgoing once he gets to know someone - His favorite foods are hamburgers and ice cream (chocolate!!)	Consumer's comments:
Case manager's signature Date	Consumer's signature Date

Figure 6.3. Case management; consumer strengths assessment.

For: <u>John Peterson</u>   Case manager: <u>Linda C.</u>   Date: 8/5/96

Planned frequency of contact: **Thursday this week/once or twice a week usually.**

Life domain focused upon:

☐ Daily living situation   ☐ Vocational/educational

☐ Social supports   ☐ Leisure/recreational supports

☐ Financial/insurance   ☒ Health

Consumer's long-term goal: **To stay in my apartment**
To remember to take medications as prescribed

Measurable short-term goals toward achievement	Responsibility	Date to be accomplished	Date accomplished	Comments
John will call his old friend Pete to ask him if he would work with him to make a buzzing medication box that will remind him to take his medication.				
1. Call Pete and ask if he would help.	John	Tues. (8/6)	Tues.	Pete was excited!
2. Visit Pete to discuss plan for building the device.	John & Linda (CM)	Thur. (8/8) 3 p.m.	Thus.	Diagram drawn.
3. List materials needed.	John & Pete	Thurs.	Thurs.	List created (about $15 needed).
4. Withdraw $20 from bank for materials.	John	Fri. (8/9)		
5. Pete will pick John up at 1 p.m. on Sat.	Pete	Sat. (8/10)		
6. Go to Ace Hardware and buy materials.	John & Pete	Sat.		
7. Work on device in Pete's basement.	John & Pete	Sat.		

Consumer's signature   Date   Case manager signature   Date

Psychiatrist signature   Date   Collateral signature   Date

Figure 6.4. Case management personal plan.

research. Clients themselves attribute part of their success to the personal planning process. This section captures the client experience in their words.

Client-Determined

- "She asked me if I wanted to write my own. That blew me away. I was afraid at first but I did it, and it felt really great, like I was in charge."
- "She told me I was in charge. Like this was my own to-do list, and I was not locked in and could change my mind whenever I wanted."
- "I was working on things that were important to me, not what somebody else said was important to me."
- "When I told her I wanted to go back to school she did not try to talk me out of it like some other people did, saying I was not ready and needed to do a whole bunch of other things before I could try this big step. She wrote it down and then we talked about all of the things that needed to get done for this to happen."

Organizing Lives

- "Before I met my case manager all my goals were up here (points to his head). Now they're more real, like I can see that I'm making progress, and it makes me feel like I can do it, and I want to do more, like when I write them down, where I can see them, it helps me to remember. I have trouble blowing things off."
- "The personal planning usually keeps it in writing, and kind of more up front for both of us [the worker and the client]. It becomes a major concern, and we try to maintain contact with people in the community, and we try to accomplish it in a certain time, we review these at least once a week, sometimes twice a week."
- "Personal planning is a process anybody could benefit from. Sometimes your life is like a rerun, it keeps going over and over, and sometimes you got to change the channel. Don't let the future be twenty years down the road, you want something a little bit sooner. Writing it down is important because sometimes my memory gets bogged down, writing it down where you don't just talk about it, where you visually see it, there's that visual contact, my personal appointments or other things I got to do, anything that helps your mind stay improved, I'm all for it."
- "I'm gonna try now to not have case management for awhile, I think I can do it. I told my case manager I'm going to keep using the personal plan as my stress management strategy."

Breaking Goals Down

- "The personal planning is pretty helpful for me. I had a hard time getting things done like the housework. We would break it up (the goal, not the house). When we do it that way I can do better. Fran [CM] has taught me to do that."

- "I get really overwhelmed real easy, and my case manager (using the personal planning tool) helped me to break them up into real small, comfortable steps that I could manage no sweat."

Collaboration

- "We set a lot of goals. We have these goal sheets, when I do my laundry, take my medication. We set goals and then we talk about it, and I usually complete all my goals, and we usually go out. Sometimes she helps me pay my bills and get them all arranged. The goal planning is, well, I'm a real restless person, and sometimes I don't want to do the things that are on my goal sheets, and she tells me, 'you don't have to do them,' but that 'they are important,' and I trust her so much that I want to do them. It's not that I do it because she wants it but because I want to do it. Those goal sheets have been really helpful."

- "I never worked this closely with anyone down here before, I've never confided my deepest thoughts, I never made out goals before or had somebody to help me make out my goals. When she [CM] came here it was kind of a miracle for me."

Sense of Achievement/Feedback

- "Completing the goals made me proud of myself, because I accomplished so much. She would say, look here, look at how much you have done, and it made me feel good because I had something to look at and something to be proud of, and I didn't feel that my life was going to waste. I felt like I can't do this, and I can't do that . . . but I can do this, and it was a great feeling. She gave me the ability to renew my mind, she taught me how to use my mind to go out and get the things I want on my level."

- "Personal planning helped me to see what I was doing in all parts of my life, and I could see the progress. It was all me. I could see how much I was doing and how much I advanced. It helped me to keep track of where I was going and to see the changes I've made. It made me feel a lot better about myself, I wasn't just existing . . . I was going someplace."

- "It felt great to actually accomplish things, I could see that I was making progress in my life."

- "I didn't want to do the plans at first, but she said she would write down what we were doing anyway and I could see what she was writing anytime I wanted. When I decided to see them, it was neat to see how far I had come."

- "I get copies of my plan, and I keep them and look back on all the things I've done when I'm feeling depressed, and it lifts me up."

- "We get together and we review the sheets and I check off all of the things that I've done, and my CM puts a sticker on the page and I love that. One time she forgot to put my sticker on and I let her have it!"

- "Normally I wouldn't have liked the goal sheets. I was afraid to have goals, but there was a sense of accomplishment. Just reminding me that there were different areas of my life. Maybe I didn't want to be that positive, maybe that day I didn't feel like I had any strengths, but I do now."

Summary

It has been said that actions sometimes speak louder than words. Such may have been the case in one particular consumer interview. A young man, who struggled with Major Depression, appeared to have difficulty responding verbally to the initial open-ended question regarding how the experience of receiving case management had been for him. He stared at the floor, for what seemed like hours, but actually was only about one minute. He then slowly got up from his chair, at which point I was certain that he was concluding the interview. He walked over to where his coat was lying on the couch, reached into his pocket, and removed a tiny piece of paper, which had been folded carefully several times over. He came back to his seat, and slowly and carefully unfolded the paper, and handed it to me without saying a word. It was a copy of his personal goal planning sheet which specified what he was currently working on with his case manager. He then went on to say:

TABLE 6.2
Personal Planning

Purpose: To create a mutual agenda for work between the client and case manager focused on achieving the goals that the client has set.

Behavior

1. The long-term goal reflects something that the person wants, desires, dreams about, hopes for, as reflected in the wants column on the strengths assessment.
2. Goals and tasks are specific, measurable, observable, reflecting as much as possible the consumer's own language.
3. Goals are broken into small, meaningful steps that have a high probability of success.
4. Target dates set for each task (no "ongoing" task); in most situations target dates are set within one week.
5. Goals and tasks are written positively: something the person will do, not what they will not do.
6. Strengths that are recorded on assessment show up in goals, action steps, and resources.
7. CM uses natural resources, (e.g., community recreational league, postsecondary educational classes, etc.), in addition to MHC resources to increase options for consumer goal achievement.
8. CM involves family, community members (non-mental-health professional), friends, partners, etc. (as wanted by consumer) to assist in achievement of action steps and goal plans.
9. The personal plan short-term goals are revised, updated, and changed, and accomplishments are celebrated in every contact between the consumer and CM.
10. A variety of ways are used to increase consumer ownership of the personal plan (e.g., consumer writes their own, consumer has a current copy, consumer signs or initials plan and changes, CM teaches consumer how to use strengths to attain goals).

Definition—goal = consumer's long-term goal
tasks, short-term goals, objectives, steps = the steps established to reach long-term goal

It's been a good experience, the goals, the sheets, make it easy for me to accomplish goals. I haven't done it like this before, it's helpful cause it's put down on paper. One time I wrote on my goal sheet. It was comfortable. Case managers need to know what the client is working on.

A summary of key case manager behaviors in developing a personal plan can be found in Table 6.2.

CHAPTER 7

Resource Acquisition: Putting Community Back into Community Mental Health

Purpose: To acquire the environmental resources desired by clients to achieve their goals and insure their rights, to increase each person's assets.

Mental health is a sense of achievement, a sense of belonging, a sense of self-worth, a sense of choices and the power to choose. Individual mental health, in this sense, is inseparable from the community. Belonging, achievement, self-worth can only occur in context and in transaction with others. The quality of the niches a person inhabits is dependent on the match between individual characteristics and the resources, opportunities, and social relations of the environment.

The mental health of people with severe mental illness will continue to suffer as long as mental health is seen as separate from community, is only seen as a group of professionals with specialized talents, is only seen as formally constituted services largely segregated from the rest of life. While the community is not the source of mental illness, it is the community that is the source of mental health. It is the community that is rich with opportunities, resources, and people. Therefore, a primary task of the strengths model case manager is to break down the walls separating clients from the community, to replace segregation with true community integration.

THE MENTAL HEALTH SYSTEM AS BARRIER

Our current system of mental health care acts as a primary barrier to integration, achievement, and decent quality of life by fostering and enforcing segregation. In many locales, a specialized program has been established for virtually all life domains:

Housing: group homes, residential treatment, nursing homes, staff-supervised apartments

Employment: sheltered workshops, prevocational skills classes, work crews at the mental health center

Recreation: partial hospital and day treatment programs

Education: GED classes at mental health center, daily living skill classes or groups

Spiritual: clergy visit congregate program (e.g., day treatment, group home)

Friendship: linkage with other clients, MHC-run socialization groups

These programs are usually delivered in groups. These programs mean that much of a person's life will be limited to interaction with other clients and paid staff. Their world becomes segregated and severely constricted or as Charlene Syx (1995) describes "an entire pretend world inside that transparent bubble" (p. 84).

Mental health workers come to believe that these programs are the service of choice for the person with severe mental illness. The range of options offered to the client are limited to these mental-health-sponsored programs. The uniformity of case plans found in most programs is derived directly from this limited view of resources. The community support program initiative was focused on creating a "caring community," but too often "community" became limited to mental health staff, other professionals (e.g., vocational rehabilitation staff), and clients. As Carling (1995) writes:

> By labeling all of the needs of individuals as originating with their "mental illness," and then by offering only treatment-oriented responses to such common human needs as housing, work, education, and social connections, these programs continued to reinforce the notion that their clients should be centrally defined by their impairment rather than their citizenship. (p. 110)

Stigma within the mental health system created the current system and continues to maintain it. Two stigmatizing myths are particularly important:

1. People with mental illness can't make reasonable choices.
2. People with mental illness are too disabled for regular housing, work, and social relationships.

These myths are used to explain failures and "difficult" clients. For example, failure to maintain a community job is presumed to be confirming evidence of their incompetence rather than due to inadequate support or to features of the job setting.

A major effect of disregarding people's choices is the widespread pattern of "treatment resistance" reported in the literature (e.g., Bachrach, 1982). The real problem, as Estroff (1987) has suggested, may actually lie in what people are offered. W. A. Anthony (1990) concurs that the problem appears to be one of unappealing programs rather than of unmotivated or resistant consumers. (Carling, 1995, pp. 111–12)

The stigma leads to "blaming the victim" and the perceived need for protective, segregated program responses.

This view is further reinforced by "blaming the environment" beliefs. The view is that the community is uncaring if not hostile to people with mental illness. The community is unaccommodating and therefore options available to other citizens are unavailable to people with mental illness. Blaming the victim combined with blaming the environment is the epoxy that adheres people with severe mental illness to segregated environments and entrapped niches where recovery is unlikely.

Mental health financing has reinforced the use and overuse of formally constituted services. Medicaid is the major source of funding for the care of people with severe mental illness. Clients in this "fee-for-service" system are viewed as income-generating. The more service provided the more income can be received up to the limit set by the state for their contribution (about 50% of the cost). Group services often bring in the most reimbursement relative to expenditures. Often, work with collaterals (e.g., landlords, employers, ministers) and transporting clients are not reimbursable activities. Sometimes, entire life domains are not reimbursable (e.g., vocational-oriented activities). So there are often powerful financial disincentives for delivering individually tailored services using natural community resources.

Another obstacle is that the identification, orchestration, and ongoing support of natural community resources is more complex and more time-consuming than reliance on formally constituted services. Referral processes for formal service (e.g., vocational rehabilitation, partial hospital) are usually well-specified and comfortable for the case manager. In contrast, work with highly idiosyncratic community settings and people places a premium on flexibility, creativity, and skills in relationship building. Some case managers, especially newer ones, find this prospect uncomfortable, if not scary.

The presence of specialized mental health programs, stigma within the mental health system, blaming the environment, financing structures, and task difficulty powerfully conspire to reduce dramatically the true integration of clients in communities.

REDEFINING THE POSSIBLE

At the root of the current system is a narrow definition of what is possible. Therefore we need to develop a new vision of the possible. A few stories may help. The first two stories reflect the success two programs have had in putting the community back in community mental health. The second two stories are specific client situations from England.

Sumner County Mental Health Center is located in rural south central Kansas. In 1991, the CSS program under the leadership of Mike Lawson had 1-1/2 staff and access to a psychiatrist and responsibility for 55 clients. They obviously did not have the client base or resources to develop specialized programs. They did not have a partial hospital or day treatment program, specialized employment program, group homes, etc. Despite this, in 1991 Sumner County had no client enter a state psychiatric hospital, had no client in nursing home or other residential placement, had 82% of their clients living in apartments, and had 42% of their clients in paid, competitive employment.

In 1991, the Horizons Mental Health Center's CSS program produced these results for the 65 clients enrolled:

1. Ninety percent were living independently

2. Sixty-two percent were receiving wages for work and only 10% were not involved in some form of vocational or educational activity

3. Only two clients were hospitalized

These results were produced by two staff members. How did they do it? They had no psychiatrist so they worked with general practitioners. They had no group homes, etc., so they worked with landlords. They had no "group room" so they used McDonald's. They had no vocational program so they worked with employers. They had no drop-in center so they worked with churches and ministers. They had limited crisis services so they worked with the police. They had no special GED program, so they organized a group of retired school teachers. They had no special social and daily living skills program, so they used the home economics department of the community college.

The staff created a CSS without walls. They turned Hutchinson, Kansas, into a CSS. They worked with police, ministers, general practitioners, the Chamber of Commerce, Hutchinson Community College, landlords, employers, and even the owner of the Seven-Eleven where some clients tended to hang out. They educated them on mental illness, told them the role and behaviors they needed to do to help, nurtured the relationship (e.g., going out in police cars, going to the 7-Eleven to shop), and always left them a card if they needed anything. The program coordinator, Cheryl Runyun, termed this the Tom Sawyer Principle: Get everyone to help you paint the fence.

Mr. D. was referred for help with self-care on the basis that he was not feeding himself properly and would probably need meals-on-wheels and close monitoring or supervision. In getting to know him, the Practitioner was told that Mr. D. spent much of his time "making a nuisance of himself" in the local pubs. The Practitioner explored the area and discovered that the publican was secretly sympathetic to Mr. D.—having had experience of mental health problems within the family. A deal was arranged whereby Mr. D. would cash his welfare check at the pub and would deposit some of the money in exchange for discounted pub meals. With Mr. D.'s agreement, the publican would also contact the Practitioner if Mr. D. failed to turn up, or appeared to be deteriorating. The

Practitioner also involved the publican in reviews of this arrangement to ensure that it was working smoothly and that neither side felt that they were being exploited. Mr. D. was delighted at the formalizing of his status as a regular, and the publican felt pleased not only about the opportunity to help out but also that the arrangement provided opportunities to put limits on Mr. D.'s eccentric behavior in the pub. (Bleach & Ryan, 1995, p. 188)

A local community center became worried about Mr. L's behavior when he used to wander around the reception area begging for cigarettes and being abusive, including shouting at his "voices." The Practitioner was able to provide them with information, resources, and strategies for dealing with the situation, and at the same time negotiate a role for Mr. L. in helping out with the cleaning and tidying up. The cleaner, a keen Union member, was resistant to the idea because of the risk of being made redundant by a volunteer. An agreement was negotiated whereby the cleaner was given permission to achieve their job targets in whatever way seemed best, and as long as the job was done it did not matter how. The cleaner, a heavy smoker, made friends with Mr. L., and they shared the work, their cigarettes, and the leisure time they created by working together. The center was no longer troubled by Mr. L.'s presence in the foyer, Mr. L. had what he regarded as a meaningful way of passing the time, and the Practitioner negotiated a mutual monitoring agreement. Mr. L. required fewer visits, because if there were any problems they would be picked up quickly by the center staff. (Bleach & Ryan, 1995, p. 101)

LESSONS

1. **People want to help.** These examples indicate that in any community there are people who want to help, to share their time and resources with people suffering from mental illness. Not everyone wants to help, nor are people equally eager to be involved. In some cases, helping is in their self-interest. For example, the mission of community colleges is to provide flexible post-secondary education to citizens. Their funding is often based on enrollment. Helping people with mental illness participate in their colleges helps them meet their needs as well. Other people give because of social or religious reasons. Some have talents that they want to share with others. Others give just because giving is a part of who they are.

2. **People need information and support.** In each of these examples, the case managers devoted considerable time to providing information on mental illness, the goals clients have, and ways of being helpful. In Hutchinson, Cheryl Runyun was part of the training program for current police officers and the orientation for new officers. The case managers also made themselves available to these community people to answer questions, check on how things are going, and to help in case of disruption or crises. The community people knew how to contact the case managers at any time. Parenthetically, these people rarely abused this privilege.

3. Client desires drive the work. In each of these examples, precise goal statements set by the clients directed the search for community involvement. When asked how to achieve such consistently high levels of client outcomes, Kathi Gale of the Family Life Center stated, "We ask the clients what they want and then we help them get it." Case managers will use natural community resources more if client desires are taken seriously. All client preference studies, whether in housing, employment, socialization, etc., overwhelmingly find that clients desire those niches that are apart from the mental health system (Tanzman, 1993).

Further evidence to support the use of natural community resources is found in the research. People with severe mental illness who work, live, and play in integrated settings spend less time in psychiatric hospitals, are more satisfied with their lives, and achieve more than others whose lives are dominated by the mental health system (Chamberlain, Topp, & Lee, 1995; Levstek & Bond, 1993).

Dimensions of Resources: The Four A's[1]

The use of naturally occurring resources entails attention to four dimensions of the resources: availability, accessibility, accommodation, and adequacy.

Consider the client who enjoys working on cars and would like to become a mechanic. As an advocate, the case manager begins with the availability issue. Are there continuing education courses at local high schools or junior colleges which provide such training? Are there mechanics in the community who would be willing to have the client help out at the service station in return for some hands-on training? Are there junk-car businesses that would provide an opportunity for the client to become familiar with car engines by stripping parts for resale? Identifying the availability of opportunities constitutes the first step in the advocacy process.

Accessibility becomes the next important area for consideration. Identifying obstacles such as lack of transportation, or expectations of the service system such as attending pre-vocational group at the center five days a week, may functionally render this resource inaccessible for the client. In such cases, efforts of the case manager may involve initially transporting the client to the resource site, or arranging for a family member, friend, or other collateral to meet this need. Additionally, efforts may need to be made to alter normal rules of access to be more responsive and supportive of the client's plan.

Once issues of availability and accessibility have been addressed, the case manager must consider how accommodating the resource will be. This refers to the nature of the relationship; the interaction and communication

---

1. Excerpted from Walter Kisthardt and Charles A. Rapp (1992), Bridging the gap between principles and practice. In S. Rose (Ed.), *Case Management and Social Work Practice*. New York: Longman.

the client will experience in any given resource context, be it the garage or the social security office. Case managers who have worked with people with mental illness know that clients who have been treated in an abusive or less than compassionate manner in a given context in the past will be reluctant to involve themselves in a similar situation. Consequently, addressing this area of accommodation frequently involves initial work in educating and supporting the potential resource person such as an employer or a landlord. Explaining any special needs the client may have may help set the stage for a more successful advocacy effort.

A focal point of work is creating a demand–competency match. Demand refers to the normal requirements of the setting or niche. Competency refers to that individual's unique configuration of desires, talents and confidence.

> A case manager was working with a particular client who wanted to have her hair permed but was extremely fearful of going in the shop to have it done. With her approval, the case manager went in to talk with the woman who ran the shop to explain the client's wishes and her particular situation. As it turned out, the beautician had experienced mental illness in her family and was very receptive to accommodating the needs of the client. She scheduled a time at the end of the day when there would be no one else in the shop, she gave the client permission to smoke if she needed to, and was reassuring and friendly in her approach to the client. The client received the perm which made her feel wonderful, and the beautician gained a regular customer.

In this situation, the normal demands of the beauty shop involved from three to seven people being present and no smoking. Competency in this case refers to the client's ability to get her hair done if there were few people and she could smoke. The case manager found a setting and helped the owner to accommodate. More traditional approaches would have been:

1. engaging a hairdresser to ply the craft at the partial hospital program,
2. using a desensitization approach with client gradually increasing the number of people in a room with the client and the length of time without a cigarette,
3. having the case manager or other professional give the perm.

For a particular client in a particular situation, these approaches could be desirable. For this client, however, the case manager made a "normal" arrangement possible. The side benefits include increasing client confidence in normal community activity, providing an opportunity for the salon owner to "give," and creating an ongoing relationship between the owner and client that in the words of Sullivan (1992) was "reusable and expandable" without cost to the service system.

A final dimension in the resource acquisition effort is that of adequacy. This issue relates to the extent that the resource meets the needs of each particular client. Is the connection giving the client a sense of personal fulfillment and satisfaction? Does their living situation meet minimal standards for decency and safety such as adequate heat, cooling, freedom from infestation, etc.? Does the client's vocational or volunteer involvement allow them to utilize their own unique talents and abilities, or are they involved exclusively in what the program has to offer?

THE PERFECT NICHE

Much of this chapter will be devoted to strategies for making naturally occurring community resources more accessible, accommodating, and adequate for clients. In many situations, the case manager is called on to help the setting adjust in some way. There are times, however, when adjustments are not needed, by the setting or the client, or are very minor. This occurs when the case manager can find the "perfect niche" where the requirements and needs of the setting are perfectly matched with the desires, talents, and idiosyncracies of the client. In the previous example, perhaps the case manager could have found a beauty salon that is rarely crowded, operated by one hairdresser, and already permits smoking. If such a setting had been found, there would have been no need for the case manager to help the salon operator to make any accommodations. The following situation vividly depicts the "perfect niche"

> Harry, a 30-year-old man, grew up in rural Kansas. Within a nine-month period, three years ago, both his parents died. Harry, with the help of his aunt and uncle who owned the contiguous ranch, continued to operate a large farming operation. After a while the relatives began noticing that Harry was "forgetting" to fulfill responsibilities or doing them wrong, and was increasingly not eating, bathing, etc. They reported that he was increasingly "talking strange." A visit to the mental health center led to a diagnosis of schizophrenia and entrance into the state psychiatric hospital.
>
> Upon discharge, Harry was placed in a group home with services provided by the local mental health center. Although not disruptive, Harry failed to meet the group home's hygiene and cleaning requirements, did not attend mental health center services, and resisted taking his medication. It was reported that Harry would pack his bags every night, stand on the porch, and announce his leaving although he never left. Over the next two years, Harry's stay at the group home was punctuated with three readmissions to the state hospital.
>
> Harry was referred to a social worker trained in the strengths model. Although Harry was largely uncommunicative, the case manager slowly began to appreciate Harry's knowledge and skill in farming. The social worker took seriously his expression of interest in farming and began working with Harry to find a place where he could use his skills.
>
> They located a ranch on the edge of town where the owner was happy to accept Harry as a volunteer. Harry and the owner became friends and Harry soon established himself as a dependable and reliable worker. After a few months Harry recovered his truck, which was being held by

his conservator, renewed his driver's license, and began to drive to the farm daily. To the delight of the community support staff, Harry began to communicate and there was a marked improvement in his personal hygiene. At the time of case termination the owner of the ranch and Harry were discussing the possibility of paid employment.

Why is this the "perfect niche?"

1. The case manager did not ask Harry or the rancher to change anything. Harry's desires and skills were a perfect match for the setting's demands and needs.
2. Harry's so-called deficits (e.g., non-communication, poor hygiene) were irrelevant to the setting. In fact, the rancher did not talk any more than Harry.
3. Both parties, the client and the key actor, benefited.
4. The "natural" resource only cost a little case management time.

That his communication and hygiene improved was never targeted by the case manager. Yet, this "radiating impact" is a consistent finding of strengths model practice where success in one area seemingly leads to sometimes dramatic successes in other areas.

Locating "perfect niches" should be a primary goal of all strengths model case managers. When successful, these niches tend to be stable, produce high levels of client satisfaction and achievement, contribute to the community, and contribute to gains in other areas. Because case managers do not have to change or "fix" the client and the resource, it is also inexpensive in terms of case manager time and auxiliary mental health services.

> Wanda was in her late 30s and had spent much of the last 10 years in and out of state hospitals. She wanted a job as a maid at a motel/hotel which she had done for two brief periods during the last decade. She had all the necessary skills. Wanda, due to tardive dyskenesia, had a rather rigid style of walking with her head always tilted to one side. She also said "Hi, how are you?" indiscriminately whenever she confronted or passed someone. If she passed you, turned around, and passed you again, she would say it twice. The hotel of choice has always been a lower scale establishment. The strengths case manager, in contrast, recognized that it was up-scale hotels that devoted considerable resources to having all employees be friendly and greet their guests. The case manager helped Wanda get a job at an up-scale hotel where her goal, her skills, and even her "inappropriate" behavior were valued.

STRATEGIES

Choose-Get-Keep

In chapter 1, the transition or continuum model of services was critiqued. The contrasting approach has been termed "choose-get-keep" by Anthony,

Cohen, and Farkas (1990). In this model, the client and case manager: (1) set a goal and choose among the alternative settings and resources, (2) getting access to the desired resource, (3) making the adjustments and providing supports to keep the desired resource (Sullivan, Nicolells, Danley, & MacDonald-Wilson, 1994). In the transition model, clients are asked to complete certain prerequisites prior to receiving (earning) the opportunity. For example, a person who wants to live in his or her own apartment may have to first demonstrate "success" in a group home, half-way house, or supervised apartment. The choose-get-keep approach avoids these hurdles and focuses on the client's goal directly and immediately.

The choosing phase includes specification of a long-term goal, the generating of options, and client selection. A long-term goal of enrolling in college or earning a bachelor's degree is the most frequent kind of beginning. With case manager assistance, the goal becomes more precise: to enroll and complete a creative writing course. The next step is the generation of options. The question is: Through what means and settings do people take a creative writing course? A list may look like the following:

1. Community college
2. University
3. Correspondence course
4. Interactive video
5. Independent study (perhaps with a local person who receives adjunct status to a community college)

Since the client's long-term goal is a degree, all alternatives should be credit-bearing. If this was not the desire, other alternatives could have been generated (e.g., pair up with retired teacher or local author). Within each of these setting options, there are other alternatives such as which creative writing course is most desirable. This step often involves the gathering of information (e.g., class schedules, course outlines, etc.). The last step within the choosing phase is the actual selection. Since fear and anxiety accompany new ventures, the client may want to visit campuses or classes, talk to current students, etc.

The getting phase is focused on gaining access to the desired resource(s). In the previous example this could include locating enrollment procedures and schedules, finding scholarships or financial support, formulating transportation plans, etc. As always, the client should do as many of the tasks as possible with help, if necessary, from people in the client's social network. Often, however, the case manager is the principal companion in "getting" activities. (Specific getting strategies will be detailed later.)

The getting phase may lead to a "rehabilitation crisis" (McCrory et al., 1980). This is described as:

> The experience of the disabled person who has accepted the challenge
> to grow, has achieved significant movement toward his goals, and is now

feeling overwhelmed by his changing/changed state. The client has advanced far enough in the process to begin to experience a transition in his activities, his relationships, his sense of himself. He is proud of his progress, yet sad for what he must give up and frightened of the uncertainties he must face. (p. 136)

The case manager needs to understand that the reaction is a rational response to fear, rather than some pathological resistance. Emotional support, reinforcement for steps already taken, slowing the pace of the "getting," and/or further breaking the goal down may be indicated.

The keeping phase is devoted to helping the client and the setting to sustain the arrangement in a satisfying and successful way for both parties. Frequently used strategies include:

1. Constructing reasonable accommodations (e.g., test-taking procedures, hours of work, etc.)
2. Pairing the client with a "travel" companion (e.g., another student, co-worker, neighbor)
3. Celebrations for achievements
4. Easy access to the case manager by the client and setting (give them a card)
5. Arranging for supplements (e.g. tutor, job coach, cleaning service)
6. Brokering the use of supportive services (e.g., community college disability service office, academic counselors, transportation services, clubs)
7. Ongoing education and consultation to the key actors in the setting.

The case manager needs constantly to assess the satisfaction with the arrangement and be prepared to help make adjustments.

In the keeping phase, the rehabilitation crisis as described above in the getting phase may also be a factor. As McCrory (1991) discusses, intense conflict can occur when the student is face-to-face with his or her own growth in connection with going to school and leaving the previous illness-related role. This may result in a recurrence of symptoms, or even possible rehospitalization. "The stronger the alliance, the easier client and practitioner will face this challenge . . . together, to acknowledge the struggle and support the [student] as decision maker in his or her own life to move ahead, to step backward, or to take a time out if it is too hard" (pp. 61–62).

Supported Living and Wrap-Around Services

Supported living refers to the collection of service approaches consistent with choose-get-keep that are called supported employment, supported housing, supported education, supported recreation, etc. A central tenet of this approach is to separate the setting of activity from the receipt of services. For example, traditionally people with severe mental illness were required to live in certain residences (e.g. group homes, nursing homes, supervised apartments) in order to receive medical care, meal preparation, case management, counseling, household maintenance and laundry services, transportation services, etc. This can be seen most vividly in total institutions like nursing homes and psychiatric hospitals. These settings provide for most needs: housing, food, socialization, medical care, etc. One of the rationales for the judgment that people with severe mental illness cannot live in their own apartments has been doubts about their ability to cook, clean, socialize, structure their lives, and at times be supervised. These services were only available in professionally operated living arrangements.

The supported living perspective separates setting from services and asserts that it is the professional's job to arrange the needed supports to make the desired setting work. In other words, services and supports are "wrapped around" the client in the settings or niches of their choice. Johnson County Mental Health Center's Community Support Program (Merriam, Kansas) used the wrap-around perspective when they closed their nursing home for people with mental illness. Most of the clients had spent much of their adult lives in psychiatric hospitals or nursing homes. Their illness was severe and many had the symptoms of being institutionalized. After nine months, 78% were still living in apartments and three people were living with families. A full 50% were involved in some kind of vocational activity. Thirty percent were working for wages and one person was attending college. Johnson County achieved these results in part through individually tailored personal plans using the wrap-around perspective. A few examples:

1. People who were erratic in taking medication—Med Drops where a nurse went to the apartment and administered medication one to three times a day
2. Self-maintenance, apartment maintenance, and supervision—attendant care up to 24 hours a day
3. People fearful of the community environment—case managers, attendant care workers, and significant others accompany people out of their apartment
4. People without transportation—client-operated van service to get people to community locations and the mental health center
5. People with meaningful social roles—heavy emphasis on vocational activity and work.

These were among the most seriously ill. For most people with severe mental illness, this level of professional service is not desired or needed but the concept still has currency.

> Joan is a 52-year-old woman who had been a resident of the RCF for about two years after being referred from a state hospital. She was diagnosed with schizophrenia in her mid-20s, after she had completed college and begun a career in civil engineering in New York City. When she became ill, her family brought her back to Kansas so they could as-

sist with her care. However, Joan's symptoms were so severe that her family could not manage her at home and she began a series of state psychiatric hospital admissions and nursing home placements that would continue for more than 20 years. Joan bounced from state hospitals to nursing homes to community hospitals back to state hospitals frequently. Typically, she would be started on medication at the hospital and seem to do very well for a time. She would then be discharged to a nursing facility where she began to refuse medications; her delusions and paranoia would increase. She would become angry and sometimes threatening and she would often begin to steal clothing from other residents. At that point she would usually be sent back to the hospital and the cycle would begin again. She was in five different nursing homes in Kansas, every state hospital in Kansas, and numerous community hospitals.

Joan had her typical ups and downs at the RCF, but the difference was we didn't send her to the hospital unless she insisted on going; then we would take her back after a short stay. We capitalized on her love of people—she developed a number of friendships with CSS clients and with staff. When we first talked about closing the RCF, Joan was pretty scared. (In fact, she had a couple of hospital stays around that time because she was so stressed out.) She really wanted to have her own place, but was fearful that she wouldn't make it. Probably the key was assuring her that she would have attendant care from someone whom she already knew on the RCF staff—for as long as she needed it. And, telling her over and over that we believed in her ability to do it. Also, we had the flexible funds to buy furniture and stuff and she really liked picking out stuff for her own place.

Joan has now lived in her own apartment for over 18 months! She still has attendant care, but only a few hours, two or three times a week. She has daily medication drops which are critical because she still thinks about stopping her meds at times. She is working with a vocational staff person trying to get a job and she was interviewed on a Kansas City TV station—they did a story about people with schizophrenia who were doing well in the community. Joan says she was able to do it because the staff were the first people who believed in her.

MULTIPLE STRATEGY METHOD OF RESOURCE ACQUISITION

A basic premise of the strengths model is that community integration and adjustment can only occur once removed from the mental health system. For example, who is better integrated: the client doing ceramics in a partial hospitalization program or the client doing ceramics in a class sponsored by the town's recreation department? Our current use of segregated services as a first choice often leads to clients never reaching the other level and to a waste of resources for those who with some help could make it in a class for "normals." Workers must begin with "normal" resources and naturally occurring supports (e.g., family, friends, neighbors), using segregated services as a last, not a first, resort. The task for the worker is to build the mechanisms necessary for the client to be able to meet the social demands such "normal" settings establish so that a client's sense of adequacy and competence can be respected. This often means engaging in environmental engineering to adapt settings to our client's needs and to providing support to both the client and environmental actors as they seek to make the adaptation work.

The general process through which a strategy is to be selected might be construed as rational problem solving. In other words, there is a goal or a set of goals that are sought and a number of avenues through which those goals can be attained. The selection of a strategy must be based on the information collected in each step of the proposed model.

The model itself contains eight steps and is portrayed in Figure 7.1.[2] The steps themselves are grouped into three phases: (1) assessment, (2) strategy selection, and (3) implementation. Although the steps are described sequentially, in operation there is considerable interaction between steps.

Resource Assessment

Too often this step is ignored because several resources may be immediately obvious. However, the obvious ones may not include all possibilities, nor are they automatically the best. It is important for the case manager and client to generate as many alternatives as possible and to assess the subjective probability that each will fulfill the goals of the client. This phase of assessment will include such tactics as interviewing, brainstorming, and researching.

Who Is in Control?   This step includes two phases determining which of the desired resources are available and identifying who is in control of them. For the available resources, the organization or person in control must be identified specifically. For those resources that are not available or not accessible, the individuals or organizations involved in the general resource area or those that are known to have an interest in the general area may provide a starting point. As in the previous step, it is necessary to push the traditional limits. Frequently, a variety of organizations, groups, or individuals provide similar resources. Again, the process calls for selecting the resource that will satisfy the desire and is most likely to be available. This step culminates in the identification and selection of an individual, group, or organization that can provide the resource in question.

Assessment of Vulnerability   The fourth step involves an assessment of those factors to which the target individual or institution would be most responsive and that would lead to the provision of the desired resources. The case manager will need to assess the target's vulnerability to positive ap-

---

2. This section has been reprinted from W. B. Davidson and C. A. Rapp (1976), Child advocacy in the justice system, *Social Work, 21,* 225–32.

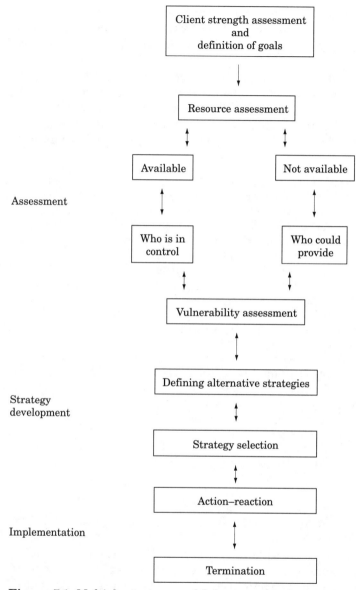

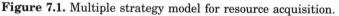

Figure 7.1. Multiple strategy model for resource acquisition.

peals and negative contingencies. Targets may consist of individuals, groups, or organizations. Sample questions that need to be answered include: (1) Does the target have an ideology that would resist or encourage the provision of the resource for the client? (2) Is there any relationship between the case manager or client and the target? (3) Does the target view the relationship as positive or negative? (4) What are the target's self-interests? (5) To whom is the target most responsive: supervisors, taxpayers, consumers, legislators, or pressure groups? (6) How accessible is the target? (7) Does the target have direct control over the provision of the desired resource or is the target only one part of the decision-making process? (8) Does the target have many potential allies and how influential are they?

This step has many implications for the effectiveness of the strategy. Therefore, adequate time and effort should be devoted to developing an accurate and complete picture of alternative targets. It should be noted that an initial positive approach strategy may be needed to attain the necessary information about the target's vulnerability. See the following case example.

> Bill Riley has been in and out of the VA hospital for 20 years for treatment of manic depressive illness precipitated by a car accident in which he sustained severe brain damage. Bill has been unable to hold a job, maintain friendships, or function in the community. The longest time spent out of the hospital during this period was 18 months.
>
> Bill was assigned to a case manager who together with Bill completed the client assessment, identified life domains in which to work, and selected getting a job as the number one priority. Bill was anxious about starting a job and the idea of a full-time job was scary. It was agreed that a part-time volunteer job in food service would be a good first step. The case manager and Bill selected the congregate meal program for senior citizens as "fitting the bill."
>
> The case manager went off to see the person who was responsible for volunteers in this program. During the conversation, the case manager described Bill's situation in some detail including the information in the first paragraph, at which time the target became worried about having "such a mentally ill person" working in their program and denied the request.
>
> Postscript: Through further negotiation, Bill was finally accepted and worked there for 10 months to everyone's satisfaction.

Selected Strategies

The multiple-strategy model suggests two dimensions of strategies. The first dimension consists of a continuum ranging from positive "salesmanship" approaches to aversive or negative approaches. In order to generate or stimulate a particular resource, the advocate must select a strategy that could be positive, negative, or somewhere in between. The points on the continuum include the following:

1. At the positive end, the case manager can attempt to gain the good favor of the person or agency in control of the desired resource.

2. At midpoint, the case manager could select a neutral strategy, often referred to as consultation, in which information would be provided to the critical individual or agency.

3. At the negative end, the case manager could decide to take direct aversive action against the critical individual or agency. If the desired re-

source is not provided, threats to take such action are also a major component of negative strategies.

The second dimension consists of a continuum of approaches to bring about change that ranges from the individual level to the societal level. The points on the continuum include the following: (1) At the individual level, the case manager could identify the critical person in control of the desired resource. (2) At the administrative level, the case manager could identify a critical agency in control of the desired resource. (3) At the policy level, strategies might include situations in which the case manager could identify some political or social system that was responsible for the resource that was lacking.

Interaction of Strategies As can be seen, the two dimensions will necessarily interact. In other words, the case manager will need to select strategies that are positive or negative and identify individuals or systems that must be changed. The examples showing the interaction of the two sets of strategies cannot be viewed as prescriptive because strategies or combinations of strategies must be executed on the basis of each client situation.

The following are a few examples of the interplay of dimensions:

SAMPLE INTERVENTIONS FROM CASE MANAGEMENT PROJECTS
Advocacy Efforts
Positive Strategy at the Individual Level

- One client wanted leisure time activities and liked to garden but the apartment complex had no provision for gardening. The case manager worked out an agreement with the landlord so that the client could plant a small garden. As an activity, gardening demands ongoing attention. Once the tulips are planted, they have to be watered and weeded. etc.

Neutral Strategy at the Individual level

- A client had cockroaches in the apartment but was afraid to contact the landlord. The case manager contacted the landlord, explained the situation and an exterminator was provided.

Positive Strategy at the Administrative Level

- A client who had been institutionalized for many years was interested in getting a job but had little experience. His family had, years ago, been in the food service business. The case manager approached the head of the city volunteer agency and arranged for the client to help serve meals to senior citizens.

- A client in tough financial straits bounced a check at a local grocery store. The client was asked to pay the store a "bounced check fee." The case manager contacted the store manager and got the fee rescinded.

Neutral Strategy at the Policy Level

- The case manager defined the lack of jobs as a prevalent client concern. They began thinking about an advocacy effort focused on eliciting job commitments from Lawrence businesses. They contacted some business organizations, presented information and sought other information which would be needed to develop a plan of action.
- Case managers became increasingly aware of the support needed by clients at the time of discharge from a psychiatric inpatient setting. A peer support program modeled after the compeer program was developed to meet this need. A grant was written and submitted for funding in order to implement and pay clients for participating in the program.

Table 7.1 is a completed strategy matrix for a client, John, whose goal was "to swim three times a week." The resource desired by John was swimming at the YMCA.

Strategy Selection

A critical element of the model is the selection of a strategy that will produce the resource needed. By necessity this will have to be accomplished in each individual situation. In the first place, at the heart of the approach is a belief in the rights of clients and the self-control of environmental resources. It is critical, then, that clients be involved in the selection of the necessary resource as well as the selection of a strategy for intervention. It is not yet possible to provide an a priori prescription as to what resources are needed, which strategies are indicated, and who should carry out the actual effort. The action–reaction sequence will provide considerable information for selecting the next strategy.

TABLE 7.1
Strategy Matrix Advocacy Focus

	Individual level	Administrative level	Policy level
Positive approach	Approach the swimming supervisor to allow John to act as his assistant swimming instructor in return for free access.	Request an exception to policy in John's case in return for the case manager applying for United Way funds for recreation scholarships to be given out by the YMCA.	Make a formal proposal to the YMCA's board to waive or reduce cost for John and those similarly situated.
Neutral approach	Engage swimming supervisor in a problem-solving session on alternative avenues for John.	Present information on the need for recreation of a group of community persons of whom John is one. YMCA and identify the barriers.	Do a study for the board highlighting groups of citizens who do not have access to the
Negative approach	Send letters to the administration, board, and national organization complaining about the supervisor's lack of cooperation.	Have the media cover the story of one individual being denied access to YMCA facilities because of administrative rules inconsistent with the Y's constitution.	Approach the United Way to reduce funds for the YMCA unless special scholarships are provided for those who can't afford.

Consequences The consequences of a strategy are multiple. Fundamentally, a strategy has consequences for three parties: the client, the case manager, and the target. Systems theory has proposed that it is not possible to affect one part of the system without affecting the whole. Therefore, depending on the nature of the resource needed and the strategy used, varying numbers of people would be affected.

A few generalizations about the relationship between the strategy and its possible consequences can be proposed. At any level, positive and neutral strategies have little chance of causing short-range negative consequences. The converse is that negative strategies have a high probability of incurring backlash or short-range negative consequences. Many strategies include combinations of positive, neutral, and negative approaches. The crucial consideration that supersedes all others is how to obtain the resource that the client needs. The client and the advocate must decide which strategy offers the highest probability of attaining the necessary resource at the same time that it minimizes any potential negative consequences. Obviously, in some instances, backlash must be risked to insure that the position of the client is not compromised.

Implementation

Once a strategy is selected, the decision of "who will do what?" becomes critical. In particular, should the case manager act for the client, act with the client, or have the client initiate the effort? Since the goal of our program is to engender empowerment, the model suggests that clients should be given as much responsibility as possible. Therefore, the client should be the primary acquirer of resources if possible. Role playing and instruction may allow clients to assume more responsibilities than would otherwise be possible. A few rules can be suggested:

1. Any case manager activity is to be discussed before and after the activity with the client.
2. The case manager should review with the client any activities the client performed on their own.
3. Positive feedback should be profusely given for any client activity, even those that may have failed. Look for the smallest increments of client competence.

A strategy that fails to produce the needed resource means either that new sources of resources need to be considered or that new strategies need to be developed. The learning that occurred during the unsuccessful effort often can be used to formulate a revised plan. If successful, the client and the case manager are ready to move to a new task related to the same goal or to a new goal. The multiple-strategy model must be construed as a set of intricately related and interacting components. However, the model does not imply that orderly execution of the phases of assessment, decision, and implementation will lead automatically to a successful disposition. The continual goal of maximizing gains while minimizing losses dictates an ongoing interplay of components. For example, the process of assessment—including assessment of strengths and aspirations, potential resources, identified individuals and institutions, and the vulnerability of these groups—continues to take place throughout the advocacy effort. In many instances, the best assessment can be carried out by initiating a particular strategy and carefully monitoring the reaction of the group providing the resources.

DEVELOPING AGREEMENT: PRINCIPLES UNDERLYING EFFECTIVE PERSUASION

Resource acquisition requires a set of perspectives and discrete skills. The premium placed on naturally occurring community resources means that case managers are interacting with a wide variety of citizens in a wide variety of settings. In their efforts to make resources available, accessible, and accommodating, case managers seek to influence these key actors.

In trying to influence others, a person may use persuasion, inducement, or constraint (Gamson, 1968). "In contrast to inducement or constraint which requires the manipulation of consequences contingent upon the target's response, persuasion involves changing the way an individual or group perceives a set of alternatives through the provision of new information" (Simons, 1987, p. 244), or as Larsen (1983) puts it, "the process of persuasion involves your presenting good reasons for a specific choice among probable alternatives" (p. 281). The following material on the principles of persuasion is based on Ronald Simons, "The Skill of Persuasion: An Essential Component of Human Service Administration," *Administration in Social Work*, Vol. 1, 3/4, 1987.

Theory and research on persuasion are concerned with identifying the characteristics of messages that persons find appealing and with discovering the nature of communications that are perceived to contain "good reasons" for adopting the position being advocated. Based upon the findings of several decades of research, the following principles appear effective persuasive appeals.

Cognitive Principle 1: Emphasize Advantages or Rewards People are constantly processing the information available to them and making decisions as to how they might best satisfy their needs and achieve their goals. Hence, the probability that individuals will change their behavior in response to a communication is increased when the message provides information indicating that the change will enable them to satisfy more effectively their needs and desires.

Several studies show that a target audience is more apt to adopt a favorable attitude toward a behavior or procedure when they perceive it to have a relative advantage over existing or alternative practices (Coleman, Katz, & Menzel, 1966; Leventhal, 1970; Rogers, 1983). Rogers (1968) notes that the advantages or reward associated with an action may not be economic or material. The benefits of adopting the line of action being advocated may be largely psychological, leading to an increase in prestige, status, or satisfaction. People must have sufficient reason for modifying their behavior or for adopting a new procedure. One good reason for doing so is because the new approach yields rewards at a level unavailable through existing practices or alternative action.

Cognitive Principle 2: Be Comprehensible   The action being advocated must be presented in a language that is readily understood by the target audience. Technical jargon should be avoided if possible. People will not adopt a line of action that they do not fully comprehend. Simple, easily understood ideas are more likely to be accepted than arguments that are complex and hard to follow (Glaser, Abelson, & Garrison, 1983; Rogers, 1983; Zaltman, 1973). Comprehension can sometimes be enhanced by augmenting verbal discussion with graphs, charts, or through site visits where the target can view the innovation in action. Clarity and comprehension are important to addressing a person's fear of the unknown.

Cognitive Principle 3: Show Compatibility of Values   There is substantial evidence that people are more apt to accept an idea if it is perceived as consistent with their present beliefs, values, and ways of doing things (Rogers, 1983; Zaltman, 1973). For instance, Woolfolk, Woolfolk, and Wilson (1977) found that students who were shown identical videotapes of a teacher using reinforcement procedures evaluated the teacher and the technique more favorably when the videotape was described as an illustration of "humanistic education" than when it was labeled behavior modification. And, Sanders and Reppucci (1977) reported that the reaction of school principals and superintendents to a program proposal varied according to whether or not the program was identified as employing a behavior modification approach. Such studies are a clear demonstration of the way that one can destroy an audience's receptivity to an idea by using words or phrases that the group perceives as representing beliefs or practices that are contrary to their value commitments.

Various groups, whether human service agencies, funding bodies, or civic organizations, are often committed to a particular sociopolitical ideology. An idea is more apt to be accepted or assimilated by a group if it is perceived to be compatible with the assumption, principles, and procedures that make up the group's ideological orientation (Glaser et al., 1983). Compatibility promises greater security and less risk to the receiver while making the new idea appear more meaningful (Rogers, 1983). Enhancing organizational performance, client-centeredness and client outcomes comprises an attractive ideology and set of values that can be difficult, but far from impossible, to disagree with.

Cognitive Principle 4: Cite Proven Results   An audience is more apt to accept an idea if its consequences have already been observed. When people can see the positive results of an action or procedure they are more likely to adopt it (Glaser et al., 1983; Rogers, 1983). Given this finding, a stepping stone approach is often the most effective way of selling an idea. First, a small group is persuaded to test the procedure. The positive results obtained in this demonstration project or pilot program are then cited in persuasive communications designed to promote the idea across a broader population.

Cognitive Principle 5: Allow for Trialability   The target group will perceive less risk if the new ideal can be tried on a piecemeal basis prior to wholesale adoption of the procedure (Rogers, 1983; Rogers & Svenning, 1969). As Glaser et al. observe:

> The extent to which a proposed change is known to be reversible if it does not prove desirable may affect its adoption. Not all innovations can be discarded later with impunity; the bridges back to the status quo may have been burned. Situations in which the user need not "play for keeps" provide more opportunity for innovation. (1983, p. 61)

People are reluctant to commit themselves to a line of action that does not allow for a later change of mind. An idea is more apt to be adopted if it can be broken into parts that can be tried one step at a time, with the group having the option of discontinuing the new procedure at any time in the process should they decide that it is not producing the anticipated results (Rogers, 1983).

Cognitive Principle 6: Link Message to Influential Others   Consistent with the predictions of Balance Theory (Heider, 1958), several studies indicate that people tend to adopt the same attitude toward an object or idea as that held by someone they like and that they tend to adopt the opposite attitude toward an object or idea as that held by someone they dislike (Tedeschi & Lindskold, 1976). In this way, individuals maintain cognitive balance.

These findings suggest that an idea is more likely to be accepted if it is linked to persons whom the target likes. The most direct method for doing this is to have someone the target likes or respects deliver the persuasive appeal. When this is not feasible, reference might be made to influential others as part of the communicated message. For instance, if a city council member is known to be a firm supporter of the state governor and the governor is known to have the same views on an issue as the case manager who is trying to influence the council member, this information could be presented to the council member. This general tactic can be used whether the favored person is the president, a movie star, a well-known expert on some topic, or the target's colleague, friend, or spouse.

The case manager might cite individuals similar to the target when information about whom the target likes or respects is lacking. This strategy is based on the extensive body of research indicating that people tend to be attracted to people they perceive as similar to themselves. Thus, when attempting to persuade a landlord to make repairs, the worker might name other landlords who have made such repairs.

Cognitive Principle 7: Avoid High-Pressure Tactics   Research based upon Reactance Theory shows that when individuals feel pressured to select a particular course of action, whether through the promise of rewards, the threat of punishment, or intense appeals, they tend to increase their valuation of alternatives to the position being advocated (Brehm, 1966; Wicklund, 1974). High-pressure tactics create a boomerang effect. The use of pressure to persuade people to adopt an idea frequently creates resistance and a determination to act in a manner that is contrary to the proposed action. Human beings value their freedom and will resist attempts to circumscribe their choice or self-determination. Therefore, messages should be presented in a manner that minimizes any threat to the target's feeling of freedom. Phrases such as "It's your decision," "But, of course, it's up to you," and "Think about it and see what you want to do" serve this function, whereas words such as "must," "should," and "have to" are likely to arouse resistance (Brehm, 1966).

Cognitive Principle 8: Minimize Threats to Security, Status, and Esteem   Case managers often commit the "rationalistic bias" of assuming that people are reasonable beings who when presented with the logic of a new and better approach will recognize its merits and embrace it without hesitation (Zaltman & Duncan, 1977). However, events frequently fail to unfold in this fashion. People's logic and reason are often distorted by less rational processes. Sound judgment may be clouded by a defensive emotional response. Emotional defensiveness may be produced because a group fears the new procedure will signal a diminution in their prestige or power (Bright, 1964; Berlin, 1968). Those persons who have benefited the most from existing practices are likely to be threatened by a change in procedures. Other individuals may fear that the new approach will devalue their knowledge and skills and that they will have a difficult time learning the new procedures (Bright, 1964; Glaser et al., 1983). In still other instances, persons may be reluctant to adopt a course of action because they feel they will lose face with their friends or some constituency.

The wise case manager will construct his or her communications in a manner that alleviates such threats. Whenever an idea might be interpreted as threatening to the target group's security, esteem, or sense of competence, these fears should be discussed and objectively examined as part of the communication process. By acknowledging and evaluating these concerns through the two-sided approach discussed below, defensiveness may be reduced and reason allowed to prevail.

DEVELOPING AGREEMENT: COGNITIVE STRATEGIES FOR PERSUASION

The previous section describes principles of persuasion, those dynamics that seem to work. This section transforms these principles into specific interpersonal strategies of documented effectiveness.

Ronald Simons (1982, 1985, 1987) has conducted an extensive review of the social psychology literature on cognitive strategies for persuasion and influence. While it is natural to think of cognitive strategies to be the exclusive realm of oral interchanges, they are also useful with written communication channels such as letters, memos, and reports. These strategies will be reviewed by describing the strategy and providing an example within the context of strengths model case management practice. This is no substitute for learning and practicing these experientially. Case managers are encouraged to practice each of these with another person (e.g., supervisor) who can observe the use of the strategy and the effect on the audience and provide feedback.

Cognitive Strategy 1: The Two-Sided Argument This strategy recognizes that there may be several points of view on any point of discussion. To use this strategy, you present the other position or positions first and then present the position you would like supported. The presentation of the other positions is more effective when it is accompanied with clear appreciation for each position. The advantage of this strategy is that it demonstrates understanding and appreciation of the other positions. It tends to reduce defensiveness and preempt counterarguments.

> We have devoted several hours of discussion over the last several days to deciding if Marge should be returned to the Welcome Group Home or placed in an apartment upon discharge from the hospital. The task today is to decide. There seems to be two positions on this issue. The first position is that Marge would be better served by placement in the Welcome Group Home. The reasons include:
>
> 1. Marge has not been responsible about taking her medications for at least two years.
> 2. Marge has not demonstrated an ability to care for herself in terms of food.
> 3. Marge tends to isolate herself and resists attending the partial hospital program; she does not know how to structure her day.
>
> Furthermore, under these conditions, we all know Marge is likely to decompensate and be rehospitalized, probably sooner rather than later. This scenario is quite possible and the reasons given are very much based on Marge's behavior over the last year and a half. If we do not address these needs, an apartment surely will not work.
>
> Discharge to an apartment, on the other hand, has some promise for the following reasons:
>
> 1. Marge wants to live in an apartment and has wanted to do so for over a year. As a program, we have increasingly respected client choice and, in fact, it is part of our mission statement.
> 2. Besides eating, Marge does possess and uses self-care skills in other areas. Her living quarters and clothing are always immaculate.
> 3. What we have been doing has not really worked. Marge had been in the Welcome Group Home for almost a year and was in another group home before that. During that 18-month period, Marge has been rehospitalized four times.

My own position is that we try the apartment and arrange for the supports needed to address the medications and food. If it does not work, we still have the group home. Remember Robbie and Gus? We had similar trepidation in their situation but for the last six months it seems to be holding. I would like to use today to brainstorm alternative ways for meeting these needs. I have brought copies of Marge's strengths assessment. As you can see, Marge is not without strengths and has a fair amount of supportive people in her life. Let's take the medication issue first.

Woven into this monologue are several ideas. First, the task before the group is made clear. Second, the contrary position is detailed first and its credibility established. Third, the group's wisdom is acknowledged and the opinion that they are the best people to work on it implied. Fourth, the desired position is described and a specific person recognized. Fifth, threats to security and control are attenuated by suggesting that a decision to go ahead is not a *fait accompli* and everyone will continue to be involved in designing it correctly. The reader may also notice how the monologue also introduced compatibility of values, cited proven results and allowed for trialability.

Cognitive Strategy 2: Cognitive Dissonance   In this strategy, when people sense a contradiction between a behavior and an attitude, they tend to want to change to resolve the dissonance. That is, if they are aware of a contradiction between a behavior and an attitude, they are likely to change the attitude or the behavior to bring the two in line with each other. There is a danger in using this strategy. Some people when they see that there is a contradiction point it out with an attitude of "I got you." Some people think about this strategy as confrontation with a negative emotional component. Our experience is that by including a negative emotional component in the delivery, that resistance results or increases. One definition of confrontation is to bring face to face, or to compare two things by placing them side by side. The challenge is to place the two contradictory items side by side within a relationship that engenders change rather than resistance. This strategy may also be used in a more active way by inducing or rewarding a person or group to perform an action that is in the direction of the desired position without examining attitudes that would contradict this behavior. When the audience sees that there were rewards from the behavior despite contradicting their original attitude, they are more likely to bring the attitude in line with the behavior. In the previous example, the case manager noted the values of the group (i.e., client choice) and used it as one of the reasons for selecting the apartment alternative.

Cognitive Strategy 3: Specify the Consequences of a Stance   With this strategy the audience is involved in exploring the consequences of a position through logical reasoning. When the consequences of the desired position are seen as more beneficial or more likely to satisfy a need, then the audience is more likely to move toward the desired position. This strategy is essentially thinking through positions and their consequences. It is more common than unusual to adopt a position without systematically thinking through the consequences. After all, we are all busy people with work loads that seldom allow time for reflection. This strategy works best when the audience or target describes their position and the anticipated consequences of this position. The case manager's job in this situation is to help clarify the position and the consequences. The case manager also has to assure that negative or possible undesired consequences are identified. In other words, the case manager must have done homework and be a skilled interviewer. When the position and consequences are clear, the leader points out how these consequences are not as desirable as those emanating from the desired position.

In the previous example, the case manager did say that the group home "solution" has not been working. The case manager could have listed other consequences such as:

1. Working with the Welcome Group Home staff is time-consuming and often not pleasant.
2. If Marge returns there, there would not be a bed available for Joe or Sam when they are discharged.
3. Since the group home is a 40-minute drive from the program, many of the transportation problems for Marge would continue.

Cognitive Strategy 4: Weight of the Evidence While specifying the consequences of a stance relies on logic, weight of the evidence relies on documentation. You present all of the evidence for your position and this suggests to people that they might adopt a new position based on the evidence. It can also be used by comparing the evidence for one position with the evidence for another position. Similar to a courtroom analogy, the position with more evidence tends to be sustained. Just as in court, you need to consider the nature of evidence. In court, there are specific rules of evidence. In the area of the social programs, evidence tends to come from empirical literature, theoretical literature, and the experiences of others.

In the previous example, the case manager pointed to Robbie and Gus as two clients in similar situations where the apartment choice worked. The case manager could also have included:

1. The research on the favorable results of supported housing
2. The success another program (familiar to the participants perhaps) has had with similar clients or a successful program that does not have access to a group home

DEVELOPING AGREEMENT: BEHAVIORAL STRATEGIES

Behavioral Strategy 1: Do Work (Tasks) with Them One of the most powerful techniques for developing a consensus with a group of people is to get them involved in doing a *task*. All too often meetings are a waste of time. The agenda is unstructured or absent and the desired outcomes are not specified. Few participants take responsibility for helping structure or lead the meeting. The meeting operates at such a level of abstraction and verbal interchange that few results could be expected. As case managers, a common strength is verbal ability. Much of case management is conducted with verbal skills. We probably selected case management in part because we had well-developed verbal skills. It is this very strength that can become a problem in the meeting. Discussion of "issues" at a conceptual level passes for doing work in the context of many meetings. We attempt to talk a participant into taking our position. We try to change minds. The variety of cognitive strategies that, in fact, may exercise influence do have a role. However, we have found that these strategies and social workers' heightened verbal abilities are even more effective within the context of doing a *task* together.

For example, you are trying to get acceptance to start a new "Med Drop" program that will deliver medications up to three times a day to clients who have great difficulty maintaining their regime. There are many concerns among the staff including potential to foster dependency, the expense of the program, and therefore the number of clients has to be limited so how will the service be rationed, and suggestions that the funds could be better used elsewhere. Your research has convinced you that such a service would dramatically increase medication compliance for a group of clients otherwise likely to require frequent hospitalization. One approach would be to use a variety of persuasion strategies (e.g., two-sided argument, cognitive decisions) to convince the people. It may, however, just continue the discussion of whether it should be done.

The *task*-centered approach in this situation would change the focus by getting the group to do work together rather than engage in verbal argument. In this case, the case manager, as the instigator, would note the difficulty in defining who will receive this service and get the group engaged in developing the criteria that will, as unambiguously as possible, determine which clients will be served and not served.

If you are successful in getting the group engaged in this *task*, you are accomplishing several things at the same time. You are building on the groups strength in terms of analytic and verbal ability by directing this into a critically important *task*. You are developing ownership for the product which enhances the implementation of the product as intended. You are drawing on the collective practice wisdom of the group which is bound to be larger than yours alone. As items are put forth as suggestions for the in-take checklist, you are provided opportunities to reward individuals as well as the group for their specific suggestions. Consequently, the group is going to experience increased feelings of competence and probably cohesion. As the group struggles with the difficulty of the *task*, you are provided with a natural opportunity to provide the group with information you acquired in your research. But most important, you have begun to change the central question from "whether to do it" to "how are we going to do it."

No single example can demonstrate the richness and variety of this strategy. However, the list of benefits is quite impressive. Of course, the group or individual members must have the specific skills required to complete the *task*. The group may simply not have any history in doing work together which may make it difficult to engage them in a *task*. You may also select a *task* that they just do not have the ability to complete. In either case it is likely that the original *tasks* can be broken down into a small *task* or set of *tasks* at which the group can be successful.

It is also frequently the case that part of the *task* cannot be finished because someone needs to do some other work outside of the group meeting. Checking case files or state policy, for example. In this situation the work is delegated to group members. The more responsibility each member can take for a part of the *task*, the more the benefits of this approach will accrue. Volunteering to do a part of the *task* shows commitment on your part as well. One advantage to the delegation of *tasks* to be done outside of the group is the natural establishment of the agenda for the next meeting as well as prior commitment to work at the next meeting.

In short, case managers who are skilled at translating issues into concrete tasks and involving others in their completion are often quite successful in change efforts.

Behavioral Strategy 2: Modeling   Modeling as a strategy for building consensus is simply doing. Much of what we want people to do is a set of behaviors that are much too complex to explain or attempt to talk people into doing. When a person does the set of behaviors (models), the components of the behavior are demonstrated. This also allows the audience to compare their behavior in similar situations to the demonstrated behavior. Not only are the behaviors demonstrated, but the rewards possible or accruing from the behavior are also demonstrated. This includes both extrinsic and intrinsic rewards. That is, modeling not only demonstrates the rewards available from others but also demonstrates the ways in which the behavior is intrinsically energizing or exciting.

This strategy is often useful in working with employers, ministers, or other people who are predisposed to helping but are uncertain how to handle a client's unusual behavior. The case manager can demonstrate how to interact with the client to get them back on task, to lower their voice, or to remind them of some expectation. Viewing the case manager interacting in a way that is effective and comfortable can reduce discomfort and fear and vividly portray the necessary behavior.

This description has several implications for use by case managers. The audience has to be able to see the behavioral components, the extrinsic rewards, and the intrinsic rewards. The audience has to believe that the rewards would also be available to them. The audience has to believe that they could perform the behavior. These conditions mean that the case manager using modeling must establish the conditions for modeling to be effective. That is, the case manager must remove any real or perceived barriers to performing the behavior. The case manager must make certain that the rewards are available to others who perform the same behavior. The case manager must explicitly demonstrate the implicit rewards through demonstrating the excitement or joy felt by performing the behavior.

Behavioral Strategy 3: Inducements and Rewards This strategy comes directly from the various behavioral schools of thought. People exhibit behavior they believe to be rewarding. Either the conditions are established to assure the person that rewards are forthcoming or the behavior is exhibited and rewards accrue which increases the frequency of the behavior. Of course, the link between the behavior and the inducement or reward must be explicit. In addition, for inducements and rewards to work they must be valued by the person and must be perceived as fair and not patronizing.

This strategy is yet another instance where the case manager must know what is valued by people in the environment and what specific individuals find rewarding.

Possible rewards for an employer could include:

1. Having a reliable worker for a job that has much turnover
2. Receiving a tax credit for hiring a person with a disability
3. Program staff try to shop at businesses that employ clients
4. The business gets free advertisement through the vocational newsletter that is distributed to over 500 people in town
5. Having on-call access to the case manager or other program staff.

The case manager must explicitly link the inducement or reward to the desired behavior. In many behavioral models this is emphasized through temporal placement of rewards and behavior. Given the environment in which case managers operate, "being there" when the behavior occurs is unlikely. Consequently, the case manager needs to be explicit in the link between the inducement, reward, and the desired behavior. Linking rewards from the case manager to rewards that occur more normally within the environment also enhances their effect. Again, being explicit about intrinsic rewards in creating a reward-based environment is a large part of this strategy.

INNOVATIVE COMMUNITY STRATEGIES

The separation of community mental health from "community" has retarded the integration and quality of life of people with severe mental illness. The community support program initiative grew from a profound recognition that to maintain people in communities with a reasonable life required attention not only to their medical (psychiatric) needs but to housing, employment, income, food and clothing, socialization, etc. The reluctance of communities to provide adequately, in part, led to mental health centers assuming major responsibility for these needs. The last 20 years have witnessed the growth of mental-health-sponsored housing, employment, education, daily living skills, socialization, transportation, and recreation programs. Mental health has assumed responsibility for functions that our society has delegated to other institutions and entities. With mental health resources being limited, such an undertaking is always limited and frustrating.

The strengths model, in its call to return "community" to our work, requires new strategies besides replacement. While much of this chapter has been devoted to case managers working on behalf of individual clients, often targeting an individual key actor, there are times when programmatic approaches are indicated. This section details four strategies for involving community stakeholders.

Data-Based Approaches

Many problems facing our clients can only or best be addressed by mobilizing a diverse group of community people. The data-based approach has several components:

1. Gathering the needed data and information
2. Identifying people and organizations who have a stake in the topic reflected by the data
3. Instigating the group to take responsibility for acting on the data

An example from Sedgwick County, Kansas (Wichita), is illustrative.

Community Support Program staff became aware that only 12 out of 874 clients were enrolled in postsecondary education. They knew that a sizable increase could not be accomplished by the program alone. The staff invited representatives from affiliate mental health agencies, the Kansas Alliance for the Mentally Ill, consumers from the program's advisory board, consumer drop-in center, representatives from universities and junior colleges, and a few employers.

At the meeting, the CSP Director, Kevin Bomhoff, distributed the data and expressed his shock and dismay. He went on to say, "We need to do something about this and the people in this group are the ones who could make it happen. The purpose of this meeting is to figure out how."

One result was the hiring of a person whose only responsibility was supported education. A liaison with each postsecondary institution was designated, and responsibility for collecting information on scholarships and financial aid and various courses of study was delegated. Methods for educating consumers, parents, and case managers were formulated. Within six months, there was a 58% increase in the number of clients enrolled in college.

This example demonstrates the three elements of a data-based strategy. One key to this strategy is that the data must be viewed as valid, accurate, and objective. If they are not, doubts will be raised and the time will be devoted to discussing whether this is a problem and where we can get better or additional data rather than strategies for correcting the situation. The results of this scenario show how community resources and energy can be mobilized with the case manager acting as but one partner.

The Caboolture Approach

An interesting experiment is occurring in Caboolture, Australia, on the outskirts of Brisbane. Under the leadership of Dr. Kalyanasundaram, community integration of people with severe mental illness has become the principal mission of the program. Their vision statement states:

> The rights, options and opportunities of the citizens of the Caboolture and Kilcoy Shires who have a mental illness shall be the same as those of all other members of the community. All citizens have the rights to be accepted, supported and respected in their choice of lifestyle as contributing members of the community. (Caboolture Adult Mental Health Services, 1995, p. 2)

Acutely aware of its limited resources, the program has had since its inception a major activity of reaching out to community people to involve them in the lives of the clients.

While individual case managers are viewed as "community resource workers" and devote much of their energy to supporting community people's efforts on behalf of individual clients, programmatically Caboolture has created the Mental Health Network of Caboolture involving community actors (see Figure 7.2). The network in turn helped create the Access Arts Program which matches artists with clients. One of their projects is to decorate a neighborhood park. Loneliness was a problem for many clients so they created the Open Door Volunteer Program that matches community people with clients. They found families for crisis services and lay people to help in respite care that became the Host Family Program. As they describe:

> . . . the emphasis is on the informal system. It is the informal system which provides the restorative experiences of friendship, understanding, and a sense of belonging. (Caboolture Adult Mental Health Services, 1995, p. 12)

Another major initiative was supporting the development and operation of a consumer organization. Under the leadership of Helen Glover and Melanie Scott this organization now offers the following:

1. Chat Line providing peer counseling
2. Community Movement Project which befriends people who are lonely
3. Building Blocks—a lunchtime socialization opportunity with a library of videos on mental health
4. Quiet Support—room in a house that people can use for respite

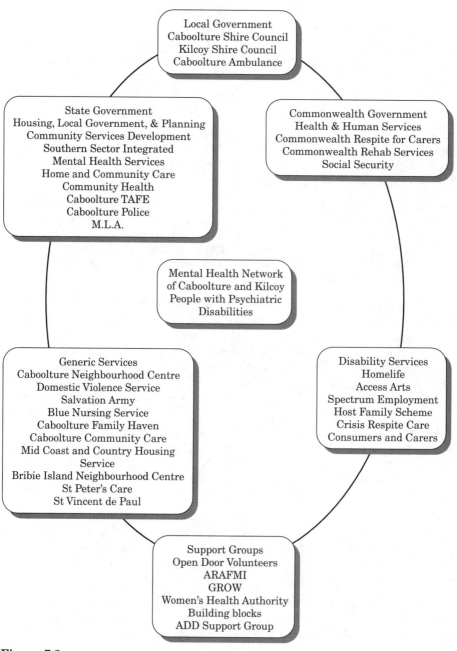

Figure 7.2.

5. Publication of an anthology of consumer poetry

6. An education program for community groups

7. Lunchtime series involving consumers and staff to discuss topics such as recovery and partnerships.

The group also does consumer advocacy, provides consultation to the professional staff, and assists consumers in finding employment and other opportunities.

One of the strategies is to funnel funds to community groups rather than using those funds to expand the mental health center services. For example, rather than applying for a grant to establish a day treatment center, Dr. Kalyanasundaram helped the Neighborhood Centers to apply for the funds. The Neighborhood Centers already served other populations and this would allow them to provide skill instruction, socialization activities, and some additional linking to other community resources.

The benefits of this approach include fostering integration and avoiding segregation, increasing access to people and resources beyond the mental health system, exploiting the talents of existing organizations, and developing new partnerships. (For more information on this exciting experiment, contact the author or Dr. Vaidyanathan Kalyanasundaram, Caboolture Adult Mental Health Services, Locked Mail Bag No. 4, Caboolture, Queensland, Australia.)

Communiversity

People desire enjoyable activities to fill their lives and opportunities to learn and be in the company of people who share common interests. These are mechanisms for growth. Day treatment centers and partial hospital programs have been established by the mental health system to contribute to this life domain. Even when done well, these programs foster segregation and oppression. Clients' interactions are with other clients and staff, the program activities are defined and supervised by staff, options and therefore choice is limited, and this is done at considerable expense to the mental health system. The increase in clubhouses and other consumer-operated programs are a desirable trend but even these are segregated and run on limited funding.

An alternative framework is to create a "program without walls" open to the public. One such effort by the University of Missouri at Kansas City is called "Communiversity." This program recruits community people to offer "classes" on hundreds of subjects including arts and crafts, cooking ethnic foods, meditation and massage, taxes, gardening, language, music, dance, computers, healing, and travel. As you can imagine, the offerings are too varied and extensive to capture here. Classes vary in schedule from six sessions of two hours each to one six-hour day. Classroom sites have been donated by libraries, churches, community centers, and universities but many of the classes occur in people's homes. The cost of each course averages about $9. If you take as many classes as you want for a semester, the cost is $40.

While mental-health-sponsored programs will always be limited, the Communiversity offers an inexpensive almost infinite array of possibilities. It taps the endless talents and strengths of citizens and provides them an opportunity to teach, to share, to give. It is integrated and provides a wide range of choices. Rather than replace community responsibility, the mental health system could join with the community to help the community meet its proper responsibility.

Creating Opportunities

Most resource acquisition activities involve identifying a community resource and then, through a variety of strategies, acquiring it for the client. Its a process of getting what is already there. Another approach has been to create opportunities. The best articulation of this community strategy is from Denise Bissonnette (1994) as applied to employment. The approach is to create jobs that clients will fill as solutions to the problems a particular business may be having. In many ways, it is a systematic attempt to create "perfect niches" which were described earlier in this chapter. Figure 7.3 contains one example. Table 7.2 summarizes the differences between "traditional job development" and the creating opportunity model. The approach is a sophisticated application of the strengths model. It places a premium

---

Samantha Travis
1424 Windswept Ave., Apt. #2
Carson, CA. 95032
(304) 354-6654

Benefit:

With a fleet of 30 cars, your business is currently paying the rate of $35–$40 per hour to have an outside auto mechanic maintain and perform simple repairs on your automobiles. I propose that you hire a full-time auto mechanic to perform the same work for one third the present hourly rate. An added benefit of having an auto mechanic on duty will be appreciated by your outside salespeople who will not have to wait for repairs from "the shop" or call a towing company to have a battery recharged, tires changed, or minor repairs.

Qualifications:

Samantha Travis is an ambitious and hard working auto mechanic who finished in the top third of her class this fall from the Carson College Auto Mechanics Training Course. She has worked on and off for several years in a family-owned gas station, and enjoys working with cars and contact with the public. Samantha looks forward to becoming part of a team where she can utilize her fine-tuned mechanical abilities.

Employment Conditions: 40 hours a week, $12 per hour

References

Deborah Callohan, Manager
Union 76 Station, Carson
(304) 654-3324

Gerald Smith, Instructor
Carson College
(304) 656-7435

Robert Wright, Counselor
Carson College Employment Project
(304) 654-7654

Figure 7.3. Beyond Traditional Job Development Training Workbook Sample Proposals: Employment proposal for a "full-time auto mechanic."

TABLE 7.2
Beyond Traditional Job Development Training Workbook
Summary of Paradigm Differences

Traditional job development	Entrepreneurial job development
Sees a limited job market	Sees a world of possibility
Views the corporate world as impenetrable, inhuman	Views the corporate world as a frame for approachable, human systems
Sees organizations as static institutions	Sees organizations as ever-changing processes
Expects organizations to make sense	Expects the unexpected from the people who make up the organization
Focuses on the decision to hire, wants to talk to the decision maker	Focuses on the need to hire, the screening and recruitment process, and the decision to hire; will talk to anybody
Recognizes employers as experts in hiring	Recognizes employers as experts in the business they are running but possible amateurs at hiring
Defines a job by the duties and minimum qualifications	Defines a job by the results produced or needs met
Works to give applicants the best edge against competing job seekers	Works to remove applicants from competition with other job seekers
Seeks openings in the open job market	Seeks opportunities in the hidden job market
Responds to job orders for existing positions	Proposes to create new employment
Utilizes resumes	Utilizes employment proposals and resumes
Sees scarcity of identified employment opportunities	Sees abundance of as of yet unidentified employment opportunities
Hears, "We're not hiring"	Hears, "We're not hiring *yet*"
Reacts to the whims of employers	Proacts to the needs of the business community
Asking	Offering

TABLE 7.3
Resource Acquisition

Purpose: To acquire the environmental resources desired by consumers to achieve their goals and insure their rights; to increase each person's assets.

Behavior

1. CM educates consumer of rights and responsibilities of citizenship.
2. CM identifies and seeks to remove policies of exclusion, stigma, and discrimination.
3. CM is persistent in using a variety of influence strategies to gain resources in a positive, collaborative manner.
4. CM assists consumer to take responsibility to accumulate resources for themselves.
5. Involves consumer and significant others in advocacy efforts.
6. CM supports and recognizes community resource people through rewards (letters, certificates, etc.).
7. CM shares knowledge of and seeks ideas and approaches to potential resources in group supervision.

on identifying client strengths and aspirations as a basis for locating vacuums in the environment.

Summary

Resource acquisition (Table 7.3) is an intrinsic part of all case management models. The strengths model, however, pushes the boundaries of traditional approaches. It requires a dramatic new set of perspectives of community, integration, and resources. It also recognizes the sophistication needed to do it. The strategies, skills, and judgment needed to successfully accomplish true community integration with clients are as complex and demanding as those required for clinical work. Despite the challenge, case managers in the United States, England, and Australia whose practice reflects the strengths model are demonstrating daily that it can be done.

CHAPTER 8

Supportive Case Management Context: Creating the Conditions for Effectiveness

The book has devoted itself to exploring the contours and textures of the client, the community, and the case manager. Case management is also powerfully influenced by the organizational context in which it is embedded. *Simply, if strengths model case management practice is to occur and flourish, producing the benefits identified throughout, the organization and its management[1] must adopt certain perspectives and practices.* This chapter seeks to describe these critical features. Of particular importance is the skillful use of group supervision.

This chapter has value at at least two levels. First, managers need to be well-grounded in the intervention methods being used by their workers (in this instance, strengths model case management) and also need to know and practice those management methods supportive of the model. This chapter speaks directly to those management methods. Second, case managers have many opportunities to influence the operation of their organizations and this chapter provides the elements that they should seek to establish. Case managers, in most organizations, are not totally passive recipients of "management." They attend meetings, sit on task forces or committees, and in a myriad of ways make suggestions or are in a position to do so.

---

1. The term "management" in this chapter refers to the people other than case managers or other direct service staff. This would include people with titles such as supervisor, team leader, coordinator, director, and administrator.

TRADITIONAL MANAGEMENT PRACTICE[2]

Current mental health management practice is characterized by separation of management from clients. Buttressed by management theory and methods, management education programs, and public tolerance, mental health management has been systematically separated from the clients it is charged to serve. As Miringoff (1980) states:

> As social welfare has grown, there has been an increasing recognition that management is needed, but such management has often been perceived, even by its own practitioners, as an activity almost divorced from the quality of service itself. In this view management is concerned almost exclusively with an organization's maintenance and political functioning; the quality and substance of service provided is seen to be outside the purview of management. Hence managerial measures of efficiency and budgetary concerns have often been viewed by service practitioners as being counterproductive to service delivery. (p. 10)

This separation between mental health manager and the client with severe psychiatric disabilities has had severe consequences. It has produced chronic and acute goal displacement, whereby the organization's means become its end. "Thus the activities that the organization engages in (interviewing clients, supervising staff, managerial tasks such as budgeting and personnel selection, etc.) are used as criteria to judge the success of the organization" (Neugeboren, 1985, p. 28). This process is characterized by concern for survival or program expansion and the loss of purpose.

Another result of the separation has been that managers frequently engage in reactive management practice; in premature embracing of snazzy new management practices, which consume large amounts of resources before they atrophy and are discarded; and in employing problem-solving modes that seem to solve problems but that never seem to lead to improved performance. The separation between management and clients also is a primary reason why management is seen either as being irrelevant or as posing an obstacle to better service delivery in so many agencies. Management continues to be seen as a major contributor to low morale and job satisfaction and as a major source of burnout (Karger, 1981).

The most profound consequence is felt by clients. Clients bring their problems, needs, pain, and suffering to the mental health agency, seeking help, direction, relief, and an increased sense of control and power. Too often, their feelings of impotence are exacerbated in the face of rules, policies, and protocols that seem unresponsive to their concerns. At times, the process of receiving service is dehumanizing, whether through the physical setting of service or through the behavior of personnel. Also, too often, our

---

2. This chapter through the material on "The Case of Estelle Richman" has been adapted from Charles A. Rapp (1993), Client-centered performance management for rehabilitation and mental health services, in Robert W. Flexer and Phyllis L. Solomon (Eds.), *Psychiatric Rehabilitation in Practice,* with permission from Andover Medical Publishers.

services are ineffective, do not help, and fail to produce benefits for the clients.

This chapter presents a framework for management practice in mental health that promises to reduce the chasm between managers and consumers and between managers and direct service staff. It does so by: (1) describing the assumptions and principles of client-centered performance management and (2) proposing a new metaphor and resultant strategies for implementing client-centered management.

ASSUMPTIONS OF CLIENT-CENTERED MANAGEMENT

One of the defining characteristics of management is that it does not directly produce or deliver goods or services. Instead, direct delivery or production of goods or services is accomplished by the teacher, the salesperson, the assembly line worker, or the direct service worker. A mental health consumer receives help through the efforts of and interaction with the therapist, the case manager, or the nurse and psychiatrist in the medication clinic. A manager's contribution to client welfare is indirect, mediated through the efforts of direct service workers. By this definition, management would include positions such as administrators, supervisors, program directors, coordinators, and so forth. The ideas in this chapter apply to all of these positions.

The first assumption of client-centered performance management is that the *raison d'être* of management is client well-being, and the principal task is to facilitate that well-being. The mental health manager is confronted with myriad constituencies (e.g., funders, licensing and regulatory organizations, advocacy groups, unions, media, staff, other agencies) that make demands on the organization. Clients are but one of these groups and often have the least power and influence. Also, these varied constituent demands are often incompatible with client goal attainment and well-being. Client-centered managers, rather than succumb to external pressures and become diverted, never lose sight of their purpose and continue to make client welfare the centerpiece of their activity with other constituents.

The second assumption is that a manager's performance is virtually identical and inseparable from the performance of the organization or organizational unit to which the manager is assigned. This perspective assumes that managers are placed in those positions to be responsible for the performance of the domain under them, whether it is a team, an office, an area, a program, a division, or an entire agency. It assumes that this is why the organization is paying the manager. It is therefore rare to have a superior manager overseeing an inadequate program or a superior team being run by an inferior manager. They are interchangeable for 80% to 90% of managers and units. This notion is more prevalent in business, where excellence in top-level management is equated with organizational performance: profit, market share, and so forth. The late Sam Walton (of Wal-Mart), Stephen Jobs (formerly of Apple), and Lee Iaccoca (formerly of

Chrysler) have achieved such high esteem in large part through the performance of their organizations. The process followed in *In Search of Excellence* (Peters & Waterman, 1982) was to identify first the high performing companies and then find the managers who made it happen.

The notion that management equates with performance is much more alien in the human services. The most typical initial response is to identify factors that seem to be beyond the influence and control of managers, which affect organizational performance. Common examples of such excuses include civil service or patronage appointments; less than adequate community services; unsympathetic judges, physicians, and other gatekeepers and decision makers; and insufficient staff in terms of amount or quality. The most frequent response is, "We don't have enough resources." For each manager, the obstacles to performance are numerous and vary in terms of type of obstacle and degree of influence. Mental health managers, however, are responsible for either mitigating the obstacles their units confront or taking such obstacles as unchangeable and seeking performance despite them.

If management equates with performance, then a clear definition of mental health service performance is necessary. The client-centered performance model posits five performance areas: client outcomes, productivity, resource acquisition, efficiency, and employees' job satisfaction. The client-centered manager is responsible for performance in each of these areas.

The centerpiece of agency and managerial performance is the benefits accrued by clients as a result of our efforts. The performance related to client outcomes focuses on the improvement in the *client's* situation or at least the curbing of a deteriorating *client* situation. Client outcomes act as the bottom line of mental health services in much the same way that profit serves business. The business executive needs to closely monitor production, acquisition of component parts, and employee morale but would never assume that happy employees who seem to be diligently working guarantee an adequate profit. In much the same way, human service managers need to perform in a variety of areas, but adequate performance in these areas is neither sufficient nor a proxy for client outcomes. It is this notion that leads Patti (1985) to argue that effectiveness (client outcomes) should be the "philosophical linchpin" of human service organizations.

PRINCIPLES OF CLIENT-CENTERED MANAGEMENT

Four principles act as the foundation for *client-centered performance management* (Gowdy & Rapp, 1989; Rapp & Poertner, 1992):

1. Venerate the people called "clients"
2. Create and maintain the focus
3. Possess a healthy disrespect for the impossible
4. Learn for a living

Principle 1: Venerate the People Called Clients

Managers play a key role in communicating the values of the program to those who use it, to those who work for it, and to the community in which it operates. Whether consciously or unconsciously, managers communicate, in their daily words and actions, how people will be viewed and treated by the program. Managers whose programs show effective results for those it serves are managers who create helping environments wherein consumers are seen and treated as human—as people who are more than mere patients or clients (Gowdy & Rapp, 1989). They are seen as whole people; each individual has a life beyond the program, comprising a variety of interests, relationships, and histories. Although schizophrenia, for example, might bring a person to a mental health center, that person is much more than "a schizophrenic." She or he is a person who happens to experience schizophrenia, along with many other life events and processes. Central to seeing people as individuals is the view that people have strengths and can grow and change over time.

Among the ways in which managers manifest this principle are: (1) knowing the clients, their stories, their history, their families, interests, and so forth; (2) having frequent contact with clients, characterized by courtesy, friendliness, and respect; (3) promoting clients as heroes; (4) assuming a client advocacy perspective toward their own jobs.

Principle 2: Create and Maintain the Focus

The organization that performs is the one that has clearly defined its mission, purpose, and performance, and that commits all its knowledge, resources, and talents to achieving those aims. The performing agency is conscientiously myopic and single-minded. It systematically excludes the irrelevant and limits the domain of organizational concern. Basically, *the performers* set out to do one or two things and to do them well. For the client-centered performance manager, that focus is defined in terms of clients and client outcomes.

Organizational focus requires the following:

1. The management's job is to select and establish an organizational focus.
2. The management should define the focus in terms of client outcomes.
3. The management's definition of a focus dictates *the elimination* of other potentially worthwhile goals and activities.
4. Management embodies a commitment, a preoccupation, an obsession with achieving that focus.

Principle 3: Possess a Healthy Disrespect for the Impossible

Mental health services suffer from a chronic lack of funds, staff, community interest, and public support. This lack of resources is simultaneously coupled with incessant demands from the program's multiple constituencies (Martin, 1980). Thus, a manager's daily work life is often typified by a continual stream of needs and demands from consumers, staff, funders, providers, courts, regulatory agents, and advocates. There are deadlines to meet, reports and grants to be written, meetings to attend, phone calls to take, questions to be answered, and crises to be resolved.

In the face of such a chaotic milieu, managers seem to evidence one of two responses: (1) surrender to such constraints and be satisfied maintaining the status quo, or (2) persist in finding opportunities to improve the program in the midst of chaos. *Both responses* mean that managers *work equally hard*, it seems, but they *work differently*. The effective managers are those who take the second course of action. Rather than remain inactive behind excuses of "not enough money," "not enough time," or "not enough staff," exceptional managers are those who say, "This is needed. Let's make it happen." They are people who instill a "make do" attitude in the workplace, in which program participants and staff members become actively involved in making good things transpire in the face of seemingly overwhelming odds. As such, the manager removes barriers to action: needless procedures, policies, meetings, and processes. The manager is willing to go with a promising idea and willing to drop one that has not worked, though the manager may have been pleased with the attempt. As Franklin D. Roosevelt stated, "But above all, try *something*." The result of this perspective is that such programs are flexible and changing, sprouting innovations based on emerging consumer needs.

Five characteristics seem to be at the root of these action-oriented managers:

1. A perception of self as powerful and responsible in the situation at hand
2. Flexibility and invention, based on a clear focus on people's needs
3. Highly developed problem-solving skills, with a premium on partializing
4. Ability to blend agendas of seemingly disparate interests
5. Persistence (Gowdy & Rapp, 1989, p. 57)

Principle 4: Learn for a Living

Managers whose program show effective results are those who seem to "learn for a living" rather than "work for a living" (Gowdy & Rapp, 1989). They actively seek out input and feedback on program performance from sources ranging from program participants and staff, to publications, performance reports, funders, and consultants. Their programs are open to visitors and observers; their offices are open to continual streams of clients and staff; their conversations are laced with stories about what they have learned from reflecting on their own practice. These managers evidence the critical skills of learning, including a total lack of defensiveness about evaluating their work; a drive to critically examine minute helping interventions and decisions to glean their impact; and the ability to brainstorm with others so that truly creative ideas can be identified and pursued.

Rather than deifying existing interventions or program models, these managers are people who approach life with the question, "What can I learn today?" They are open to experimentation. They create learning environments for their staff by paying attention to client outcome data, by constantly putting the work of the program under a critical (but non-blaming) microscope, by encouraging contact with a diversity of people, and by providing support for risk takers.

The Traditional Organization

The most resilient symbol of management is the organizational chart. Originally devised for the military and borrowed by manufacturing companies during the Industrial Revolution, the hierarchical and pyramidal organization chart (sometimes referred to as a table of organization) is ubiquitous in human service organizations. The basic configuration is portrayed in Figure 8.1. The chart typically includes three types of personnel. The first is the *line staff*, the people who actually make the product or deliver the service. The second type is *supervisory and management*, who are responsible for controlling and coordinating the work to be done. The third type of personnel is *support staff*, who perform specialized roles for the organization, such as budgeting and accounting, legal services, information systems, housekeeping, etc. In the pure sense, these support personnel have no direct authority over the line and managerial personnel.

This traditional organizational configuration was designed to enhance the manufacture and distribution of products. Efficiency was the ultimate

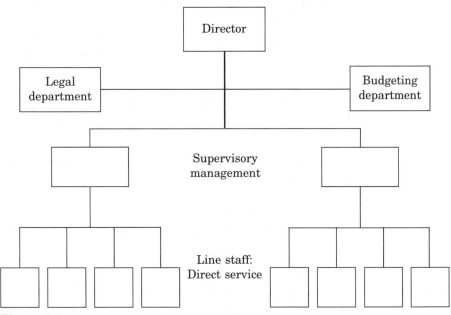

Figure 8.1.

criterion, and control was the principal function of management. The organizational chart portrayed the positions that exist in the organization, how these are grouped into units, and how formal authority and communication flows among them (Mintzburg, 1979). This vertical hierarchy depicts the division of labor and establishes that power is centered at the top.

The criticisms of this organizational configuration are legion. For the client-centered performance manager, the most pertinent consequence is the inherent separation of managers from front-line workers and clients. Furthermore, the larger the organization, the greater the distance between day-to-day client contact and the policy decisions affecting these clients. "The vertical, one-way hierarchy tends to separate and give precedence to goals of organizational maintenance over client-oriented goals" (Altshuler & Forward, 1978, p. 58). While this seems to occur in business, with profound consequences (Peters & Waterman, 1982), mental health services—with their plethora of constituencies—make it that much easier to forget about the clients. The typical organizational structure reinforces the tendency to maximum non-responsiveness to clients and their welfare.

A second implicit consequence of this configuration is that control remains the major managerial function, with its assumption that employees in the trenches will engage in actions that are wrong or bad or inadequate unless their behavior conforms to the letter of the management-established policies and procedures, and that close monitoring is required. Unfortunately, many organizational rules (i.e., policies and procedures) were developed not based on the needs of clients but, rather, on the needs of the organization. For example, most paperwork was not designed to help front-line workers provide better service but, to control who is to receive what form of help for how long, in order to please other constituencies. Another problem with rules in mental health organizations is that they assume that clients are the same, or at least similar enough that a rule can be implemented uniformly, with rather uniform results. The worker trying to help a particular client knows how farcical this assumption is. The agendas for managers, workers, and clients are, therefore, widely discrepant. Managers seek to control and maintain adherence to the rule book, while workers seek to help individuals, who are unique. It is no wonder that management in so many mental health organizations is seen as irrelevant or as the major obstacle to quality service.

A third consequence of the typical organizational configuration is symbolic. Clients are rarely included in the chart. The power is at the top, and all others are subordinate. Subordinate means "inferior to or placed below another in rank, power, importance, etc.; subservient or submissive" (*Webster's New World Dictionary*, 1972). These concepts are abhorrent to the client-centered performance manager. The need for a new symbol, a new metaphor for the human service manager, is needed.

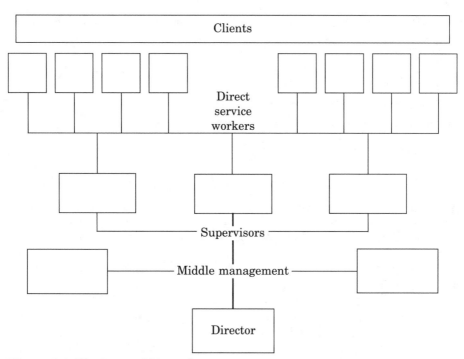

Figure 8.2. The inverted hierarchy.

THE INVERTED HIERARCHY: A NEW MANAGEMENT METAPHOR[3]

Mental health organizations that are producing superior rates of client outcomes seem to turn the typical organizational configuration upside-down in everyday practice (Rapp & Poertner, 1992). It is from this observation that the inverted hierarchy was created (Figure 8.2). This organizational configuration is a more accurate portrayal of a client-centered organization and has more fidelity with concepts underlying the client-centered performance model of management. First, at the pinnacle of the chart are the clients, and all organizational personnel are subservient to them. In fact, supervisors are subservient to front-line workers and the person who may be called the "boss" is subservient to supervisors and front-line workers.

The assumption central to the inverted hierarchy is that the principal function of management at any level is *not to control*, but *to help the next higher rung do their jobs more effectively. Subservient* then relates not only to power and authority but also to service. The service provided by management is to help others who want to do the best job possible to do their

3. Please see Charles A. Rapp and John Poertner (1992), *Social Administration: A Client-Centered Approach*, New York: Longman, for a detailed description of the strategies and methods summarized in this section.

job better. How do managers help? There seem to be four major categories of organizational helping:

1. Clearly laying out the job to be done and the expectations of how it should be done (providing direction)
2. Providing the tools to get the job done
3. Removing obstacles and constraints to the desired performance
4. Creating a reward-based environment

Providing Direction

One way in which managers can help those who provide direct services is to lay out clearly the job to be done and the expectations of how it should be done. This guidance also includes providing clarity about how a particular employee's job fits into a larger context of program, agency, and society. The cluster of managerial strategies would include the development and use of an inspiring vision, a mission statement, and a well-crafted program design that provides a variety of direction-setting elements such as goals and objectives, target population, and a service plan.

The *service plan* itself describes where the help will be provided, what will be the natural flow of helping phases, what are the existing expectations of clients and workers, and how the emotional elements will be accommodated. It also prescribes the minimum behaviors required of key actors for the program to meet its goals.

If done with precision and tied to client outcomes, *job descriptions* are the most direct source of job prescription for the individual employee. While direct service worker positions come to mind first, it is equally important to write supervisory and managerial job descriptions that are precise.

If "what gets measured gets done," the data that are collected by personnel and are reported also send a powerful message concerning what is important to the organization. The *selection and reporting of client outcomes* defines the priority domains of the work. The selection and reporting of those worker behaviors most influential in producing these outcomes establishes the most important behaviors. In this respect, the data help guide and direct behavior. Performance appraisal and interpersonal feedback similarly direct behavior and provide a set of tools for improving performance.

A powerful technique for directing behavior is the *modeling* of supervisors and managers. Does their behavior consistently embody the values of the organization? Are they models of client-centeredness? This modeling helps guide others in how to make decisions and how to behave. There is no more destructive element in an organization's culture than supervisors and managers who pronounce one set of values or prescriptions and then behave in incompatible, inconsistent, or opposite ways.

The modeling of client-centeredness is particularly important. The following are but nine examples that are often within the control of managers:

1. Interact with clients in the hallway or waiting rooms; find opportunities to do so—have an open-door policy concerning clients
2. Institutionalize a variety of client feedback mechanisms (e.g., client satisfaction surveys, focus groups, suggestion boxes) and respond to them
3. Insure client representation on the board of directors or advisory board
4. Provide membership dues for staff and consumers so that they can join consumer organizations and advocacy groups
5. Arrange for advocacy group representatives to regularly address staff meetings
6. Donate honoraria to consumer organizations
7. Talk about clients in every interaction; make them heroes
8. Ensure that the manager's personal staff acts as an extension of that manager, in treating clients with the highest degree of courtesy, respect, and dignity
9. Hire former clients

Another opportunity for providing direction occurs in many of the myriad day-to-day interactions. The most obvious are those in which staff come to you for advice and suggestions. Others are more subtle. A worker frustrated by a client who has not followed through on a series of agreements will have a natural tendency to be angry with or to blame the client. While acknowledging the frustration, the manager can reframe the client's behavior as being a result of fear or lack of confidence. The manager can emphasize the heroic mission the program has established to work with clients confronting the most difficult situations.

Providing the Tools

With expectations clarified and a variety of mechanisms established to reinforce them, the tools required to meet the expectations must be provided. It is often the discrepancy between expectations and tools that causes job dissatisfaction and low levels of effectiveness—for example, setting ambitious goals for clients and workers and then requiring services on 50 clients at one time.

For the client-centered manager, there are two general strategies for facilitating employees in their meeting of expectations. First, the client-centered performance manager seeks to place as many resources as possible in the trenches, where the help occurs. Overhead costs should be kept to the minimum, which usually means reducing the levels of managerial and staff positions. In many agencies, especially public bureaucracies, there are simply too many employees who do not provide service as their primary responsibility. Second, the client-centered performance manager should constantly be asking employees, "How can I help you with your job?" Furthermore, the employees responses should be written down, and the manager should find a way to implement their requests. An eminently worthwhile question that the manager could ask every day while driving home is, "What did I do today that made the jobs of my workers more effective or easier?" Tools can be categorized into three groups: (1) information, (2) structural supports, and (3) tangible resources.

Am I asking the staff to do something they do not know how to do? The answer is too often yes. Information as tools includes training, technical assistance and consultation, interpersonal feedback, and information system feedback especially that concerning client outcomes.

Structural supports include reasonable case loads (i.e., 20 to 1 or less), and interagency agreements that detail the reciprocal responsibilities in behavioral language between agencies and organizations. Structural supports include the design of assessment and case-planning forms that help case managers do their jobs rather than to just meet documentation requirements. The forms included in this book were developed from this perspective. Volunteers, emergency transportation services, case manager assistants, and adequate clerical support can help case managers focus on the job they have to do.

Structural supports also include supportive policies and procedures. Organizations often develop policies and procedures in response to a perceived problem that no longer exists, or these policies and procedures are contradictory to expectations the same organization has for its workers. For example, the agency may expect workers to be available for crisis situations after hours but then places limits on the use of compensatory time. If the expectation is for an outreach mode of service delivery yet billable service hours do not include transportation time, major disincentives are created. The best source of identifying organizational anomalies is the workers themselves. If we *listen* to them, we will be able to identify the areas of change.

Tangible resources for the worker and client are important tools. Tangible resources for the worker can vary widely, depending on the agency and the particular job, so a few examples will have to do. A classic situation concerns the case manager who is expected to do work outside of the agency. Resource supports would include cars, adequate travel reimbursement, liability insurance, a beverage holder and trash bag for the car, clipboards or laptop computers for recording in cars or parks, a roll of quarters to check in with the agency, and either cellular phones or beepers. For many workers, easy-to-use resource guides, Rolodex® files, adequate office supplies, and so on, would help them to do their jobs more effectively or efficiently.

Tangible resources for the client can vary widely also, but in many agencies, access to a "slush fund" for emergencies would be critical. These are monies not tied to bureaucratic controls (e.g., forms, permissions, meetings, and several layers of review) but almost immediately available for such things as rent deposits, food, clothing, registration fees for community activities, and so forth. It could mean a *lending closet*, where clients who could not afford to buy could borrow items, such as vacuum cleaners, kitchen supplies, furniture, or even fishing poles.

Removing Obstacles and Constraints

The third category of managerial behaviors required by the inverted hierarchy is the constant and conscientious removal of barriers to performance. In a sense, the lack of any of the previously mentioned tools acts as an obstacle. For example, inadequate job descriptions detailing work expectations are an obstacle. Large caseloads are an obstacle. The major theme is "less is more": less paperwork, fewer meetings, fewer priorities, fewer permissions, fewer organizational levels, fewer excuses, less noise.

Reward-Based Environment

The fourth cluster of management behaviors composing the inverted hierarchy concerns creating a reward-based environment in which to work. Mental health practice provides an opportunity to touch others—to make a difference in people's lives. It provides rich opportunities for learning and collegiality. Work should be a source of satisfaction, esteem, achievement, and pride. Work should be enjoyable. Yet, for too many human service personnel, work is frustrating, depressing, punishing, and joyless. The agency environments are often oppressive, and management is often perceived to be part of the problem. Clients and employees *require* a reward-based environment, which contributes to each person feeling that he or she is a winner.

Positively reinforced behavior slowly comes to occupy a larger and larger share of time and attention, and less desirable behavior begins to be dropped. Yet, most managers appear not to understand the power of this concept; the reward structure is inadequate in terms of the amount and the way in which it is implemented. The first rule of reinforcement is that the rewards need to be valued by the person being rewarded. While it is true that all persons have their own sets of job values and unique reinforcement menus, there are probably more similarities among people than differences. For example, most of us respond positively to written and verbal praise, and to formal recognition through awards. Based on the work of B. F. Skinner, Peters and Waterman (1982) observed that high-performing managers follow five additional rules in using positive reinforcement:

1. The reinforcement should be specific as to the behavior being rewarded
2. The reinforcement should have immediacy—close time proximity between the behavior and the reward
3. Small achievements (e.g., one client got a part-time job) warrant rewards (try to make everyone a winner)
4. The reinforcement should be unpredictable or intermittent (this happens naturally in large organizations because no manager can be aware of all behavior that warrants reward)
5. A fair amount of the reinforcement comes from top management (not just from your immediate supervisor)

What this portrays is an environment where people are receiving many rewards for many different behaviors at a variety of times from many different sources. This also suggests that those reward systems that are at set times (annual reviews or employee of the month) and are based on general criteria (made the greatest contribution to the agency) are less potent for meeting personal or organizational needs. The most prevalent obstacle to the creation of reward-based environments is the manager's belief that money, promotions, and other tangible rewards are the only or the most powerful rewards. The problem is that these rewards are limited, delayed, and often not under the manager's control. The evidence, however, is that the aforementioned rewards are as powerful as tangible rewards and are controlled by the manager. William Manchester, in describing his World War II experiences as a foot soldier, said, "A man wouldn't sell his life to you, but he will give it to you for a piece of colored ribbon." Not only are they powerful, but they have a nice effect on the giver as well.

THE CASE OF ESTELLE RICHMAN: PROVIDING TOOLS AND REMOVING OBSTACLES

Case management had been a lower level priority in this Ohio community mental health center for several years. Case managers were given little support and recognition. In early 1986, the executive director, Estelle Richman, identified case management as a number one priority and became committed to providing case management effectively.

Various stakeholders were first identified: the county mental health board, the agency's board of trustees, agency administrators, and case managers. Each group of stakeholders was seen as a team that needed to interact with another group of stakeholders or team. Ms. Richman acted as a facilitator between the county board of mental health and the agency board of trustees and between the agency board of trustees and the agency administrators. The case manager supervisor acted as a facilitator between the agency administrators and the case managers. Once stakeholders had been identified, the process of education began.

Educating the board of trustees was effective due to its simplicity and honesty. First, case management was added as an agenda item every month, as part of the director's report. Topics included: meaning of Community Support Program (CSP), importance of case management, the need for case management, evaluation based on outcome rather than productivity standards, empowerment versus enablement. The result of this education process was the board's approval of a new organizational structure that created a case management unit separate from the outpatient department. The unit was staffed with a supervisor and 16 case managers.

Second, both the executive director and the case management supervisor took advantage of every opportunity to attend county and state conferences, workshops, or seminars on case management. Articles, books, and other materials on case management were collected, read, and discussed.

Policies and procedures began to develop. Simultaneously with their self-education program, Ms. Richman and her program director began an energetic education program for the case managers. This training included teaching a model for effective case management and making workers feel like stakeholders with a voice in determining how the program would function. After a couple of months, these workers were able to contribute invaluable feedback.

The following items were presented by the case managers and, with Ms. Richman's influence, policies were successful adopted or changed to make the program more effective:

1. *The case managers expressed a need for an agency-owned vehicle for them to use if their own car was not available.* Ms. Richman requested that the finance committee of the board of trustees approve leasing a car. The committee learned that aggressive outreach was the preferred mode of treatment and availability of an agency-owned vehicle would facilitate this. Further, statistics showed that case managers spent 50% of their direct service time in the field. The committee was impressed by the data and the commitment of "meeting the client on the client's turf" and recommended approval to the board. The leased car arrived two months after the request. The finance committee has continued its support by approving the leasing of additional vehicles.

2. *Punching a time clock acted as a barrier to case management work.* The time clock had been placed in the agency by the board of trustees, and all staff were required to punch in except the highest level administrators. Data were presented to the personnel committee by the director, showing that case managers were frequently needed by clients prior to 9:00 A.M. and after 5:30 P.M. Each time they came in early or left late, special recordings needed to be done. Large accumulations of compensatory time developed. The paperwork flow through the personnel department tripled. The personnel director and Ms. Richman requested that case managers be permitted to work flexible hours. The personnel committee of the board enthusiastically endorsed flexible time and removal of the time clock for case managers. This was achieved in three months. The removal of the time clock for case managers not only removed an obstacle to their work but also became a symbol of the organizational importance assigned to case management services, case managers, and their clients.

3. *Visual display pagers became a necessity, as case managers spent an increasing percentage of time out of the agency.* Pagers cost the agency $200 per pager plus air time. The fiscal director had not planned for them in his budget and was apprehensive as to their value. Ms. Richman's program director spent time explaining case management, aggressive outreach, and community resources. The budget director began to understand that case managers working with clients and collaterals in the community were more productive than when in the agency. All 16 case managers received their own pagers.

4. *Case managers frequently complained about required paperwork.* They noted that some forms were redundant and others appeared useless.

All paperwork not relevant to the client was reviewed by the county mental health board and the agency quality assurance coordinator. All paperwork that could not be documented as necessary by a primary funding body was eliminated. If the only funding body requesting the document was the county mental health board, negotiations were held to eliminate the document. Required paperwork frequently is reviewed. An agency goal to maintain documentation time at less than 20% remains strong. Clerical workers have been retrained to help with non-clinical documentation and routine paperwork.

5. *Caseload size was an immediate problem as the agency sought to do effective case management.* It was apparent that caseload size had to be reduced. The board of trustees made the commitment to shift resources and to hire additional case managers to effect an overall caseload ratio of 43:1 from the original 75:1. With the identification of priority clients, 3 case managers have 10 to 12 clients, 10 have 35 clients, 2 have 60 to 80 clients, and 1 has 150 clients. (Clients on the 150-person caseload require only medication monitoring. Clients on the 60–80 caseloads are currently stabilized and working but have periodic needs for support. These caseloads are the next priority to be reduced to 35:1.)

6. *Many clients have a payee for their disability checks, which is frequently an outside agency with minimal understanding of the mental health system.* The program director and billing coordinator approached Ms. Richman and the fiscal director about the feasibility of the agency becoming representative payee for clients requesting this service. Case managers felt strongly that they would be better able to advocate for clients in the community if the agency was the payee. While very new territory, Ms. Richman and the fiscal director determined that clinically it would be worth the risk. Financially, the agency loses money on this project, but case management successes have far outweighed any fiscal negatives. Currently, the agency is the representative payee for 100 clients.

In conclusion, the agency has been successful in implementing a comprehensive case management system, and this is due to an executive director who was single-minded in her pursuit, who set the direction (e.g., specify client outcomes, job descriptions, designed a model of intervention), provided the tools to do the job (e.g., training, leased cars, pagers, quality supervision), and assertively removed obstacles to performance (e.g., paperwork, time clock, caseload size).

GROUP SUPERVISION

The once-a-week, 1- to 1 1/2-hour meeting between a front-line practitioner (e.g., case manager) and supervisor continues to be the centerpiece of supervisory practice in mental health and the human services more broadly. Since the late 1930s, the principal focus of supervision has shifted from the case to the worker (Burns, 1958). The notion is that by supporting and educating the worker, clients will be better assisted. Unfortunately the evidence suggests that worker perceptions of supervisory helpfulness are not associated with planning cases or developing practice skills (Shulman, Robinson, & Lucky, 1981), that worker satisfaction with supervision is uncorrelated with worker performance (Olmstead & Christensen, 1974), and that case discussions may be the smaller part of supervision (Kadushin, 1974; Munson, 1979). In fact, Shulman et al., (1981) found case consultation representing only 43% of supervision, and Kadushin (1974) found that case discussion-dominated supervision was practiced by less than 20% of the supervisors.

Teams vs. Individuals

There continues to be considerable controversy in the field between proponents of team versus individual models of case management service delivery. The use of interdisciplinary or otherwise configured teams has been a hallmark of Assertive Community Treatment (ACT) and has often been used as a point of demarcation with other models. The arguments for a team approach include: reduced burnout (Boyer, 1991), enhanced continuity of care (Bond, Witheridge, Dincin, & Wasner, 1991; Test, 1979), increased availability of someone who knows the client (Bachrach, 1992), more creative service planning (Test, 1979). The advantages of individual case managers that have been proffered include: a single point of accountability (Degen et al., 1990; Bond et al., 1991), more efficiency of case management time through less meetings (Degen, Cole, Tamayo, & Dzerovych, 1990; Bond et al., 1991), increased clarity of task assignment (Degen et al., 1990), and one person to develop a professionally intimate relationship (Bachrach, 1992).

The team versus individual dichotomy tends to camouflage the similarities between these two models. For example, since its inception the strengths model has stipulated a group supervision/team approach for the purpose of creative case planning, problem solving, sharing knowledge of resources, and support to team members (Modrcin, Rapp, & Chamberlain, 1985; Rapp & Chamberlain, 1985; Rapp & Wintersteen, 1988; Modrcin et al., 1988). Responsibility for actual service delivery is lodged with an individual case manager although the supervisor, or even other team members, often act as backup. The distinction between models is further blurred when one considers that several of the reported sites for ACT research were dominated by single-case-manager service provision (Bond, McDonel, & Miller, 1991; Santos et al., 1993; Borland, McRae, & Lycan, 1989).

Both ACT and Strengths prescribe that an experienced mental health professional without preference for discipline act as team leader. PACT (the Wisconsin variant of ACT) recommends that a psychiatrist act as team leader.

The evidence of effectiveness is equivocal. McGrew, Bond, Dietzen, & Salyers, (1994) found that "shared caseloads" were significantly correlated with a reduction in days hospitalized. In the one study that sought to examine this variable, Bond et al., (1991) found less burnout and staff turnover for teams than individuals and reduced hospitalization as time went on although overall no differences were found on program dropouts and hospital admissions. Bond et al. (1995) hypothesized that lack of overall differences may be attributable to the control group also receiving intensive case management, although not using a team approach. In another study, Sands and Cnaan (1994) studied two team approaches where a difference was "corporate responsibility for cases" versus "individual caseloads with team backup." There were no outcome differences although the authors commented that both groups of subjects were "faring relatively well." The criticalness of a team approach in service delivery also gets tempered by the favorable outcomes found in the strengths model research that uses individual case managers.

One report (Degen et al., 1990) from a project that used the team approach reflected:

> The team method of case management is time consuming and manpower intensive. Staff over-saturation with frequently changing information often results in long or incessant meetings, or communication attempts that are sometimes spurious. Staff have a tendency to "tune out" because of overarousal or overflow. Additionally, another problem with team case management is accountability in a system where there is no primary case manager except for charting, with resultant ambiguity about who will do the follow-up after treatment planning. (p. 268)

In contrast, one study found that team case managers provided more hours of service than did single case managers (Bond, personal communication, 1995). Teams also may be impractical for rural areas (McGrew & Bond, 1995; Santos et al., 1993).

The conclusion is that both models prescribe a team approach under the leadership of a seasoned professional for the purposes of planning and support. They differ, however, in that service delivery is the responsibility of a single case manager in the Strengths model with supervisory backup but shared responsibility in ACT. The evidence suggests that team-delivered services are no more successful in producing client outcomes than individually delivered services. But the consensus is that the team is needed for backup, support, and service-planning ideas. In fact, ACT experts surveyed by McGrew and Bond (1995) "rated shared caseloads for treatment planning as more important than shared caseloads for treatment provision" (p. 117).

Purpose of Group Supervision

Group supervision began for us 14 years ago with the very first strengths model case management demonstration project (Rapp & Chamberlain, 1985). The reason we chose this approach was for efficiency. We did have the resources to adequately supervise four case managers using the traditional approach of supervision with its once-1-week 1 1/2-hour meeting with each manager. Within four months, it was clear that it was not only efficient but more effective. All the case managers delighted in the approach and could point to specific advantages. We have come to believe that group supervision is indispensable to effective case management practice.

Group supervision is designed to accomplish three purposes:

1. Support and affirmation
2. Ideas
3. Learning

Strengths model case management is a demanding job that requires high levels of skills and energy in the face of heretofore incorrigible situations to achieve ambitious ends. Furthermore, this work is often done alone. Group supervision is a mechanism for case managers to feel connected to a group sharing the same mission and challenges. Its aim is to affirm case managers: their efforts, their ingenuity, and their accomplishments. Group supervision is a good mechanism for exchanging feedback.

The central task of group supervision is the generation of promising ideas to more effectively work with clients. Even the most skilled strengths model case manager will run into a situation where "nothing seems to be working." It is one order of business to know the perspectives and methods of the strengths model, and another to apply these to the myriad of idiosyncratic client situations. Brainstorming is central to group supervision. Groups are more likely to generate the "right" answer or richer alternatives than people acting alone or in dyads. This is a major advantage of group supervision over individual supervision.

The third purpose of group supervision is to facilitate learning. By placing individual client situations "under the microscope," case managers have an opportunity to learn things that would apply to similar situations. In fact, an important task of the supervisor is to help the team generalize from idiosyncratic client situations to other client situations. Group supervision provides information on community resource alternatives that could be useful for other clients.

What Is Group Supervision?

The inverted hierarchy framework avers that the central purpose of supervision is to help case managers do their jobs on behalf of clients in an effective, efficient, and satisfying way. Group supervision has been found to be a principle mechanism for achieving these supervisory purposes.

In its most frequent form, group supervision involves a unit or team of case managers (usually four) and their supervisor. At times, specialists (e.g., medical personnel, vocational staff, substance abuse experts) may be called to participate. Occasionally family members or key actors (e.g., friend, minister, employer) may be invited. The group meetings vary in length and frequency. The recommended and most frequent scheduling is once a week for two hours.

During this two-hour period, two to four difficult client situations are intensely discussed. The selection of client situations is usually delegated to case managers with perhaps consultation by the supervisor. The selection is based on client situations on which the case manager desires new ideas. Typically, these are clients who have been unable to achieve their goals. Other situations particularly amenable to group supervision are:

1. Lack of progress in engaging with a client or developing a relationship
2. Situations where case managers are having difficulty identifying client strengths or developing personal plans
3. Difficulties with particular key actors in gaining access or accommodation
4. Client goals where identification of community resources has been lacking or where the "perfect niche" has not been found

Crisis situations are rarely appropriate for group supervision; instead, the case manager should consult directly with the supervisor or specialist at the time of the crisis.

Each discussion of a client situation begins with the distribution of the client's strengths assessment and most recent personal plan(s) and a presentation of the particular situation by the case manager. This presentation should include:

1. A statement of the difficulty or problem
2. A statement of what the case manager would like to see instead (desired state) and how the group can help
3. A complete list of strategies and efforts already tried to achieve the desired state

This presentation is then followed by questions from the group and brainstorming solutions or alternative. Statements of empathy and support are often exchanged. Minimum standards for brainstorming usually include that at least three potential alternatives be generated. Each discussion of a client situation closes with the case manager repeating the alternatives and perhaps indicating the one believed to be most promising. The case manager should also tell the group what the next discrete step is (e.g., consult with client on Thursday; phone Ms. Harris at the Garden of Eden nursery; write on paper the information needed to employ a two-sided argument with the landlord). Each client situation discussion usually lasts between 25 and 40 minutes.

Once the client situations have been discussed, group supervision concludes with each case manager sharing one or more achievements from the past week, some of which could be derived from past group supervision brainstorming. This kind of "celebration" is found to be uplifting and energizing for case managers as they return to their work.

The Methods of Group Supervision

Logistics   Group supervision is essential to competent strengths model case management. As such, the time set aside for it needs to be protected.

The session should start on time. Interruptions and distractions should be avoided whether from other staff entering the room, telephone calls, or client demands. If interruptions cannot be totally eliminated, the *specific* situations warranting interruptions need to be written and all staff and perhaps clients notified.

The setting for the group supervision should be large enough for the members to arrange themselves comfortably in a circle. Some teams benefit from having a chalk board or flip chart present. While the location is most often a room within the case management agency, some group supervisions have occurred in a church or other community facilities or in the supervisor's home. One case management team had their weekly group supervision in a gazebo located in a cemetery across from the mental health center. The supervisor said that it was quiet, there were no interruptions, it was convenient, and it modeled an outreach mode of service delivery.

The selection of the case situations to be presented and the order should be established before the group supervision or within the first few minutes of beginning. The case manager should have copies of the client's strengths assessment and recent personal plan(s) sufficient for each person in the group. Group supervision is about clients and the work with them. Discussion of policies, new procedures, or other agency topics should be rigorously avoided unless they directly pertain to the client situation under discussion. These topics need to be transmitted and often discussed but this should occur at some other opportunity.

Affirmation and Support

Group supervision is to be an uplifting experience, enjoyable if not fun. Supervisors and case managers should laugh. Energy that case managers make on behalf of clients (whether they succeed or not), creative or particularly skillful methods that were employed (whether they succeeded or not), and specific achievements (including small ones) should be recognized if not celebrated. When group supervision is really working, the exchange of "pats on the back" come from all team members, not just the supervisor.

The ambiance of group supervision should be characterized as positive and optimistic. This does not mean that frustrations (and even anger) are not permitted or attended to. They surely must be. But group supervision needs to help a particular case manager get beyond that by reminding the person of how far the client has come, by recognizing the efforts made to date, by helping the case manager "see the forest through the trees" and regaining a focus on client achievement, and by generating alternative ideas and strategies.

Ideas

There are certain conditions that facilitate creativity and idea generation, and obstacles. One facilitating condition is for everyone to be clear on the desired outcome. This is why the case manager is required to tell the group what the desired state would be and how the group can be helpful. At times, this requires the case manager to do some thinking ahead of time. Its often easier to say "Joe needs to stop swearing in the cafe" than specifying what Joe should be doing. Like work with clients, setting goals as the presence of something rather than absence is more conducive to achievement. At times a case manager may have difficulty doing this. In these situations, the case manager should state this and instruct the group that this is what he or she wants help with.

Another facilitating condition is for members to have the necessary information. Over the last 15 years, we have found three pieces of information to be critical. First, a clear statement of the dilemma or problem and why it's a problem for the client and others. Second, information on the client's strengths and the client goals, efforts, and achievements reflected in the personal plans. What the client wants in the particular situation is often forgotten and is critical to generating ideas and selecting the ones to try. This is not always obvious. For example, the person who loudly swears in the cafe and therefore will not be permitted to return may want to continue eating lunch at the cafe or wants to talk to someone while eating. Third, all the strategies already tried by the case manager with some level of detail. This last set of information is important to reduce or eliminate some of the "yeah—but I already tried that." "Yeah—buts" waste time and place a pall over brainstorming. Other information, specific to the client situation being examined, can be gathered through questioning.

One particularly productive source of questions is the strengths model fidelity items included at the end of chapters 4 through 7. Often even the most skilled strengths case manager has not followed all the methods specified in the model (e.g., goals are not broken down enough; strategies of interpersonal influence have not been used or have been done inadequately; goals and steps are established that do not employ client strengths). Reviewing the fidelity items may prompt a series of questions that may later produce promising ideas.

Once the desired state has been precisely described and relevant information shared, only then does idea generation commence. The two stages of information gathering and idea generation should be kept separate when possible, otherwise time will be wasted prematurely generating ideas just to have them discounted because all the information was not taken into account.

The brainstorming phase of client situation discussions should be characterized by the free flow of ideas. Evaluation of the ideas should be left to the next phase. The aim is to generate as many different ideas by as many people as possible, not to evaluate or select the best. Often the most "crazy" idea, if allowed to be shared, can provoke a similar but perhaps more feasible idea. Some teams even have an award (one is named the Twilight Zone Award which when given is accompanied by the rest of the team humming the theme song) for the wackiest or most non-traditional idea. If brainstorming is to flourish, evaluation and selection need to be kept separate from idea generation.

The case manager is responsible for recording all the ideas generated. The use of a flip chart is often helpful because it allows everyone to keep track of ideas already generated. Brainstorming continues until the group has exhausted its ideas and the case manager has at least three promising or "reasonable" ideas to try. The evaluation and selection of ideas are the case manager's and clients' responsibility although the group surely can comment and suggest. Options that require the least change by the client and resource, *if they are attractive to the client*, should be given extra consideration since they often have the most probability of success both short-term and long-term (see the section on the perfect niche).

The discussion of a particular client situation concludes by the case manager identifying the "best" ideas and specifying the first (next) discrete step they will take.

Learning

The group supervision format, with its difficult client situation focus and group involvement, enhances professional learning beyond that allowed by individual form of supervision. Learning can be further enhanced by the supervisor (or others) helping the group to generalize from the discussion of specific clients. The supervisor would point out similarities with other client situations or strategies used successfully by other case managers. Supervisors should exploit every opportunity to frame and feed back to group members that the use of the fidelity behaviors will produce client outcomes.

Learning also occurs in terms of community resources. Except in the smallest of communities, will any case manager be fully apprised of all the resources available? Often a resource is identified in group supervision that is eventually rejected for that particular client situation but gets used for another client.

The Power of Group Supervision

Group supervision is clients, clients, clients. Nothing else should be allowed to intrude. Rather than "talk about" cases, the team works together—generating specific alternatives to be implemented. The overall effect is one of empowerment, not continued frustration. The alternatives may not work, but the team will learn from it and other alternatives will be produced.

The advantages of group supervision include the following:

1. Generate more ideas regarding creative alternatives in working with challenging circumstances
2. Ethnic and cultural diversity present in the group may help in understanding consumer behavior from a cultural perspective
3. Support and affirmation from colleagues who understand how challenging, frustrating, and disappointing the work can be
4. Having others with whom you can share successful helping efforts and consumer success stories
5. Can help with the "can't see the forest for the trees" phenomenon. One

may get a different perspective from a colleague who is not as intimately involved with the consumer

6. When circumstances suggest difficult treatment decisions (such as petitioning for involuntary commitment), case managers may feel a sense of sharing and consensus; in effect, the decision becomes a team decision rather than an individual one

7. May be more efficient in terms of time allotted to supervision and communicating information and ideas to each case manager

8. The entire team becomes familiar with consumers, and on-call crisis coverage may be shared and individualized response delivered

9. Case managers may gain support in the face of opposition from other providers or family regarding treatment decision

10. Team may enjoy sessions and have fun while helping each other

11. There may be generalized learning—ideas or resources discussed for one consumer may have relevance for others

12. Case managers may feel a sense of respite—a time away from the telephone calls, consumer requests, other demands on their time

At the end of this chapter are two tools that have been developed to help guide and evaluate group supervision. The first one, "Case Managers Group Supervision Feedback," was designed for case managers to evaluate the sessions and provide feedback to the supervisors and other case managers. The second one, "Supervisor's Group Supervision Monitor," allows the supervisor to evaluate the session and his or her performance. Teams are urged to use these as a basis for exchanging feedback and for fulfilling group supervision's promise of increased efficiency, satisfaction, and effectiveness.

OTHER CONDITIONS FOR EFFECTIVENESS

Adapting the perspectives and methods of the inverted hierarchy and using group supervision as an integrating centerpiece of the framework will increase client outcomes and the job satisfaction of case managers. The research on case management with people suffering from severe mental illness suggests several other necessary features to create the conditions for effectiveness. The following material is based on the outcome research on the Active Community Treatment (ACT) and strengths model of case management, the two models with evidence of effectiveness.

Staffing

Both ACT and Strengths use teams of "generalists" with consultation by medical professionals and other experts as needed. The strengths model sees BA-level case managers as adequate. In fact, in three strengths model studies, the case managers were undergraduate or graduate students in social work. The PACT model (Wisconsin variant of ACT) prescribes inter-disciplinary teams including psychiatrists (recommended team leader), nurses, and social workers and could include vocational counselors, substance abuse counselors, etc.

ACT research has found that only the degree of nurse participation on the team was correlated with client outcomes (McGrew et al., 1994). The study of ACT experts found "relatively low interjudge agreement for the team subscale with wide variance in size, make-up, and operation" (McGrew & Bond, 1995).

Reports of consumers as case managers or as case manager extenders seem promising (Solomon & Draine, 1994; Porter & Sherman, 1988). Both Solomon and Draine (1994) and Kisthardt (1993) found consumers to value the interpersonal characteristics (emotional engagement, personal support) as more important than credentials or consumer/non-consumer status.

The evidence is that case managers can be selected from a wide pool of people (professionals, BA-level generalists, students, consumers) but need high-quality supervision (see previous section) from a seasoned professional, and easy access to medical personnel and other experts. Considerable pre-service and in-service training and technical assistance has been recommended (Bond, 1991; Sullivan & Rapp, 1991; Modrcin et al., 1988). A benefit of this staffing configuration is that it would be less expensive than requiring case managers to be fully credentialed.

Caseload Size and Frequency of Contact

The expectations of case managers concerning the direct provision of services, the outreach mode of service delivery, involvement with client crises, highly individualized service, the breadth of life domains to be attended to, and the work with naturally occurring community resources inevitably requires a rather high staff-to-client ratio. High staff-to-client ratios received virtually unanimous agreement of ACT experts (McGrew & Bond, 1995). The ACT programs recommended 1:10 ratio (Test, 1992; Witheridge, 1991). The strengths model suggests caseload sizes between 1 to 12 (Rapp & Wintersteen, 1988) and 1 to 20 (Macias et al., 1994). Both approaches suggest tailoring caseload size to the "needs presented by clients and the outcomes or benefits sought by the intervention" (Witheridge, 1991, pp. 52–53). No study, however, has found positive client outcomes with caseloads exceeding 20:1.

While not the only reason, small caseload sizes are prescribed to allow increased intensity of case manager contact with the client. On one hand, Rife, Greenlee, Miller, and Feichter (1991) found that "the strongest predictor of client [homeless mentally ill] engagement in case management was frequency of case management contacts. Clients who received more frequent monitoring were more likely to remain engaged in case management services and not to return to a homeless condition" (p 65). Similarly, Quinlivan et al. (1995) found a strong inverse association between frequency of contact and in-patient utilization. Another study (Dietzen & Bond, 1993) found that "the four [ACT] programs with moderate or substantial impact in reducing hospital days also had moderate to high levels of service intensity, together averaging 11 contacts per client per month. The three programs that had minimal impact on hospital use had moderate to low service intensities, together averaging 6.3 contacts per client per month" (p. 841). Others (McGrew et al., 1994) found that number of contacts, not number of hours of contact, were significantly related to hospital outcomes. This study also found a significant relationship between frequency of telephone contacts and contacts with collaterals and hospital outcomes.

Three conclusions seem warranted:

1. Frequency of case manager–client contact rather than hours of contact makes a difference; the use of telephone may be a helpful supplement, not a replacement.

2. Frequency of contact and hospital outcomes will never be truly linear since those who are most ill will often receive the most contact but may also have higher rates of hospitalization (even if reduced compared with similar control subjects).

3. The quality of the contact, not just frequency, may be a mitigating factor. For example, small caseloads employing ineffective methods or skill-deficit case managers would probably be ineffective. The study by Hornstra et al. (1993) is illustrative. A brokerage model intervention with small caseloads and significantly more caseworker contact produced no client outcomes differences compared with the control group.

Length of Service

Each of the models prescribes time-unlimited case management services. Mental illness is lifelong with cyclical exacerbation of symptoms. Because of their serious and ongoing difficulties, the members of this group are likely to need lifelong or very long-term access to a broad range of services, delivered in a highly personalized fashion, to maintain their previous gains and make further progress (Ridgeway & Zipple, 1990; Talbott, 1988). In the study of ACT experts (McGrew & Bond, 1995), "time-limited services for some clients, was rated very low 93.7, reflecting the experts' opinions that short-term services were contrary to the ACT model" (p. 118).

The evidence suggests that short-term case management can produce short-term client outcomes in hospitalization prevention, acquiring stable housing, and adequate money management (Bond, 1991). Impressive results have been attained in the strengths model for as little as six months' worth of case management. However, other research strongly suggests that while immediate gains can be made, without long-term services client gains can evaporate and others do not have time to occur (Goering, Wasylenki, Farkas, Lancee, & Ballantyne, 1988; McGrew et al., 1994; Strauss, Hafes, Lieberman, & Harding, 1985). The seminal work by Stein and Test (1980) showed that when services were removed, many clients relapsed or showed loss of gain.

The conclusion is that case management services should be of indefinite duration. Given the importance of continuity of relationship and service, the case manager or team should be constant, not requiring clients to switch to different case managers as needs change.

The preference of these models is to have the ultimate *service* responsibility for the clients assigned to the case manager rather than sharing responsibility with other programs or agencies. The PACT and Strengths programs were started as semiautonomous alternatives to the then current service systems. As Turner and Shifren (1979) argued: Case management is the "integrative mechanism at the client level" (p. 9). Fragmented responsibility is generally the rule and the polar opposite of integration. This does not mean that referrals to other programs do not occur (although the strengths model prioritizes non-programmatic resources), but that authority is not delegated. As Bond (1991) concluded: "Outreach teams are likely to have less impact if they are viewed as components of a mental health system than if they have functional autonomy" (p. 77).

24-Hour Availability

Each model argues that case managers should be accessible 24 hours a day, 7 days a week. One of the reasons for team approaches is to spread this responsibility across team members. The ACT experts, however, reached relatively low levels of agreement on this element while the early Wisconsin efforts and some subsequent ACT programs adhere to this rigidly. Some ACT programs are nine to five. Since the client outcomes have been positive, the great variation in this dimension seems to make it optional.

What is not optional is that clients need access to crisis and emergency services 24 hours a day, 7 days a week. The effectiveness of crisis services is probably enhanced by access to staff who have familiarity and a relationship with the client. This would necessarily include the case manager, the team leader or supervisor, the team members, or in some (probably smaller areas) the crisis staff themselves.

Summary of Structural Features

1. Team structure for the purpose of creative case planning, problem solving, sharing knowledge of resources and support to team members
2. Team leaders/supervisors should be experienced, mental health professionals
3. Case managers can be BA-level workers but need access to specialists; involvement of nurses seems particularly important
4. Caseload sizes can vary based on client severity, geography, etc., but should never exceed 20:1. The average across-program clients should probably be 12 to 1 to 15 to 1
5. Efforts should be made to enhance the continuity of relationship between the client and case manager

6. Clients need 24 hour, 7 days a week access to crisis and emergency services. That service should require access to staff who have familiarity and a relationship with the client (can be and perhaps should be the case manager)

7. Preservice, in-service, and technical assistance should be available

8. Length of case management service should be indeterminate and expected to be ongoing (although intensity at any point in time would vary)

9. Case managers should have ultimate responsibility for client services (with the exception of medication). They retain authority even in referral situations

Case Managers Group Supervision Feedback

Your group supervision has been specifically designed as a major source of help in your work with clients and as a means of providing mutual support. The items below represent the kinds of help and support you can and should expect from your supervisor and each other. Once completed it provides a snapshot for you and your supervisor as to how well these purposes are being met. Please complete this at the end of the supervisory session and return it to your supervisor.

1. Did you receive help in the following areas:

    a. Using the strengths assessment to identify goals, tasks or strategies.

                                                                               YES NO

    b. Identifying non-mental health resources for my client(s).   YES NO

    c. Identifying the activities I am doing for or with my client(s) that could/should be done by someone in the community or by themselves.   YES NO

    d. Breaking client goals into smaller tasks.   YES NO

    e. Translating "problems" into "goals."   YES NO

    f. Identifying patterns and similarities between cases to enhance learning.

                                                                               YES NO

    g. Identifying what the client wants.   YES NO

    h. Engaging clients and developing a relationship.   YES NO

    i. Identifying client strengths.   YES NO

2. Did the discussion on your case close with at least 3 options in which you identified for the group your next tasks?

3. Was the supervision atmosphere optimistic and positive (i.e., focused on what can be done rather than what cannot be done)?

4. What did you receive positive feedback for?

5. What successes were identified in your work?

6. Were any of your conscientious efforts which failed acknowledged?

7. Did you laugh during the session?

Any Other Comments or Feedback

Supervisor's Group Supervision Monitor

Group supervision is a critical element in supervisory practice and indispensable to a high performing case management program. The following items warrant careful monitoring. It is divided into two sections: I. Group Interaction; II. Client Situation Discussion. Supervisors can use this instrument a prompt to themselves before and during group supervision and as a self-evaluation tool after the section.

I. Group Interaction

1. Did the session start on time? YES NO
2. Is the seating arrangement circular (everyone can see everyone else) and comfortable? YES NO
3. Was the discussion among all the participants or was it predominantly directed toward the supervisor? YES NO
4. Did the supervisor laugh during the session? YES NO
5. During the session, did the case managers laugh? YES NO
6. Was the supervision atmosphere optimistic and positive (i.e., focused upon what can be done rather than what cannot be done)? YES NO
7. What interruptions occurred during the supervisory session?
8. Which client situations were reviewed?
9. Which case manager dominated (if any)?
10. Who is generating alternatives?
11. Who made excuses to shoot down a potential resource or idea?
12. What conscientious efforts which failed were celebrated?
13. Who left group supervision feeling energized?

II. Client Work

1. For each client situation, were at least three alternative solutions or strategies generated? YES NO
2. Did each client situation discussion end with a specific plan for case manager action or strategy? YES NO
3. Did each client situation discussion close with the case manager identifying the specific tasks to be done? YES NO
4. If any case manager was frustrated with a client or others, did the supervisor help him/her make more realistic expectations and/or break tasks into smaller steps? YES NO
5. Who used the strengths assessment to identify goals, tasks or strategies?
6. For each client situation discussed, what natural resources and helpers in the community were identified?
7. For each client situation discussed, what strategies for involving natural helpers were generated?
8. If words like "problems" and "deficits" used rather than "interests," "strengths," "goals," etc., how did the supervisor reframe them?

9. What patterns and similarities between client situations were identified to enhance learning?

10. What successes did group members celebrate?

11. Who received positive feedback for

    use of client strengths?

    use of natural helpers?

    specific client achievements and goal attainment?

12. Did the group identifying policies within the agency or within other agencies or programs which indicate supervisory advocacy?

13. Any other observations?

CHAPTER 9

Strengths Model Epilogue: Commonly Asked Questions (Objections) and Managed Care

During the last 15 years, the mental health team at the University of Kansas School of Social Welfare has presented the strengths model before tens of thousands of people in over 40 states, England, Ireland, and Australia. The challenging questions we have received helped instigate and direct our efforts to better understand the strengths perspective and refine its methods. In this section, the six most frequently asked questions are addressed. Since managed care is a source of increasingly frequent questions, a separate section on this topic follows.

QUESTIONS AND OBJECTIONS

What About Real Problems and Crises?

Since all the helping professions and our society as a whole continue to be preoccupied with problems, deficits, pathololgy, etc., it is no wonder that this is the most frequently asked question about the strengths model. The incessant focus on problems prevents attention to achievement and usually creates more problems or crises. The following vignette (Weick & Chamberlain, 1997) is illustrative:

> Loretta, age 34, is diagnosed as having a borderline personality disorder. She had multiple hospitalizations yearly following suicidal threats, gestures such as cutting of wrists, other forms of self-injury, overdosing on medications, and two more serious suicide attempts. In recent years, she had also begun to threaten to hurt other people. Loretta had been in treatment for many years. Creative social workers and psychiatrists

had worked diligently with her to help her get jobs and move from her family home into her own apartment. In spite of years of treatment focused on understanding and coping with her depression and suicidal impulses, exploring different ways of managing her feelings, each job or new living arrangement ended abruptly with a dramatic crisis involving threats and/or self-destructive behaviors and subsequent hospitalizations.

A newly assigned social worker decided that Loretta's destructive behaviors dominated not only her life but also the years of case planning. In an attempt to rid both she and the client of the emphasis on "the problem," they worked together to arrive at a detailed crisis plan involving a crisis team to respond to Loretta's calls and threats, and arrange immediate hospitalization during crises. Once the crisis plan was put into effect, the worker's only job became assisting Loretta in defining her considerable talents and helping her to find ways to express them in work, her home life, and social activities. In the four years that this plan has been in place, Loretta has had two brief hospitalizations. Fortunately, they were not accompanied by the usual spectacle of mental health professionals and emergency vehicles so she has been able to return to her job and apartment following discharge. With the social worker's refusal to be involved in the problem, Loretta has slowly learned to shift her attention to building more satisfying activities in her daily life. For Loretta, putting the problem in its place may, in fact, have saved her life.

The strengths model, as reflected in Loretta's case, did not ignore the problems but "instead of being the star performer in a play, they became minor characters with small roles." (Weick & Chamberlain, 1997). There are three ways for putting problems in their proper place: (1) we recognize problems only in their proper context, (2) we adopt simpler ways of talking about problems, and (3) we pay less attention to the problem (Weick & Chamberlain, 1997).

On the other hand, when called on to intervene in crises or with severe situations, the case manager is probably not implementing the strengths model. For example, when a person is dangerous to themselves and others, the case manager and the entire mental health team is often forced to make decisions such as commitment. Even during these episodes, the case manager should explore less extrusive options with the client, but in large part the strengths model does not apply. Lack of food, clothing, shelter, the basics of life requires different approaches. If really dangerous to themselves or others (e.g., children, parents, spouse), the above discussion applies. In most cases, however, the client desires these basics, and as has been already noted, the case manager should help in their acquisition. Doing this is not necessarily the strengths model. Although maximizing options is desirable, any form of decent practice or even basic human kindness would ask no less. You do not need an assessment of strengths or a personal plan.

The point here is that while discrete elements of the strengths model are often applicable, not every situation is amenable or can benefit from the full application of the strengths model nor should proponents claim that it is. The core of case management practice is not these episodic crises but helping clients create lives that they desire, to minimize these episodes, to mitigate losses due to these situations (e.g., lost apartment, job, etc.) and allow them to rebound more quickly from them.

What About the Illness?

People who pose this question are often reacting to the relative deemphasis of the mental illness in most treatises and presentations on the strengths model as applied to people with severe mental illness. Given the dominance of medically oriented professional education and training, the strengths model is perceived as virtually "ignoring" the illness. While in no way does the strengths model "ignore" the illness, it is true that its etiology, symptoms, etc., play a more modest role in its theory and practice. There are several reasons for this.

First, strengths model case management is about habilitation and rehabilitation; its focus is on achievement, empowerment, and the quality of one's life, not on curing the illness. Second, our experience and that of others suggest that the "failure" to achieve is due less to the illness than to social and personal processes that are common to the human experience, albeit sometimes exaggerated with people of serious mental illness. Nature creates mental illness, society creates disabilities. For example, the most frequent explanations of why clients fail to achieve goals are the illness and its symptomatology or processes such as "resistance." Our experience, in contrast, suggests that far more prevalently goals fail for the same reasons all people fail to achieve (see Chapter VI).

Having said this, the strengths model does "honor the reality of, say, schizophrenia and the damage this neurological, psychosocial disorder can do." (Saleebey, 1996). Strengths model case managers are encouraged to work with clients and medical personnel to find the proper medication regime, to help clients to follow that regime, and to identify side effects of the medication and seek solutions. Of critical importance is the work done with clients to identify the earliest possible precursors and indications of symptom exacerbation and to develop plans for early efforts to prevent further exacerbation.

Isn't the Strengths Model Just Positive Reframing?

Absolutely not, although many people who claim to be strengths-based practitioners are doing merely this. Positive reframing refers to the technique of redefining a destructive or an inappropriate behavior of the client or a failure situation into a positive action or characteristic. Angry outbursts become examples of assertiveness. "Manipulative" behavior becomes creative strategies to get attention. For sure, some modest reframing is useful. A client who says "I only completed one year of college" has in fact completed 13 years of education with the latter years completed while likely confronting the onset of the illness.

The foundation of the strengths model, however, is that everyone has real talents, skills, competencies, etc. It posits that human behavior is purposeful and goal-directed. Furthermore, human behavior is powerfully affected by the resources and opportunities available from the environment. The strengths model has been designed to help case managers identify these *real* things. Sure, the person has schizophrenia but also *real* talent in the arts, sports, mechanics, etc. This is not reframing but identifying the elements that comprise the well-part of the individual.

What About Stigma and Discrimination?

This is the environmental corollary to "What about the illness?" People with serious mental illness are stigmatized and discriminated against in employment, housing, recreation, religion, etc. This is real although some progress continues to be made. While education can contribute to a reduction in stigma, the most powerful method is integration. Barriers, whether religious, racial, economic, etc., are most effectively destroyed when diverse people are asked to work together, play together, learn together, or live together. Nowhere has the hatred, separation, stigma, and discrimination been greater for a longer period of time than that between Israelis (Jews) and Palestinians (Arabs):

> **Nablus, West Bank (AP)**—The two officers, one Israeli and the other Palestinian, fought each other in the 1982 war in Lebanon. Now, they command joint security patrols to protect the shaky peace.
>
> Despite the many upheavals of recent months—suicide bombings by Islamic militants, a protracted Israeli blockade of the West Bank and Gaza Strip, a new Israeli government—the two commanders and their men have become friends. They ride in convoys by day and drink coffee by night.
>
> "Now, some of the teams are really friends and talk about going into future businesses together," said Buganim, a 22-year-old from the Israeli coastal town of Nahariya.
>
> "Day by day, our respect grows," he said. "They are like family now."
> (July 14, 1996, *Lawrence Journal World*)

Having said this, it is equally true that every community contains numerous people and organizations that want to help or will readily do so if approached. Just as in the case of individuals where achievement is enhanced by exploiting real strengths, the same is true in communities. While case managers should be aggressive in attacking discrimination and insuring clients' rights, more frequently, better lives are fostered by using the community resources that are there for the asking.

What Is New Here? (We Already Do This)

This can be answered on two levels. First, I admit that the strengths model legacy is long-standing. Each element or idea or method has its roots in the experience, research, and ideas of many others. The uniqueness, if it exists, is in the borrowing, synthesis, and packaging of these ideas.

At a second level, that of actual mental health and case management practice, the strengths model is a dramatic break. Many case managers and mental health organizations "argue that they already abide by the stricture of a strengths orientation. A review of the actual practice reveal that they fall short of full endorsement and application of a strengths-based practice." (Saleebey, 1996, p. 303). As Saleebey writes:

> For example, in many mental health agencies around the country, Individual Service Plans are devised to "incorporate" the strengths of client and family in the assessment and planning. But most ISPs are rife with diagnostic assessments and elaborations, narratives about decompensation, and explorations of continuing symptomatic struggles and manifestations Axes I and II of the D.S.M. are usually prominently featured. Often, the strengths assessment is consigned to a few lines at the end of the evaluation and planning form. The accountings rendered on these forms are, for the most part, in the language of the worker and employ the mental health system lexicon. (p. 303)

A recent study of supported housing where "client choice" was a linchpin found that few clients were provided few if any options (Srebnik, Livingston, Gordon, & King, 1995). This is not the strengths model. If a mental health agency has more than a few people working in sheltered workshops or living in group homes, the strengths model is not being practiced. If most clients spend the majority of time interacting with other clients or staff, the strengths model is not being practiced. If most (written or oral) descriptions of clients start, end, and are dominated by their problems, weaknesses, deficits, and inadequacies rather than their talents, dreams, and achievements, the strengths model is not being practiced.

Client Goals Are Fine but What About Needs?

The answer depends on one's definition of "need." In the strengths model, needs are defined as human needs necessary to sustain life such as food, shelter, absence of self-harm, or dangerousness to others. Addressing these may contain elements of the strengths model, but a full application is unwarranted. "Needs" beyond this should be at the discretion of the client who is helped to convert the need to a statement of what he or she desires.

This approach is different than that generally practiced. Need is often defined more broadly to include not only the basics of life but "needs" for structure, or less isolation, or in terms of services, "she needs partial hospital," "he needs a group home." The position here is that no human or person with mental illness "needs" these. Some may desire them and the task becomes to generate options and formulate a plan to be implemented.

MANAGED CARE AND STRENGTHS-BASED CASE MANAGEMENT

I have been urged by reviewers and colleagues to include material on managed care and its fit with the strengths model of case management. I was reluctant to do so for several reasons, the main one being that this is a practice text not a policy book. I finally was convinced, however, when I concluded that the conditions that augured managed care will only be exacerbated in the future and those conditions may effectively bury not only the strengths model but other reasonable approaches to case management.

Background

Managed care continues to be seen as the most prevalent solution to the problem of rapidly escalating health care costs and entitlement programs in general. In fact, as I write, the consensus projection of federal budget trends from the General Accounting Office and the Congressional Budget Office is that by the year 2007 (10 years away), the entire federal budget will be used to pay for entitlement programs (e.g., Medicare, Medicaid, AFDC, Veterans Benefits) and interest on the national debt. Of all the entitlement programs the growth of health related expenditure far outstrips all others.

Managed care is, at its core, a financing strategy that caps expenditures for a given period (most often a year). While each managed care approach is unique, the one common denominator is a fixed amount of money to provide a set of services to a predetermined target population. The state determines the specifications, accepts bids and proposals, and selects the contractor responsible for the funds, the services, and the clients. Under most plans, the contractor assumes "the risk" of spending above the contracted amount. Contractors therefore establish risk pools to protect themselves from such circumstances. Any money not spent is kept by the contractor as "profit."

The results of managed care in public mental health has led to these conclusions:

1. The state authority controls the nature and quality of the mental health system through the design of the managed care contract.
2. Managed care will control expenditures no matter how it is done.
3. Money is the primary motivator; financial incentives dictate client service.
4. There will be competition for the contract no matter how rigorous the contract requirements.

Beyond this, generalization is fraught with danger since each managed care plan is unique and those in mental health are only a few years old. It is fair to say, however, that there is no evidence that suggests people with severe mental illness are receiving better service nor are they achieving better outcomes. In fact, most analysis seem to emphasize less service, less timely service, less personal service, less access to appropriate services, less client choice, and huge profits for the contractors (especially for-profit entities).

Incentives

A critical facet of all social policy, financing or otherwise, is the incentive structure it contains. The still dominant fee-for-service mode provides incentives for more service (especially the most profitable) and therefore increased spending. It leads to overuse of services that accrue the most reimbursement compared with cost. For example, partial hospital/day treatment in many venues has been a major source of income for providers despite the lack of evidence demonstrating its efficacy. Since fee-for-service systems by necessity specify "fundable" services, other services or approaches are excluded. Most Medicaid plans do not reimburse supported work, supported education, or consumer-operated services despite the evidence of effectiveness. Flexibility to tailor service packages to individuals is constrained by detailed specifications of who can be served with what approaches.

The fee-for-service financing mechanism tends to result in costs continuing to increase; some outcomes (e.g., employment and education) remain stagnant; some people not receiving the most effective services in the intensity needed; and some people receiving services that are not effective or needed including hospitalization.

In contrast, the financial incentives in the typical mental health managed care system include:

1. Reduced use of expensive institutional care (e.g., state hospitalization, nursing facilities) for those facilities included in the managed care contract

2. Increased use of inexpensive natural resources and a reduction in formal services since services are an expense rather than income-generating

3. Increased use of services provided and paid for by others not included in the managed care contract (e.g., nursing homes, jails, shelters) known as cost-shifting

4. Flexibility in the array of services and options due to reduction in program- specific rules—unfortunately this incentive is attenuated by item 5

5. Increased administrative costs for controlling client utilization of services

6. Disincentives to serve the most disabled because they cost more

7. Disincentive to client choice to curtail short-term costs

8. Incentives for crisis response and client maintenance and disincentives for rehabilitation

The negative results of the typical managed care financing structure can be predicted: (1) a dramatic increase in the amount of money diverted from services to administrative costs and profits; (2) people with the most serious disabilities not getting served; (3) many clients underserved; (4) some cost shifting to other entities (e.g., nursing facilities, jails, police, etc.); (5) individualized care reduced; and (6) when no financial incentives exist, desired client outcomes decrease.

On the positive side, managed care provides powerful incentives to reduce the use of hospitalization and other forms of expensive and segregated institutional programs. Relatedly, managed care encourages the use of natural community resources since they are free or of little cost. Although rare, managed care systems could be based on achieving client outcomes rather than units of service with their attendant onerous recording requirement. In this case, dramatically increased flexibility would occur to create client-tailored service packages.

Managed Care and Strengths Model Case Management

First-generation managed care operations in mental health suggest strongly that neither strengths model case management nor other approaches with indicated effectiveness, like assertive community treatment teams or the rehabilitation model, will be used. Rather, practice guidelines for case management in managed care are assuming a utilization review function focused on limiting expenditures in the short term. As the GAO (1996) notes: "By using practice guidelines, plans are making a conscious decision about the care they intend to provide, reflecting the trade-off between costs and benefits" (p. 13).

Bill Anthony (1996) has contrasted this utilization review approach with the community support services (CSS) approach that includes strengths model care management (Table 9.1). The irony is that of the four major approaches to case management in mental health, the only one with a compelling track record of failure in terms of client outcomes, is the broker model that has many parallels with the utilization review depiction.

Can Managed Care Support Strengths Model Case Management?

CSS case management (including strengths) is not being implemented by first-generation managed care programs. Given the early experiences with mental health managed care, it can be anticipated that costs will be controlled, hospitalization will be reduced, clients will be underserved, and client outcomes will decrease. Are managed care and strengths model case management mutually exclusive or can they be mutually supportive? I think the latter is possible.

First, CSS case management and UR case management are two distinct services (with very little but the superficial in common) yet have the same label. This must change. One alternative is to rename UR case management to just utilization review or benefits manager, which are more descriptive of function. Another alternative is to rename CSS case management. While none of the present candidates seem comfortable (e.g. community consultant, integration specialist, care worker), there are two good reasons to do

TABLE 9.1

Case Management Differences Between Community Support Systems and Utilization Review

CSS	UR
Working alliance with consumer	Working alliance with professional
Ongoing interactions with consumer	No interactions with consumer
Decision making usually on-site	Decision making usually off-site
Consumer involved in decision making	Consumer not involved in decision making
Decision makers are case manager and consumer	Decision makers are case manager and professional
Decision making with same group of consumers	Decision making with different consumers
Case manager may perform other therapeutic functions with consumer	Case manager performs no other therapeutic functions with consumer
Case manager trained in case management knowledge and skills	Case manager trained in utilization review knowledge and skills
Tends to have experience working with people with severe mental illness	May not have experience working with people with severe mental illness
Has helping orientation	Has benefit management orientation
Accesses services directly	Grants permission to access services
Cuts through red tape	Adds to red tape
Recovery vision	Medical necessity vision
Wellness model	Illness model
Community support system values	Managed care values
Research shows improved consumer outcomes	No research support for improved consumer outcomes
Consistent with current trends in business reengineering	Inconsistent with current trends in business reengineering
History of using case management team approach	No history of using case management team approach
Underlying comprehensive service system design articulated	No underlying comprehensive service system design articulated

so. First, "case management" is an awful term that almost everybody, professionals and consumers, dislikes or even resents. We seek to *help people* not "manage cases." Unfortunately, for historical and reimbursement reasons combined with lack of consensus on an alternative, "case management" continues to be used.

A second reason to change the label is that it is not accurate and misleads. Case management formally entered mental health in 1978 with the onset of the community support program. Under this program, case management was to ensure that needed services were provided to people suffering from serious mental illness. The early formulation of case management and early implementation of the service were of the broker model type (Levine & Fleming, undated). It was not long, however, before this arid linkage to a service model was being replaced by enriched approaches (ACT, strengths, rehabilitation) that included direct service elements such as skill training, detailed rehabilitation plans, and work with naturally occurring community resources with all approaches requiring a close relationship with the client and increased authority for case manager decision making within the mental health agency.

The point here is that CSS case management is a multifaceted service that seeks to help clients achieve the goals they set for themselves. They are responsible across life domains. It is the one service not limited in focus. It is not limited to formal services but is encouraged to look beyond these. In many locales, especially rural areas, CSS case management acts as a replacement or substitute for specialized programs (see Cheryl Runyan story in Chapter 7). Therefore, CSS case management under managed care could be renamed and purchased as a separate service by UR case managers.

There are strengths and dangers in this approach. First, although compared with hospitalization and usual service approaches, CSS case management is significantly less expensive. Since controlling costs predominates in managed care, CSS case management seems to be a perfect match. In Solomon's (1992) review of the case management research, she identified 10 studies that attended to "cost effectiveness/savings." Of these 10, 8 found the experimental case management group to be less expensive than the control condition, and one reported no differences. The one reporting no difference (Borland et al., 1989) had most of their clients living in residential treatment where costs paralleled state hospital costs. The only study finding increased costs for the case management group was the study employing a broker model (Franklin et al., 1987).

Second, most people in mental health believe that CSS case management, like medication services and crisis services, should be universally available for individuals with serious disabilities for an undetermined length of time. Under this recommendation, the UR case manager would not have discretion over the rationing of this service. Perhaps states could make universal accessibility to CSS case management a mandated element of their contracts.

The strengths of this approach, beyond "calling a spade a spade," include moving CSS case management to a new level of prominence. Given its efficacy, CSS case management should be able to compete well with other service approaches. The strengths model, in particular, with its focus on community strengths offers the promise of a highly cost-effective service. Initial evidence from the application of the strengths model to older adults requiring long-term care has indicated reduced costs due to "increased levels of informal support, a more sustainable balance of formal and informal services, and fewer transitions between home and health care facilities" (Fast, Chapin, & Rapp, 1994; Fast & Chapin, 1996).

A second step needed for managed care and strengths model case management to be mutually supportive is for managed care contracts to be outcome-based rather than service-based. In other words, managed care contracts could place a premium on achieving the core outcomes of CSS: reducing hospitalization and increasing community tenure; improving vocational, educational, and living arrangement status; and increasing community activity and participation. Achievement standards could be set for each. While some service reporting and standards would necessarily be included, the emphasis could change from carefully counting units of service to "here's your money, and here's your clients, and here are the client outcomes you need to produce." How it is done is less important. Since no mental health service has a better record of efficacy, CSS case management would likely be at a premium.

REFERENCES

Altshuler, S. C., & Forward, J. (1978). The inverted hierarchy: A case manager approach to mental health. *Administration in Mental Health, 6*(1), 57–68.

American Psychological Association (APA). (1977). *Ethical Standards of Psychologists.* Washington, DC: American Psychological Association.

Anthony, W. A. (1979). *Principles of psychiatric rehabilitation.* Baltimore, MD: University Park Press.

Anthony, W. A. (1994). Recovery from mental illness: The guiding vision of the mental health system in the 1990's. In IAPSRS (Eds.), *An Introduction to Psychiatric Rehabilitation* (pp. 557–67). Boston, MA: International Association of Psychosocial Rehabilitation Services.

Anthony, W. A. (1996, April). Managed care case management for people with serious mental illness. *Behavioral Healthcare Tomorrow,* pp. 67–69.

Anthony, W. A., Cohen, M. R., & Farkas, M. D. (1990). *Psychiatric rehabilitation.* Boston, MA: Boston University, Center for Psychiatric Rehabilitation.

Arns, P., & Linney, J. (1993). Work, self, and life satisfaction for persons with severe and persistent mental disorders. *Psychosocial Rehabilitation Journal, 17*(2), 63–79.

Axelrod, S., & Wetzler, S. (1989). Factors associated with better compliance with psychiatric aftercare. *Hospital and Community Psychiatry, 40,* 397–401.

Axinn, J., & Levin, H. (1975). *Social Welfare: A History of the American Response to Need.* New York: Harper & Row.

Bachrach, L. L. (1982). Young chronic patients: An analytic review of the literature. *Hospital and Community Psychiatry, 33,* 189–97.

Bachrach, L. L. (1992). Case management revisited. *Hospital and Community Psychiatry, 43*(3), 209–10.

Barker, R. (1968). *Ecological Psychology.* Stanford, CA: Stanford University Press.

Bartlett, H. M. (1958). Toward clarification and improvement of social work practice. *Social Work, 3,* 3–9.

Beisser, A. (1990). *Flying without wings: Personal Reflections on Loss, Disability, and Healing.* New York: Bantam.

Berg, I. K., & Miller, S. D. (1992). *Working with the Problem Drinker: A Solution-Focused Approach.* New York: W. W. Norton.

Berlin, I. N. (1968). Resistance to change in mental health professionals. *American Journal of Orthopsychiatry, 69,* 109–15.

Bissonnette, D. (1994). *Beyond Traditional Job Development. The Art of Creating Opportunity.* Chatsworth, CA: Milt Wright and Associates.

Blanch, A., & Parrish, J. (1993). *Alternatives to Involuntary Treatment: Results of Three Roundtable Discussions.* Bethesda, MD: Community Support Program, Center for Mental Health Services.

Bleach, A., & Ryan, P. (1995). *Community Support for Mental Health: A Handbook for the Care Programme Approach and Care Management.* London: The Sainsbury Centre for Mental Health.

Bleuler, M. (1978). *The Schizophrenic Disorders* (p. 409). New Haven, CT: Yale University Press.

Bond, G. R. (1991). Variations in an assertive outreach model. *New Directions for Mental Health Services, 52,* 65–80.

Bond, G. R., & Dincin, J. (1986). Accelerating entry into transitional employment in a psychosocial agency. *Rehabilitation Psychology, 31,* 143–45.

Bond, G. R., McDonel, E. C., & Miller, L. D. (1991). Assertive community treatment and reference groups: An evaluation of their effectiveness for young adults with serious mental illness and substance abuse problems. *Psychosocial Rehabilitation Journal, 15*(2), 31–43.

Bond, G. R., McGrew, J. H., & Fekete, D. M. (1995). Assertive outreach for frequent users of psychiatric hospitals: A meta-analysis. *Journal of Mental Health Administration, 22*(1), 4–16.

Bond, G. R., Witheridge, T. F., Dincin, J., & Wasner, D. (1991). Assertive community treatment: Correcting some misconceptions. *American Journal of Community Psychology, 19*(1), 41–51.

Borland, A., McRae, J., & Lycan, C. (1989). Outcomes of five years of continuous intensive case management. *Hospital and Community Psychiatry, 40,* 369–76.

Boyer, S. L. (1991). *A Comparison of Three Types of Case Management on Burnout and Job Satisfaction.* Doctoral dissertation, Department of Psychology, Indiana University–Purdue University, Indianapolis.

Brehm, J. W. (1966). *A Theory of Psychological Reactance.* New York: Academic.

Bright, J. R. (1964). *Research, Development, and Technological Innovation: An Introduction.* Homewood, IL: Irwin.

Brower, A. M. (1988). Can the ecological model guide social work practice? *Social Service Review, 62*(3), 411–29.

Bryer, J. B., Nelson, B. A., Miller, J. B., & Krol, P. A. (1987). Childhood sexual and physical abuse as a factor in adult psychiatric illness. *American Journal of Psychiatry, 144,* 1426–30.

Bulhan, H. A. (1985). *Frantz Fanon and the Psychology of Oppression.* New York: Plenum Press.

Burgess, E. (1939). Introduction. In R. Faris & H. W. Dunham (Eds.), *Mental Disorders in Urban Areas* (pp. 1–3). Chicago: University of Chicago Press.

Burns, M. (1958). *The Historical Development of the Process of Casework Supervision as Seen in the Professional Literature of Social Work.* Unpublished doctoral dissertation, University of Chicago.

Caboolture Adult Mental Health Services. (1995). *Community Connections: The Cor-*

nerstone of Community Services Development for People with a Psychiatric Disability in Caboolture. Caboolture, Queensland, Australia: Author.

Carling, P. J. (1995). *Return to Community.* New York: Guilford Press.

Center for Mental Health Services. (1993). *Mental Health Statistics.* Rockville, MD: Author.

Chamberlain, R., & Rapp, C. A. (1991). A decade of case management: A methodological review of outcome research. *Community Mental Health Journal, 27*(3), 171–88.

Chamberlain, R., Topp, D., & Lee, R. (1995). *Kansas Mental Health Reform: Progress as Promised.* Lawrence, KS: The University of Kansas School of Social Welfare.

Chambers, D. (1993). *Social Policy & Social Programs.* New York: Macmillan.

Chapin, R. K. (1995). Social policy development: The strengths perspective. *Social Work, 40*(4), 506–14.

Coleman, J. W., Katz, E., & Menzel, H. (1966). *Medical Innovation: A Diffusion Study.* New York: Bobbs-Merrill.

Compton, B., & Galaway, B. (1984). *Social Work Process* (3rd ed.). Homewood, IL: Dorsey.

Cowger, C. (1989). Assessment guidelines for clinical practice: A strengths perspective. *University of Illinois School of Social Work Newsletter, 2*(2), 4–5.

Cowger, C. D. (1992). Assessment of client strengths. In D. Saleebey (Ed.), *The Strengths Perspective in Social Work Practice* (pp. 139–47). New York: Longman.

Crapanzano, V. (1982). The self, the third, and desire. In B. Lee (Ed.), *Psychosocial Theories of the Self* (pp. 179–260). New York: Plenum Press.

Curtis, J. L., Millman, E. J., & Struening, E. (1992). Effect of case management on rehospitalization and utilization of ambulatory care services. *Hospital and Community Psychiatry, 43,* 895–99.

Curtis, L. C., & Hodge, M. (1994). Old standards, new dilemmas: Ethics and boundaries in community support services. In The Publication Committee of IAPSRS (Eds.), *An Introduction to Psychiatric Rehabilitation* (pp. 339–56). Boston: The International Association of Psychosocial Rehabilitation Services.

Davidson, W. S., & Rapp, C. A. (1976). Child advocacy in the justice system. *Social Work, 21,* 225–32.

Deegan, P. E. (1988). Recovery: The lived experience of rehabilitation. *Psychosocial Rehabilitation, 11*(4), 11–19.

Deegan, P. E. (1996). Recovery as a journey of the heart. *Psychiatric Rehabilitation Journal, 19*(3), 91–97.

Degen, K., Cole, N., Tamayo, L., & Dzerovych, G. (1990). Intensive case management for the seriously mentally ill. *Administration and Policy in Mental Health, 17*(4), 265–69.

Deitchman, W. S. (1980). How many case managers does it take to screw in a light bulb? *Hospital and Community Psychiatry, 31,* 788–89.

DeJong, P., & Miller, S. D. (1995). How to interview for client strengths. *Social Work 40*(6), 721–864.

de Shazer, S. (1988). A requiem for power. *Contemporary Family Therapy, 10,* 69–76.

Dietzen, L. L., & Bond, G. R. (1993). Relationship between case manager contact and outcome for frequently hospitalized psychiatric clients. *Hospital and Community Psychiatry, 44*(90), 839–43.

Dion, G., & Anthony, W.A. (1987). Research in psychiatric rehabilitation: A review of experimental and quasi-experimental studies. *Rehabilitation Counseling Bulletin, 30,* 177–203.

Dodd, P., & Gutierrez, L. (1990). Preparing students for the future: A power perspective on community practice. *Administration in Social Work, 14*(2), 63–78.

Elton, C. (1927). *Animal Ecology.* London: Sidgewick and Jackson.

Estroff, S. E. (1987). No more young adult chronic patients. *Hospital and Community Psychiatry, 38*(1), 5.

Estroff, S. E. (1989). Self, identity and subjective experiences of schizophrenia: In search of the subject. *Schizophrenia Bulletin, 15*(2), 189–96.

Ewalt, P. L., & Honeyfield, R. M. (1981). Needs of persons in long-term care. *Social Work, 25,* 223–31.

Fanon, F. (1968). *The Wretched of the Earth.* New York: Grove Press.

Faris, R., & Dunham, H. W. (1939). *Mental Disorders in Urban Areas.* Chicago: University of Chicago Press.

Fast, B., & Chapin, R. (1996). The strengths model in long-term care: Linking cost containment and consumer empowerment. *Journal of Case Management 5*(2), 51–57.

Fast, B., Chapin, R., & Rapp, C. (1994). *A Model for Strengths-Based Case Management with Older Adults: Curriculum and Training Program.* Unpublished manuscript, School of Social Welfare, The University of Kansas, Lawrence, KS.

Fergeson, D. (1992). In the company of heroes. *The Journal, 3*(2), 29.

Fischer, J. (1978). *Effective Casework Practice.* New York: McGraw-Hill.

Franklin, J., Solovitz, B., Mason, M., Clemons, J., & Miller, G. (1987). An evaluation of case management. *American Journal of Public Health, 77,* 674.

Freire, P. (1973). *Education for Critical Consciousness.* New York: The Seabury Press.

Friedrich, R. M. (July, 1995). *Is There Hope for Those Who Require Long-Term Care?* Paper presented at the National Alliance for the Mentally Ill Annual Convention, Washington, DC.

Gamson, W. A. (1968). *Power and Discontent.* Homewood, IL: Dorsey.

General Accounting Office. (1996). *Practice Guidelines: Managed Care Plans Customize Guidelines to Local Interests.* Washington, DC: General Accounting Office.

Germain, C., & Gitterman, A. (1980). *The Life Model of Social Work Practice.* New York: Columbia University Press.

Germain, C. B. (1991). *Human Behavior in the Social Environment: An Ecological View.* New York: Columbia University Press.

Glaser, E. M., Abelson, H. H., & Garrison, K. N. (1983). *Putting Knowledge to Use.* San Francisco: Jossey-Bass.

Glater, S. I. (1992). The journey home. *The Journal, 3*(2), 21–22.

Goering, P., Wasylenki, D., Farkas, M., Lancee, W., & Ballantyne, R. (1988). What difference does case management make? *Hospital and Community Psychiatry, 39,* 272–76.

Goffman, E. (1961). *Asylums.* Garden City, NY: Anchor Books

Goldstein, H. (1943). *Social practice: A Unitary Approach.* Columbia, SC: University of South Carolina.

Goldstein, H. (1992). Victors or victims: Contrasting views of clients in social work practice. In D. Saleebey (Ed.), *The Strengths Perspective in Social Work Practice* (pp. 27–38). New York: Longman.

Gowdy, E., & Rapp, C. A. (1989). Managerial behavior: The common denominators of effective community based programs. *Psychosocial Rehabilitation Journal, 13,* 31–51.

Grimmer, D. (1992). The invisible illness. *The Journal, 3*(2), 27–28.

Grinnell, J. (1917). Field tests of theories concerning distribution control. *American Naturalist, 51,* 115–28.

Gutride, M. E., Goldstein, G. P., & Hunter, G. F. (1973). The use of modeling and role playing to increase social interaction among social psychiatric patients. *Journal of Consulting and Clinical Psychology, 40,* 408–15.

Hackney, H., & Cormier, L. (1979). *Counseling Strategies and Objectives.* Englewood Cliffs, NJ: Prentice-Hall.

Harding, C. M., Brooks, G., Ashikaga, T., Strauss, J. S., & Breier, A. (1987a). The Vermont longitudinal study of persons with severe mental illness II: Long-term outcome of subjects who retrospectively met DSM-III criteria for schizophrenia. *American Journal of Psychiatry, 144*(6), 727–35.

Harding, C., Brooks, G., Takamaura, A., Strauss, J., & Brier, A. (1987b). The Vermont longitudinal study of persons with severe mental illness I: Methodology, study sample, and over all status 32 years later. *American Journal of Psychiatry, 144*(6), 718–26.

Harding, C., Zubin, J., & Strauss, J. (1987). Chronicity in schizophrenia: Fact, partial fact, or artifact? *Hospital and Community Psychiatry, 38*(5), 477–86.

Hatfield, A. B., & Lefley, H. P. (1993). *Surviving Mental Illness: Stress, Coping and Adaptation.* New York: Guilford Press.

Heider, F. (1958). *The Psychology of Interpersonal Relations.* New York: Wiley.

Hepworth, D., & Larsen, J. A. (1986). *Direct Social Work Practice.* Chicago: Dorsey.

Hollingshead, A. B., & Redlich, F. C. (1958). *Social Class and Mental Illness.* New York: Wiley.

Hornstra, R. K., Bruce-Wolfe, V., Sagduyu, K., & Riffle, D. W. (1993). The effect of intensive case management on hospitalization of patients with schizophrenia. *The Journal of Hospital and Community Psychiatry, 44*(9), 844–53.

Huxley, P., & Warner, R. (1992). Case management, quality of life, and satisfaction with services of long-term psychiatric patients. *Hospital and Community Psychiatry, 43*(8), 799–802.

Jacobson, A., & Richardson, B. (1987). Assault experiences of 100 psychiatric inpatients: Evidence of the need for routine inquiry. *American Journal of Psychiatry, 144,* 908–13.

Jaffe, P. G., & Carlson, P. M. (1976). Relative efficacy of modeling and instructions in eliciting social behavior from chronic psychiatric patients. *Journal of Consulting and Clinical Psychology, 44,* 200–207.

Jansson, B. (1990). *Social Welfare Policy.* Belmont, CA: Wadsworth.

Kadushin, A. (1974). Supervisor-supervisee: A survey. *Social Work, 19*(3), 288–97.

Kagle, J. D., & Cowger, C. D. (1984). Blaming the client: Implicit agenda in practice research. *Social Work, 29*(4), 347–52.

Kaplan, L., & Girard, J. (1994). *Strengthening high-risk families.* New York: Lexington Books.

Karger, H. J. (1981). Burnout as alienation. *Social Service Review, 55*(2), 270–83.

Kaufman, J., & Zigler, E. (1987). Do Abused Children Become Abusive Parents? *American Journal of Orthopsychiatry, 57,* 186–92.

Keil, J. (1992). The mountain of my mental illness. *The Journal 3*(2), 5–6.

Kieffer, C. H. (1984). Citizen empowerment: A developmental perspective. In *Studies in Empowerment* (pp. 9–36). New York: The Haworth Press.

Kirk, S., & Kutchins, H. J. (1988). Deliberate misdiagnosis in mental health practice. *Social Service Review, 24,* 225–37.

Kisthardt, W. (1992). A strengths model of case management: The principles and functioning of helping partnerships with persons with persistent mental illness.

In D. Saleebey (Ed.), *The Strengths Perspective in Social Work* (pp. 59–83). New York: Longman.

Kisthardt, W. (1993). The impact of the strengths model of case management from the consumer perspective. In M. Harris & H. Bergman (Eds.), *Case management: Theory and Practice* (pp. 165–82). Washington, DC: American Psychiatric Association.

Kisthardt, W. E., & Rapp, C. A. (1992). Bridging the gap between principles and practice: Implementing a strengths perspective in case management. In S. M. Rose (Ed.), *Case Management and Social Work Practice* (pp. 112–25). New York: Longman.

Kisthardt, W. E., & Rapp, C. A. (1996). *Reconsidering Social Isolation from a Strengths Perspective.* Lawrence, KS: The University of Kansas School of Social Welfare.

Kretzmann, J. B., & McKnight, J. L. (1993). *Building Communities from the Inside Out.* Evanston, IL: Northwestern University.

Lamb, R. H. (1980). Therapist-case managers: More than brokers of service. *Hospital and Community Psychiatry, 31,* 762–64.

Larson, C. U. (1983). *Persuasion: Reception and Responsibility* (3rd ed.). Belmont, CA: Wadsworth.

Lee, J. A. B. (1994). *The Empowerment Approach to Social Work Practice.* New York: Columbia University Press.

Leete, E. (1988). A consumer perspective on psychosocial treatment. *Psychosocial Rehabilitation, 12*(2), 45–62.

Leete, E. (1989). How I perceive and manage my illness. *Schizophrenia Bulletin, 15,* 197–200.

Leete, E. (1993). The interpersonal environment: A consumer's personal recollection. In A. B. Hatfield & H. P. Lefley (Eds.), *Surviving Mental Illness* (pp. 114–28). New York: Guilford Press.

Leiby, J. (1978). *A History of Social Welfare and Social Work in the United States.* New York: Columbia University Press.

Leventhal, H. (1970). Findings and theory in the study of fear communication. In L. Berkowitz (Ed.), *Advances in Experimental Social Psychology, 5* (pp. 119–86). New York: Academic.

Levine, I. S., & Fleming, M. (undated). *Human resource development: Issues in Case Management.* Baltimore: University of Maryland Center of Rehabilitation and Manpower Services.

Levstek, D. A., & Bond, G. R. (1993). Housing cost, quality, and satisfaction among formerly homeless persons with serious mental illness in two cities. *Innovations and Research, 2*(3), 1–8.

Liberman, R. P. (1992). *Handbook of Psychiatric Rehabilitation.* New York: Macmillan.

Liberman, R. P., Massel, H. K., Mosk, M. D., & Wong, S. E. (1985). Social skills training for chronic mental patients. *Hospital and Community Psychiatry, 36,* 396–403.

Locke, E., Shaw, K., Saari, L., & Latham, G. (1981). Goal setting and task performance: 1969–1980. *Psychological Bulletin, 90*(1), 125–52.

Macias, C., Kinney, R., Farley, O. W., Jackson, R., & Vos, B. (1994). The role of case management within a community support system: Partnership with psychosocial rehabilitation. *Community Mental Health Journal, 30*(4), 323–39.

Maluccio, A. (1979). *Learning from Clients: Interpersonal Helping as Viewed by Clients and Social Workers.* New York: Free Press.

Maluccio, A. N. (1981). *Promoting Competence in Clients.* New York: Free Press.

Martin, P. Y. (1980). Multiple constituencies, dominant social values, and the human services administrator: Implications for service solving. *Administration in Social Work, 4*(2), 15–27.

McClelland, D. C., Atkinson, J. W., Clark, R. W., & Lowell, E. L. (1953). *The Achievement Motive.* New York: Appleton-Century-Crofts.

McCrory, D. (1991). The rehabilitation alliance. *Journal of Vocational Rehabilitation, 1*(3), 58–66.

McCrory, D., Connoly, P., Hanson-Mayer, T., Sheridan-Landolfi, J., Borone, F., Blood, A., & Gilson, A. (1980). The rehabilitation crisis: The impact of growth. *Journal of Applied Rehabilitation Counseling, 11*(3), 136–39.

McGrew, J. H., & Bond, G. R. (1995). Critical ingredients of assertive community treatment: Judgments of the experts. *The Journal of Mental Health Administration, 22*(2), 113–25.

McGrew, J. H., Bond, G. R., Dietzen, L., & Salyers, M. (1994). Measuring the fidelity of implementation of a mental health program model. *Journal of Consulting and Clinical Psychology, 62*(4), 670–78.

McKnight, J. L. (undated). *Beyond Community Services.* Evanston, IL: Northwestern University Center for Urban Affairs.

Mills, R. C., & Kelly, J. G. (1972). Cultural adaptation and ecological analogies: Analysis of three Mexican villages. In S. E. Golann & C. Eisdorfer (Eds.), *Handbook of Community Mental Health* (pp. 61–75). New York: Appleton-Century-Crofts.

Mintzberg, H. (1979). *The nature of managerial work.* Englewood Cliffs, NJ: Prentice- Hall.

Miringoff, M. L. (1980). *Management in Human Service Organizations.* New York: Macmillan.

Modrcin, M., Rapp, C., & Chamberlain, R. (1985). *Case Management with Psychiatrically Disabled Individuals: Curriculum & Training Program.* Lawrence, KS: University of Kansas School of Social Welfare.

Modrcin, M., Rapp, C., & Poertner, J. (1988). The evaluation of case management services with the chronically mentally ill. *Evaluation and Program Planning, 11,* 307–14.

Moore-Kirkland, J. (1981). Mobilizing motivation: From theory to practice. In A. Maluccio (Ed.), *Promoting Competence in Clients* (pp. 27–54). New York: Free Press.

Munson, C. (1979). An empirical study of structure and authority in social work supervision. In C. Munson (Ed.), *Social Work Supervision* (pp. 286–96). New York: Free Press.

Naylor, J., & Ilgen, D. (1984). Goal setting: A theoretical analysis of a motivational technology. In B. Staw & L. L. Cummings (Eds.), *Research in Organizational Behavior,* (Vol. 6, pp. 95–140). Greenwich, CT: Jai Press.

Neugeboren, B. (1985). *Organization, Policy, and Practice in the Human Services.* New York: Longman.

Olmstead, J., & Christensen, H. (1974). *Research Report No. 2—Effects of Agency Work Contexts: An Intensive Field Study* (SRS No. 74-05416). Washington, DC: U.S. Government Printing Office.

Park, R. (1952). *Human communities.* Glencoe, IL: Free Press.

Patti, R. (1977, Spring). Patterns of management activity in social welfare agencies. *Administration in Social Work, 1*(1), 548.

Patti, R. (1985, Fall). In search of purpose for social welfare administration. *Administration in Social Work, 9*(3), 1–14.

Peele, S., & Brodsky, A. (1991). *The Truth About Addiction and Recovery.* New York: Simon & Schuster/Fireside.

Peters, T. J., & Waterman, R. H. (1982). *In Search of Excellence.* New York: Harper & Row.

Peterson, C., Maier, S., & Seligman, M. E. P. (1993). *Learned Helplessness: A Theory for the Age of Personal Control.* New York: Oxford.

Pincus, A., & Minahan, A. (1973). *Social Work Practice: Model and Method.* Itasca, IL: F. E. Peacock Publishers.

Porter, M., & Sherman, P. S. (1988). *The Denver Case Management Project.* Denver: Colorado Division of Mental Health.

Quinlivian, R., Hough, R., Crowell, A., Beach, C., Hofstetter, R., & Kenworthy, K. (1995). Service utilization and costs of care for severely mentally ill clients in an intensive case management program. *Psychiatric Services, 46*(4), 365–75.

Rapp, C. A. (1992). The strengths perspective of case management with persons suffering from severe mental illness. In D. Saleebey (Ed.), *The Strength Perspectives in Social Work* (pp. 45–58). New York: Longman.

Rapp, C. A. (1993). Client-centered performance management for rehabilitation and mental health services. In R. W. Flexer & P. L. Solomon (Eds.), *Psychiatric Rehabilitation in Practice* (pp. 173–92). Boston: Andover Medical Publishers.

Rapp, C. A. (1993). Theory, principles, and methods of strengths model of case management. In M. Harris & H. Bergman (Eds.), *Case Management: Theory and Practice* (pp. 143–64). Washington, DC: American Psychiatric Association.

Rapp, C. A. (1995). The active ingredients of effective case management: A research synthesis. In L. Giesler (Ed.), *Case Management for Behavioral Managed Care* (pp. 5–45). Washington, DC: Center for Mental Health Services.

Rapp, C. A., & Chamberlain, R. (1985). Case management services to the chronically mentally ill. *Social Work, 30*(5), 417–22.

Rapp, C. A., & Poertner, J. (1992). *Social Administration: A Client-Centered Approach.* New York: Longman.

Rapp, C. A., & Wintersteen, R. (1989). The strengths model of case management: Results from twelve demonstrations. *Psychosocial Rehabilitation Journal, 13*(1), 23–32.

Rappaport, J. (1977). *Community Psychology.* New York: Holt, Rinehart & Winston.

Rappaport, J. (1985). The power of empowerment language. *Social Policy, 16*, 15–21.

Rappaport, J. (1990). Research methods and the empowerment social agenda. In P. Tolan, C. Keys, F. Chertok, & L. Jason (Eds.), *Researching Community Psychology* (pp. 51–63). Washington, DC: American Psychological Association.

Rappaport, J., Davidson, W., Mitchell, A., & Wilson, M. N. (1975). Alternatives to blaming the victim or the environment: Our places to stand have not moved the earth. *American Psychologist, 30*, 525–28.

Reilly, S. (1992). Breaking loose. *The Journal, 3*(2), 20.

Richmond, M. (1922). *What is Social Casework?* New York: Russell Sage.

Ridgway, P., & Zipple, A. M. (1990). The paradigm shift in residential services: From the linear continuum to supported housing approaches. *Psychosocial Rehabilitation Journal, 13*, 11–31.

Rife, J. C., Greenlee, R. W., Miller, L. D., & Feichter, M. A. (1991). Case management with homeless mentally ill people. *Health and Social Work, 16*(1), 58–67.

Risser, P. A. (1992). An empowering journey. *The Journal, 3*(2), 38–39.

Robinson, G., & Bergman, G. T. (1989). *Choices in Case Management.* Washington, DC: Policy-Resources Incorporated.

Rogers, C. R. (1959). A theory of therapy, personality and interpersonal relationships as developed in the client-centered framework. In S. Koch (Ed.), *Psychology: A Study of a Science, Vol. II*. New York: McGraw-Hill.

Rogers, E. M. (1968). *Diffusion of Innovations* (3rd ed.). New York: Free Press.

Rogers, E. M. (1983). The communication of innovations in a complex institution. *Educational Records, 48*, 67–77.

Rogers, E. M., & Svenning, L. (1969). *Managing change*. Washington, DC: U. S. Office of Education.

Rose, S. M. (1991). Acknowledging abuse backgrounds of intensive case management clients. *Community Mental Health Journal 27*(4), 255–63.

Rose, S. M., & Black, B. L. (1985). *Advocacy and Empowerment: Mental Health Care in the Community*. Boston: Routledge & Kegan, Paul.

Rose, S. M., Peabody, C. G., & Stratigeas, B. (1991). Responding to hidden abuse: A role for social work in reforming mental health systems. *Social Work, 36*(5), 408–13.

Rothman, D. (1971). *The Discovery of the Asylum*. Boston: Little, Brown.

Ryan, C. S., Sherman, P. S., & Judd, C. M. (1994). Accounting for case management effects in the evaluation of mental health services. *Journal of Consulting and Clinical Psychology, 62*(5), 965–74.

Ryan, W. (1971). *Blaming the Victim*. New York: Random House.

Rydman, R. J. (1990). More hospital or more community? *Administration and Policy in Mental Health Services, 17*(4), 215–34.

Saleebey, D. (1996). The strengths perspective in social work practice: Extensions and cautions. *Social Work, 41*(3), 296–305.

Sanders, J. T., & Reppucci, N. D. (1977, October). Learning network among administrators of human service institutions. *American Journal of Community Psychology, 5*, 269–76.

Sands, R. G., & Cnaan, R. A. (1994). Two modes of case management: Assessing their impact. *Community Mental Health Journal, 30*(5), 441–57.

Santos, A. B., Doci, P. A., Lachanace, K. R., Dias, J. K., Sloop, T. B., Hiers, T. G., & Belvilacqua, J. J. (1993). Providing assertive community treatment for severely mentally ill patients in a rural area. *The Journal of Hospital and Community Psychiatry, 44*(1), 34–39.

Scheie-Lurie, M. (1992). Recovery: It takes more than finding the right pill. *The Journal, 3*(2), 36.

Sheafor, B. W., Horejsi, C. R., & Horejsi, G. A. (1991). *Techniques and Guidelines for Social Work Practice* (2nd ed.). Boston: Allyn & Bacon.

Shulman, L. (1979). *The Skills of Helping Individuals and Groups*. Itasca, IL: F. E. Peacock.

Shulman, L. (1992). *The Skills of Helping* (3rd ed.). Itasca, IL: F. E. Peacock.

Shulman, L., Robinson, E., & Lucky, A. (1981). *A Study of the Content, Context, and Skills of Supervision*. Vancouver, Canada: University of British Columbia.

Simon, B. L. (1994). *The Empowerment Tradition in American Social Work*. New York: Columbia University Press.

Simons, R. L. (1982). Strategies for exercising influence. *Social Work Journal, 27*(3), 268–74.

Simons, R. L. (1985). Inducement as an approval to exercising influence. *Social Work, 30*(1), 56–68.

Simons, R. L. (1987). The skill of persuasion: An essential component of human services administration. *Administration in Social Work, 11*(3/4), 241–54.

Smalley, R. E. (1967). *Theory for Social Work Practice*. New York: Columbia University Press.

Snyder, C. R. (1994). *The Psychology of Hope.* New York: Free Press.

Solomon, P. (1992). The efficacy of case management services for severely mentally disabled clients. *Community Mental Health Journal, 28,* 163–80.

Solomon, P., & Draine, J. (1994). Satisfaction with mental health treatment in a randomized trial of consumer case management. *Journal of Nervous and Mental Disease, 182,* 179–84.

Srebnik, D., Livingston, J., Gordon, L., & King, D. (1995). Housing choice and community success for individuals with serious and persistent mental illness. *Community Mental Health Journal, 31*(2), 139–52.

Stanley, R. (1992). Welcome to reality—Not a facsimile. *The Journal 3*(2), 25–26.

Stein, L., & Test, M. A. (1980). Alternative to mental hospital treatment 1 conceptual model: Treatment program, and clinical evaluation. *Archives of General Psychiatry, 37,* 392–97.

Strauss, J. B., Hafey, H., Lieberman, P., & Harding, C. M. (1985). The course of psychiatric disorder, III: Longitudinal principles. *American Journal of Psychiatry, 142,* 289–96.

Strauss, J. S. (1989). Subjective experiences of schizophrenia: Toward a new dynamic psychiatry. *Schizophrenia Bulletin, 15,* 177–78.

Strickberger, M.W. (1990). *Evolution.* Boston: Jones & Bartlett.

Sullivan, A. P., Nicolellis, D. L., Danley, K. S., & MacDonald-Wilson, K. (1994). Choose-Get-Keep: A psychiatric rehabilitation approach to supported education. In IAPSRS (Eds.), *An Introduction to Psychiatric Rehabilitation* (pp. 230–40). Boston: International Association of Psychosocial Rehabilitation Services.

Sullivan, W. P. (1989). Community support programs in rural areas: Developing programs without walls. *Human Services in the Rural Environment, 12*(4), 19–24.

Sullivan, W. P. (1992). Reconsidering the environment as a helping resource. In D. Saleebey (Ed.), *The Strengths Perspective in Social Work* (pp. 148–57). New York: Longman.

Sullivan, W. P. (1994a). A long and winding road: The process of recovery from severe mental illness. *Innovations and Research 3,* 19–27.

Sullivan, W. P. (1994b). Recovery from schizophrenia: What we can learn from the developing nations. *Innovations and Research, 3*(2), 6–7.

Sullivan, W. P., & Rapp, C. A. (1991). Improving client outcomes: The Kansas technical assistance consultation project. *Community Mental Health Journal, 27*(5), 327–36.

Syx, C. (1995). The mental health service system: How we've created a make-believe world. *Psychiatric Rehabilitation Journal, 19*(1), 83–85.

Szasz, T. S. (1970). *The Manufacture of Madness: A Comparative Study of the Inquisition and the Mental Health Movement.* New York: Harper & Row.

Talbott, J. A. (1979). Deinstitutionalization: Avoiding the disasters of the past. *Hospital and Community Psychiatry, 30*(9), 621–24.

Talbott, J. A. (1988). The chronically mentally ill: What do we now know, and why aren't we implementing what we know? In J. A. Talbott (Ed.), *The Perspective of John Talbott. New Directions for Mental health Services, No. 37* (pp. 43–58). San Francisco: Jossey-Bass.

Tanzman, B. (1993). An overview of surveys of mental health consumers' preferences for housing and support services. *Hospital and Community Psychiatry, 44,* 450–55.

Taylor, J. (1997). Niches and practice: Extending the ecological perspective. In D. Saleebey, (Ed.), *The Strengths Perspective in Social Work Practice* (2nd ed.). New York: Longman.

Tedeschi, J. T., & Lindskold, S. (1976). *Social Psychology: Interdependence, Interaction and Influence.* New York: Wiley.

Test, M. A. (1979). Continuity of care in community treatment. In L. I. Stein (Ed.), *Community Support Systems for the Long-Term Patient. New Directions for Mental Health Services, 2* (pp. 15–23). San Francisco: Jossey-Bass.

Test, M. A. (1992). Training in community living. In R. P. Lieberman (Ed.), *Handbook of Psychiatric Rehabilitation* (Vol. 166, pp. 153–70). Needham Heights, MA: Allyn & Bacon.

Trickett, E. J., Kelly, J. G., & Todd, D. M. (1972). The social environment of the high school: Guidelines for individual change and organizational redevelopment. In S. E. Golann & C. Eisdorfer (Eds.), *Handbook of Community Mental Health* (pp. 98–115). New York: Appleton-Century-Crofts.

Truax, C. B., & Carkhuff, R. R. (1967). *Toward Effective Counseling and Psychotherapy.* Chicago: Aldine.

Truax, C. B., & Mitchell, K. (1971). Research on certain therapist interpersonal skills in relation to process and outcome. In A. Bergin & S. Garfield (Eds.), *Handbook of Psychotherapy and Behavior Change* (pp. 299–344). New York: Wiley.

Turner, J. C. (1977). Comprehensive community support systems for mentally disabled adults: Definitions, components, guiding principles. *Psychosocial Rehabilitation Journal, 1*(3), 39–47.

Turner, J. E., & Shifren, I. (1979). Community support system: How comprehensive? *New Directions for Mental Health Services, 2,* 1–13.

U.S. Department of Health and Human Services. (1983). *Statistical Profile.* Washington, DC: U.S. Government Printing Office.

Watzlawick, P., Weakland, J., & Fisch, R. (1974). *Change: Principles of Problem Formation and Problem Resolution.* New York: W. Norton.

Webster's Third New International Dictionary. (1976). Springfield, MA: G.C. Merriam.

Weick, A., & Chamberlain, R. (1997). Putting problems in their place: Further explorations in the strengths perspective. In D. Saleebey (Ed.), *The Strengths Perspective in Social Work Practice* (2nd ed.). New York: Longman.

Weick, A., & Pope, L. (1988). Knowing what's best: A new look at self-determination. *Social Casework, 69*(1), 10–16.

Weick, A., Rapp, C. A., Sullivan, W. P., & Kisthardt, W. (1989, July). A strengths perspective for social work practice. *Social Work, 89,* 350–54.

Wells, C., & Masch, M. (1986). *Social Work Ethics: Guidelines for Professional Practice.* New York: Longman.

Werner, E., & Smith, R. (1982). *Vulnerable but Invincible.* New York: Adams, Bannister, Cox.

Werner, E., & Smith, R. (1992). *Overcoming the Odds.* Ithaca, NY: Cornell University Press.

White, R. W. (1959). Motivation reconsidered: The concept of competence. *Psychological Review, 66,* 297–333.

Wicklund, R. A. (1974). *Freedom and Reactance.* Hillsdale, NJ: Erlbaum.

Wilson, W. J. 1987). *The Truly Disadvantaged: The Inner City, the Underclass, and Public Policy.* Chicago: University of Chicago Press.

Wirth, L. (1964). *On Cities and Social Life.* Selected papers edited by A. Reiss. Chicago: University of Chicago Press.

Witheridge, T. F. (1991). The "active ingredients" of assertive outreach. *New Directions for Mental Health Services, 52,* 47–64.

Wolin, S. J., & Wolin, S. (1993). *The Resilient Self.* New York: Villard Books.

Woolfolk, A. E., Woolfolk, R. L., & Wilson, G. T. (1977). A rose by any other name: Labeling bias and attitudes toward behavior modification. *Journal of Consulting and Clinical Psychology, 45,* 184–91.

Zaltman, G. (1973). *Processes and Phenomena of Social Change.* New York: Wiley.

Zaltman, G., & Duncan, R. (1977). *Strategies for Planned Change.* New York: Wiley.

INDEX